Tick..

Hear that clock ticking? It's the c̶[...]̶ Exam, and it'll be here before you know i[...] or one day to go, now's the time to start maximizing your score.

The Test Is Just a Few Months Away!

The rest of us are jealous—you're ahead of the game. But you still need to make the most of your time. Start on page 249, where we'll help you devise **classroom and homework strategies** so you'll be well-prepared for the big day. You can even keep tabs on your class by following our **progress charts**, just in case you need to start forging ahead on your own.

Actually, I Only Have a Few Weeks!

That's plenty of time for a full review. Turn to page 51, where you'll find a **comprehensive review** of all the key calculus topics. Then learn how to beat the test using our **Multiple Choice Strategies** (page 230).

Let's Be Honest. The Test Is Tomorrow and I'm Freaking Out!

No problem. Read through the **20 Problems You Must Be Able to Solve** (page 3). If you find you're rusty on a certain topic, look it up in the review section beginning on page 51. Then get a quick tutorial on how to maximize your score with our **Strategies for Maximizing Your Score** (page 31).

But I Don't Even Know What I'm In For!

Grab a pencil and take a **Practice Test** (page 255). Don't worry about the scores—just focus on getting to know the test. Before you go to bed, go through the **Checklist for Test Day** (page 48) and keep it close. It'll walk you through the next 24 hours.

Relax. Everything you need to know, you've already learned. We're just here to keep it fresh in your mind for test day.

My Max Score

AP CALCULUS AB/BC

Maximize Your Score in Less Time

Carolyn Wheater

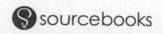

Copyright © 2011 by Sourcebooks, Inc.
Cover and internal design © 2011 by Sourcebooks, Inc.
Series design by The Book Designers

Sourcebooks and the colophon are registered trademarks of Sourcebooks, Inc.

This publication is designed to provide accurate and authoritative information in regard to the subject matter covered. It is sold with the understanding that the publisher is not engaged in rendering legal, accounting, or other professional service. If legal advice or other expert assistance is required, the services of a competent professional person should be sought.—*From a Declaration of Principles Jointly Adopted by a Committee of the American Bar Association and a Committee of Publishers and Associations*

Published by Sourcebooks, Inc.
P.O. Box 4410, Naperville, Illinois 60567-4410
(630) 961-3900
Fax: (630) 961-2168
www.sourcebooks.com

Library of Congress Cataloging-in-Publication Data

Wheater, Carolyn C.
  My max score AP calculus AB/BC : maximize your score in less time / by Carolyn Wheater.
      p. cm.
    1.   Calculus--Examinations--Study guides 2.   Advanced placement programs (Education)--Examinations--Study guides. I. Title.
  QA309.W44 2011
  515.076--dc22
                              2010039348

Printed and bound in the United States of America.
                    VP 10 9 8 7 6 5 4 3 2 1

Contents

Introduction

Everybody comes to an AP test from a different place. For some, it's the one AP test of their high school career, while for others, it's just one of many. Some students have been focused on it all year, supplementing their classwork with extra practice at home. Other students haven't been able to devote the time they would like—perhaps other classes, extracurricular activities, after-school jobs, or other obligations have gotten in the way. Wherever you're coming from, this book can help. It's divided into three sections: a last-minute study guide to use the week before, a comprehensive review for those with more than a week to prepare, and a long-term study plan for students preparing well in advance.

Think of these sections as a suggestion rather than a rigid prescription. Feel free to pick and choose the pieces from each section that you find most helpful. If you have time, review everything—and take as many practice tests as you can.

Whether you have a day or a year to study, there are a few things you know before diving in. Let's start by getting to know the AP Calculus Exam.

About the Test

The AP Calculus Exam is 3 hours 15 minutes long and is divided into two main sections, with two parts to each. Each main section is given equal weight in scoring. Here's how the test is broken down:

Section	Questions	Time Allowed	Calculator Allowed?
Multiple Choice Part A	28 questions	55 minutes	No
Multiple Choice Part B	17 questions	50 minutes	Yes
Free Response Part A	2 questions	45 minutes	Yes
Free Response Part B	4 questions	45 minutes	No

Note that the number of items in the free response section was changed in May 2011. In the past, there were 3 questions in each part, though the time allotted to each section was the same.

Exam Scoring

The multiple choice and free-response sections are each worth half of your total grade. For the multiple choice section, your score is calculated by adding up all your correct answers. Unlike in the past, an incorrect answer and a blank answer are scored the same, so it makes sense to guess randomly even if you have no idea of the answer. In the free-response section, you rack up points for each step you correctly write out toward the correct answer. You won't score much if you just write down the correct answer, and you can still earn lots of points even if you get the answer wrong, if you follow the correct steps along the war.

Exam graders add up your raw score and use it to award you one of five AP grades:

5   Extremely well qualified

4   Well qualified

3   Qualified

2   Possibly qualified

1   Not recommended for AP credit

It would be great if everyone could get a 5, but unfortunately it doesn't work out that way. In 2009, about 42 percent of students got a 4 or a 5 on the Calculus AB Exam, and 51 percent of students got a 4 or a 5 on the Calculus BC Exam. For each, another 18 or 19 percent got a 3.

You don't need to answer every question to get a good score. On a typical year, getting 70 percent of questions right will earn you a 5, and you can usually earn a 3 by correctly answering just 40 percent. The goal is not to answer every question correctly, but to answer as many as you can.

Visit mymaxscore.com for an additional practice test for the AP Calculus AB/BC Exam, as well as practice tests for other AP subjects.

THE ESSENTIALS: A LAST-MINUTE STUDY GUIDE

It's one night before the AP Calculus Exam, and you're just opening this book now. Panic time, right? Not so fast. If you've been studying calculus all year, then you're already well prepared. All you need now is to settle your nerves, review a few key ideas to refresh your mind, and line everything up for test day. We'll help you make the most of the precious hours you have available before the test, and we promise to have you in bed at a reasonable hour—you'll need your beauty sleep tonight.

You don't have much time, so you'll want to make the most of the time you have. That means turning off distractions and getting focused. Turn off your cell phone, TV, and any music you can sing along to. Ask your family not to bother you unless it's really important, and then close the door. If you get distracted by the Internet and instant messaging, turn off those programs. In other words, do whatever you need to focus like a laser on AP Calculus for the next few hours.

Getting Started

You won't be able to review everything the night before the test, so here's your crash course:

- Start by reviewing the 20 Problems You Need to Solve in the next section. If you find any areas that you really need to review, read over that topic in the Review section and do the sample problems at the end.

- Review the test-taking strategies on page 31.

- If you still have time, take the practice test at the end of the book. Time yourself strictly to simulate an actual test, and practice using the test-taking strategies as you work.

- Go over the checklist for test day, making sure you have all your materials ready.

- Go to bed and get a good night's sleep.

Now let's start maximizing your score!

20 Problems You Must Be Able to Solve

Thnere are certain questions that show up on almost every AP exam, whether in the free response sections or in the multiple choice sections. They represent the essential skill set, the big ideas you must understand. These twenty questions review the fundamental tasks you'll need to perform if you want to score well on the AP exam.

1. Area of the Region Between Two Curves

Let R be the region bounded by the graph of $f(x) = x^3 - x + 1$ and $g(x) = 2 - x^2$. Find the area of the region R.

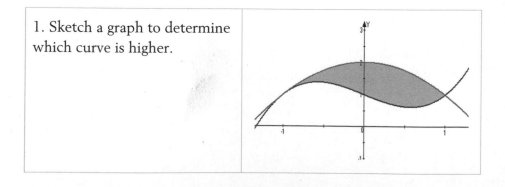

1. Sketch a graph to determine which curve is higher.

2. Find points of intersection or other limits of integration.	$x^3 - x + 1 = 2 - x^2$ $x^3 + x^2 - x - 1 = 0$ $x^2(x+1) - 1(x+1) = 0$ $(x^2 - 1)(x+1) = 0$ $x = \pm 1$
3. Set up the integral $$\int_a^b [g(x) - f(x)]dx$$	$$\int_{-1}^{1} [(2 - x^2) - (x^3 - x + 1)]dx$$
4. Simplify, if possible.	$$= \int_{-1}^{1} [1 + x - x^2 - x^3]dx$$
5. Find the antiderivative.	$$= x + \frac{x^2}{2} - \frac{x^3}{3} - \frac{x^4}{4} \Big|_{-1}^{1}$$
6. Evaluate.	$$= \left(1 + \frac{1}{2} - \frac{1}{3} - \frac{1}{4}\right) - \left(-1 + \frac{1}{2} + \frac{1}{3} - \frac{1}{4}\right)$$ $$= \left(\frac{11}{12}\right) - \left(-\frac{5}{12}\right) = \frac{16}{12} = \frac{4}{3}$$

2. Area in Polar Form

Let R be the shaded region inside the graph of $r = 5\sin\theta$ but outside the graph of $r = 2 + \sin\theta$. Find the area of R.

1. Sketch a graph.	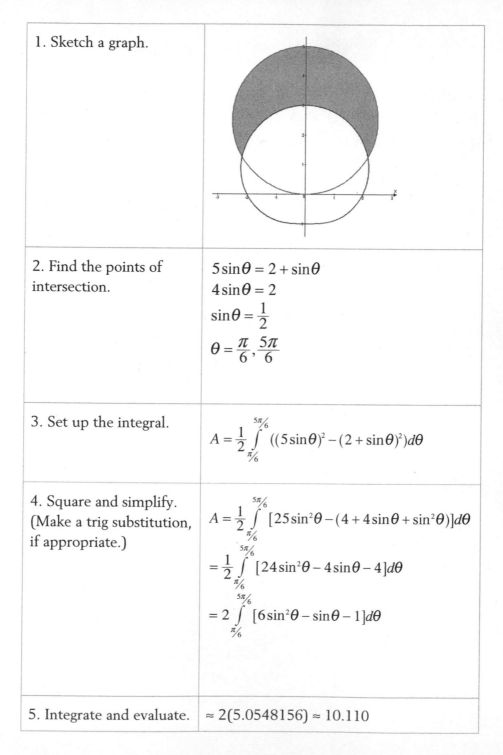
2. Find the points of intersection.	$5\sin\theta = 2 + \sin\theta$ $4\sin\theta = 2$ $\sin\theta = \dfrac{1}{2}$ $\theta = \dfrac{\pi}{6}, \dfrac{5\pi}{6}$
3. Set up the integral.	$A = \dfrac{1}{2}\displaystyle\int_{\pi/6}^{5\pi/6} ((5\sin\theta)^2 - (2+\sin\theta)^2)d\theta$
4. Square and simplify. (Make a trig substitution, if appropriate.)	$A = \dfrac{1}{2}\displaystyle\int_{\pi/6}^{5\pi/6} [25\sin^2\theta - (4 + 4\sin\theta + \sin^2\theta)]d\theta$ $= \dfrac{1}{2}\displaystyle\int_{\pi/6}^{5\pi/6} [24\sin^2\theta - 4\sin\theta - 4]d\theta$ $= 2\displaystyle\int_{\pi/6}^{5\pi/6} [6\sin^2\theta - \sin\theta - 1]d\theta$
5. Integrate and evaluate.	$\approx 2(5.0548156) \approx 10.110$

3. Volume of Solid of Revolution

Let R be the region in the first quadrant enclosed bounded by the graphs of $y = \frac{2}{x}$, $y = \sqrt{x+3}$, and $x = 3$. Find the volume of the solid generated when R is rotated a) about the x-axis and b) about the y-axis.

a) To find the volume when the region is rotated about the x-axis:

1. Sketch a graph.	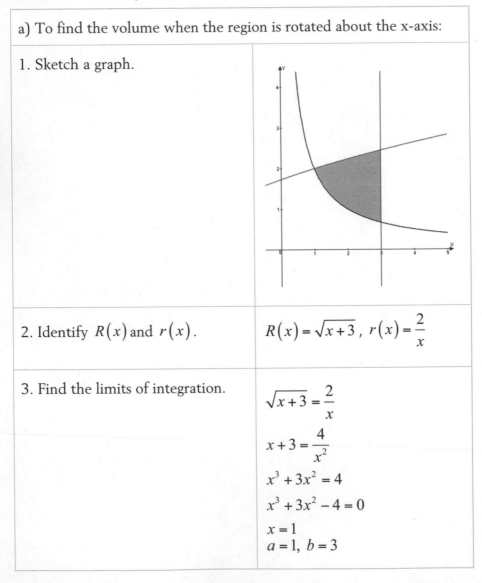
2. Identify $R(x)$ and $r(x)$.	$R(x) = \sqrt{x+3}$, $r(x) = \dfrac{2}{x}$
3. Find the limits of integration.	$\sqrt{x+3} = \dfrac{2}{x}$ $x+3 = \dfrac{4}{x^2}$ $x^3 + 3x^2 = 4$ $x^3 + 3x^2 - 4 = 0$ $x = 1$ $a = 1,\ b = 3$

4. Set up the integral. $\int_{a}^{b} (\pi R(x)^2 - \pi r(x)^2)\,dx$	$\pi \int_{1}^{3} \left(x + 3 - \frac{4}{x^2} \right) dx$
5. Find the antiderivative.	$= \pi \left[\frac{x^2}{2} + 3x + \frac{4}{x} \right]_{1}^{3}$
6. Evaluate.	$= \pi \left(\frac{9}{2} + 9 + \frac{4}{3} \right) - \pi \left(\frac{1}{2} + 3 + \frac{4}{1} \right)$ $= \frac{89\pi}{6} - \frac{15\pi}{2}$ $= \frac{22\pi}{3}$

b) To find the volume when the region is rotated about the y-axis:

1. Sketch a graph.	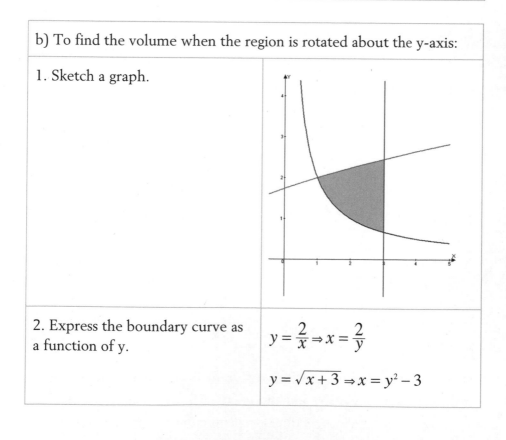
2. Express the boundary curve as a function of y.	$y = \frac{2}{x} \Rightarrow x = \frac{2}{y}$ $y = \sqrt{x+3} \Rightarrow x = y^2 - 3$

3. Find the limits of integration.	The shape of the region requires that the volume be found in two parts. The three intersection points are $(3, \frac{2}{3})$, $(1, 2)$, and $(3, \sqrt{6})$. The first integral will be from $y = \frac{2}{3}$ to $y = 2$, and the second from $y = 2$ to $y = \sqrt{6}$.
4. Express r (and, if necessary, R) as functions of y.	From $y = \frac{2}{3}$ to $y = 2$, $$R(y) = 3 \text{ and } r(y) = \frac{2}{y}.$$ From $y = 2$ to $y = \sqrt{6}$, $$R(y) = 3 \text{ and } r(y) = y^2 - 3.$$
5. Integrate with respect to y.	$$\pi \int_{2/3}^{2} \left(9 - \frac{4}{y^2}\right) dy + \pi \int_{2}^{\sqrt{6}} (-y^4 + 6y^2) dy$$ $$= \pi \left[9y + \frac{4}{y}\right]_{2/3}^{2} + \pi \left[-\frac{y^5}{5} + 2y^3\right]_{2}^{\sqrt{6}}$$
6. Evaluate.	$$= 8\pi + \left(\frac{24}{5}\sqrt{6} - \frac{48}{5}\right)\pi$$ $$\approx 31.911$$

4. Volume by Cross Sections

Let R be the region in the first quadrant bounded by the graphs of $y = 2\cos x$, $y = 1 + 3\cos x$, and the y-axis. The region R is the base of a solid with square cross sections perpendicular to the x-axis. Find the volume of the solid.

1. Sketch a graph.	
2. Determine the limits of integration.	$2\cos x = 1 + 3\cos x$ $\cos x = -1$ $x = \pi$ The limits of integration are 0 and pi.
3. Express the critical dimension of the cross section in terms of the boundary functions.	The side of the square cross sections will be $(1 + 3\cos x) - 2\cos x$ or $1 + \cos x$.
4. Express the area of the cross section.	$A = (1 + \cos x)^2$ $= 1 + 2\cos x + \cos^2 x$
5. Integrate the area from a to b.	$V = \int_0^\pi (1 + 2\cos x + \cos^2 x)\,dx$ $= \int_0^\pi \left(1 + 2\cos x + \dfrac{1 + \cos 2x}{2}\right)dx$ $= \dfrac{1}{2}\int_0^\pi (3 + 4\cos x + \cos 2x)\,dx$ $= \dfrac{1}{2}\left[3x + 4\sin x - \dfrac{1}{2}\sin 2x\right]\Big|_0^\pi$

6. Evaluate.	$= \dfrac{3\pi}{2}$

5. Particle Motion

A particle moves along the x-axis so that its velocity at time $0 \le t \le 5$ is given by $v(t) = \sin t + 2\cos t$. The position of the particle at time t is $x(t)$ and $x(0) = 1$.

a) Find the acceleration of the particle at time $t = 3$.

b) Find the total distance traveled by the particle from time $t = 0$ to $t = 3$.

c) Find the position of the particle at time $t = 3$

a) 1. Acceleration is the derivative of velocity.	$v(t) = \sin t + 2\cos t$ $a(t) = \cos t - 2\sin t$
2. Evaluate. (Remember: t is in radians!)	At $t = 3$, $a(3) = \cos(3) - 2\sin(3) \approx -1.272$

b) 1. Determine where particle changes direction.	$v(t) = \sin t + 2\cos t = 0$ $t \approx 2.034$
2. To find distance traveled, take the absolute value of the integral of velocity, evaluated between the changes in direction.	$\left\| \int_{0}^{2.034} (\sin t + 2\cos t)dt \right\| + \left\| \int_{2.034}^{3} (\sin t + 2\cos t)dt \right\|$ $= \left\| -\cos t + 2\sin t \,\big\|_{0}^{2.034} \right\| + \left\| -\cos t + 2\sin t \,\big\|_{2.034}^{3} \right\|$
3. Evaluate.	$\approx 3.236068 + 0.9638355$ ≈ 4.200

c) 1. The position of the particle is its initial position plus the displacement.	$x(3) = 1 + \int\limits_{0}^{3} (\sin t + 2\cos t)dt$ $= 1 + [-\cos t + 2\sin t]\big\|_{0}^{3}$
2. Evaluate.	$= 1 + [(-\cos 3 + 2\sin 3) + 1]$ ≈ 3.272

6. Particle Motion in Parametric or Vector Form

The position of a particle moving in the xy-plane at any time t, $0 \le t \le 2\pi$, is given by the parametric equations $x(t) = e^{t}$ and $y(t) = e^{2t} - 4e^{t} + 3$.
a) Find the velocity vector for the particle at any time t, and at the point $t = 0$
b) Write an equation for the path of the particle in terms of x and y.

a) 1. Velocity is the derivative of position.	$x(t) = e^{t} \Rightarrow x'(t) = e^{t}$ and $y(t) = e^{2t} - 4e^{t} + 3 \Rightarrow y'(t) = 2e^{2t} - 4e^{t}$. The velocity vector is $\langle e^{t}, 2e^{2t} - 4e^{t} \rangle$.
2. Evaluate.	At $t = 0$, the velocity is $\langle 1, -2 \rangle$.

b) 1. Solve $x(t)$ for t.	$x(t) = e^{t} \Rightarrow t = \ln x$
2. Substitute into $y(t)$.	$y(t) = e^{2t} - 4e^{t} + 3$ $y = e^{2\ln x} - 4e^{\ln x} + 3$
3. Simplify.	$y = x^{2} - 4x + 3$

7. Particle Motion in Polar Form

A particle moving with nonzero velocity along the polar curve given by $r(\theta) = 1 - 2\cos\theta$ has position $(x(t), y(t))$ at time t, with $\theta = 0$ when $t = 0$. This particle moves along the curve so that $\frac{dr}{dt} = \frac{dr}{d\theta}$.

a) Find the value of $\frac{dr}{dt}$ at $\theta = \frac{\pi}{2}$ and interpret your answer in terms of the motion of the particle.

b) Find the total distance traveled by the particle from $\theta = 0$ to $\theta = \pi$

a) 1. Differentiate $r(\theta)$ with respect to θ.	$r(\theta) = 1 - 2\cos\theta$ $\frac{dr}{d\theta} = 2\sin\theta$
2. Evaluate.	$\left.\frac{dr}{d\theta}\right|_{\theta=\frac{\pi}{2}} = 2\sin\frac{\pi}{2} = 2$
3. Interpret.	Since $\frac{dr}{dt} = \frac{dr}{d\theta}$, $\frac{dr}{dt} = 2$. At the time when $\theta = \frac{\pi}{2}$, r is increasing at 2 units per second. At the same moment, the position of the particle is $r\left(\frac{\pi}{2}\right) = 1 - 2\cos\frac{\pi}{2} = 1$. The particle is moving away from the origin.

b) Distance traveled is the integral of speed over time. In the case of a polar equation, the arc length is $L = \int \sqrt{r^2 + \left(\frac{dr}{d\theta}\right)^2}\, d\theta$.

1. Square r.	$(1-2\cos\theta)^2 = 1 - 4\cos\theta + 4\cos^2\theta$
2. Find $\dfrac{dr}{d\theta}$.	$\dfrac{dr}{d\theta} = 2\sin\theta$
3. Square $\dfrac{dr}{d\theta}$.	$(2\sin\theta)^2 = 4\sin^2\theta$
4. Simplify $r^2 + \left(\dfrac{dr}{d\theta}\right)^2$.	$1 - 4\cos\theta + 4\cos^2\theta + 4\sin^2\theta$ $1 - 4\cos\theta + 4$ $5 - 4\cos\theta$
5. Set up the integral.	$L = \displaystyle\int_0^\pi \sqrt{5 - 4\cos\theta}\, d\theta$
6. Integrate and evaluate.	≈ 6.682

8. Curve Sketching

Let f be a function defined on the closed interval $-3 \le x \le 3$ with $f(x) = \ln(x^2 - 2x + 6)$. Find all values of x in $[-3,3]$ at which

a) f has a relative minimum.

b) the graph of f has a point of inflection.

a) 1. The critical points occur when $f' = 0$ (or f' does not exist).	
2. Find the derivative.	$f(x) = \ln(x^2 - 2x + 6)$ $f'(x) = \dfrac{2x - 2}{x^2 - 2x + 6}$

3. Set the derivative equal to zero.	$f'(x) = \dfrac{2x-2}{x^2-2x+6} = 0$
4. Solve for x.	$2x-2 = 0$ $x = 1$
5. Use a first derivative test to determine whether the critical number is a minimum.	$f'(0) = \dfrac{-2}{6} = -\dfrac{1}{3}$ and $f'(2) = \dfrac{2}{6} = \dfrac{1}{3}$ Since the first derivative is negative for $x < 1$ and positive for $x > 1$, the function changes from decreasing to increasing at $x = 1$. The function has a minimum at $x = 1$.

b)
1. Points of inflection occur when $f'' = 0$ (or f'' does not exist).

2. Find the second derivative.	$f'(x) = \dfrac{2x-2}{x^2-2x+6}$ $f''(x) = \dfrac{2(x^2-2x+6)-(2x-2)^2}{(x^2-2x+6)^2}$ $f''(x) = \dfrac{-2(x^2-2x-4)}{(x^2-2x+6)^2}$
3. Set the second derivative equal to zero.	$f''(x) = \dfrac{-2(x^2-2x-4)}{(x^2-2x+6)^2} = 0$

4. Solve for x.	$-2\left(x^2 - 2x - 4\right) = 0$ $x = \dfrac{2 \pm \sqrt{20}}{2} = \dfrac{2 \pm 2\sqrt{5}}{2} = 1 \pm \sqrt{5}$ $x \approx 3.236$ or $x \approx -1.236$ Only $x \approx -1.236$ is in the stated interval.
5. Test f'' on both sides to verify a change in concavity.	$f''(-2) = \dfrac{-8}{14^2}$ and $f''(0) = \dfrac{8}{6^2}$ The second derivative changes from negative to positive at $x \approx -1.236$, indicating that the function changes from concave down to concave up. The function has a point of inflection at $x \approx -1.236$.

9. Linear Approximation

The volume of a spherical balloon changes as air is pumped into the balloon and released from the balloon. The radius of the balloon, in centimeters, is modeled by a twice-differentiable function $r(t) = -t^2 + 4t - 1$, where t is measured in seconds, over the time interval $0 \le t \le 5$. Estimate the volume of the balloon at $t = 3.1$ seconds using the tangent line approximation at $t = 3$ seconds. Note that the volume of a sphere of radius r is given by $V = \dfrac{4}{3}\pi r^3$.

1. Find the derivative.	$V(t) = \dfrac{4}{3}\pi [r(t)]^3$ $\dfrac{dV}{dt} = 4\pi [r(t)]^2 \dfrac{dr}{dt}$ $\dfrac{dV}{dt} = 4\pi (-t^2 + 4t - 1)^2 (-2t + 4)$

2. Find the slope of the tangent.	$\dfrac{dV}{dt}\Big|_{t=3} = 4\pi(-9+12-1)^2(-6+4)$ $= 4\pi(2)^2(-2) = -32\pi$
3. Find the equation of the tangent line.	$y - \dfrac{32\pi}{3} = 32\pi(t-3)$
4. Use the tangent to approximate the function.	$y - \dfrac{32\pi}{3} = -32\pi(3.1-3)$ $y = \dfrac{32\pi}{3} - 32\pi(0.1)$ $y \approx 23.457$

10. Graphical Analysis

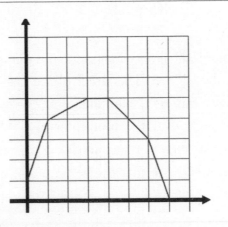

The graph of the function f shown consists of 5 line segments. Let g be the function given by $g(x) = \int_0^x f(t)\,dt$. Find $g(5)$, $g'(5)$, and $g''(5)$.

1. If $g(x) = \int_0^x f(t)\,dt$, then $g'(x) = f(x)$.

2. $g(5)$ can be found by the area under the curve.	$A = \frac{1}{2}(1)(1+4) + \frac{1}{2}(2)(4+5) + 5 + \frac{1}{2}(1)(5+4)$ $= \frac{5}{2} + 9 + 5 + \frac{9}{2} = 21$
3. $g'(5)$ is the value of the derivative of g at $x = 5$, which is $f(5)$.	The point (5, 4) is on the graph of f, so $g'(5) = 4$.
4. $g''(5)$ is the slope of the graph of $g'(x)$ at $x = 5$, or the slope of $f(x)$ at $x = 5$.	From the graph, $g''(5) = \frac{-2}{2} = -1$.

11. Analysis of Data

A projectile is launched from an initial height of 0 meters at time $t = 0$ seconds. The velocity of the projectile is recorded at intervals over the first minute of its flight, and the data is shown in the table.

t	0	10	20	27	34	40	46	53	60
$v(t)$	13	16	17	19	22	24	27	31	35

a) Find the average acceleration of the projectile over the first minute (60 seconds) and indicate units of measure.

b) Use a midpoint Riemann sum with 4 subintervals to approximate $\int_0^{60} v(t)dt$. Using correct units, explain the meaning of $\int_0^{60} v(t)dt$ in terms of the flight of the projectile.

a) Average acceleration is change in velocity over time.	$\dfrac{v(60)-v(0)}{60-0} = \dfrac{35-13}{60} = \dfrac{22}{60} = \dfrac{11}{30}$ meters per second
b) 1. Use 4 subintervals. #1 $\Delta t = 20$, midpoint value $= 16$ #2 $\Delta t = 14$, midpoint value $= 19$ #3 $\Delta t = 12$, midpoint value $= 24$ #4 $\Delta t = 14$, midpoint value $= 31$	$\displaystyle\int_{0}^{60} v(t)dt = 20\cdot 16 + 14\cdot 19 + 12\cdot 24 + 14\cdot 31$ $= 320 + 266 + 288 + 434$ $= 1308$ meters
2. The integral of velocity is distance.	$\displaystyle\int_{0}^{60} v(t)dt$ represents the total distance traveled by the projectile over the first 60 seconds, in meters.

12. Differential Equations

Consider the differential equation $\dfrac{dy}{dx} = 2xy$. Sketch a slope field for the given differential equation at the points indicated and find the particular solution $y = f(x)$ to the differential equation with the initial condition $f(0) = 3$.

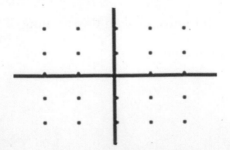

1. Evaluate $\dfrac{dy}{dx}$ for each point in the region.

x \ y	-2	-1	0	1	2
-2	8	4	0	-4	-8
-1	4	2	0	-2	-4
0	0	0	0	0	0
1	-4	-2	0	2	4
2	-8	-4	0	4	8

2. Sketch the slopes at each point.

3. Manipulate the equation algebraically so that each side of the equation contains only one variable.

$$\frac{dy}{dx} = 2xy$$

$$dy = 2xy\,dx$$

$$\frac{dy}{y} = 2x\,dx$$

4. Integrate each side of the equation. Add a constant of integration to complete the general equation.

$$\ln|y| = x^2 + C$$

$$y = e^{x^2 + C}$$

$$y = e^{x^2} \cdot e^C$$

$$y = Ce^{x^2}$$

5. If an initial condition is given, substitute for each of the variables.	$f(0) = 3$ $3 = Ce^0$
6. Solve for C.	$C = 3$
7. Write the particular equation.	$y = 3e^{x^2}$

---

13. Exponential Growth

Oil is being pumped continuously from a certain oil well at a rate proportional to the amount of oil left in the well; that is, $\dfrac{dy}{dt} = ky$, where y is the amount of oil left in the well at any time t. Initially there were 3,500,000 gallons of oil in the well, and 5 years later there were 750,000 gallons remaining. Write an equation for y, the amount of oil remaining in the well at any time t.

1. The rate at which oil is being pumped is $\dfrac{dy}{dt} = ky$. To find an equation for y, the amount of oil remaining in the well, solve the differential equation.	
2. Separate the variables.	$\dfrac{dy}{dt} = ky$ $\dfrac{dy}{y} = kdt$
3. Integrate both sides. Don't forget the C.	$\ln\lvert y\rvert = kt + C$

4. Convert to exponential form.	$\ln\lvert y \rvert = kt + C$ $y = e^{kt+C}$ $y = e^{kt} \cdot e^{C}$ $y = Ce^{kt}$
5. Use the initial condition to solve for C.	$3,500,000 = Ce^{0}$ $C = 3,500,000$
6. Use the additional information to solve for k.	$750,000 = 3,500,000e^{5k}$ $e^{5k} = \dfrac{3}{14}$ $5k = \ln\left(\dfrac{3}{14}\right)$ $k = \dfrac{1}{5}\ln\left(\dfrac{3}{14}\right) \approx -0.308$
7. Write the particular equation.	$y = 3,500,000e^{-0.308t}$

14. Riemann Sums and Trapezoidal Rule

A train travels along a straight track with positive velocity $v(t)$, in miles per hour. Selected values of $v(t)$ are shown in the table.

t	0	0.5	1	1.5	2	2.5	3
$v(t)$	0	25	45	60	80	55	60

a) Use a right-hand Riemann sum with 3 subintervals of equal length and values from the table to approximate $\int_0^3 v(t)dt$. Show the computations that lead to your answer. Using correct units, explain the meaning of $\int_0^3 v(t)dt$ in terms of the train's travel.

b) Use the Trapezoidal Rule to approximate $\int_0^3 v(t)dt$. Show the computation that leads to your answer.

a) 1. Divide the interval into 3 subintervals of equal size.	Each subinterval will be 1 hour long.
2. Use the right-hand value of $v(t)$, that is, the value of v for the highest value of t in the subinterval.	$\int_0^3 v(t)dt = 1\cdot 45 + 1\cdot 80 + 1\cdot 60 = 185$ miles is the approximate distance traveled by the train in the first 3 hours.

b) The trapezoidal rule approximates $\int_0^3 v(t)dt$ by the area of a collection of trapezoids. $A_{trapezoid} = \frac{1}{2}h(b_1 + b_2)$. Since the trapezoids share sides, the sum becomes $\frac{1}{2}\Delta x\left[v_0 + 2v_1 + 2v_2 + 2v_3 + 2v_4 + 2v_5 + v_6\right]$.

1. The height of each trapezoid is Δx.	
	$\Delta x = 0.5$ for all the trapezoids.
2. The bases of the trapezoids are adjacent values in the table.	
	0 & 25, 25 & 45, 45 & 60, 60 & 80, 80 & 55, 55& 60

3. Set up the sum.

$$\frac{1}{2}\Delta x[v(0)+2v(0.5)+2v(1)+2v(1.5)+2v(2)+2v(2.5)+v(3)]$$

4. Evaluate.

$$\frac{1}{2}\cdot\frac{1}{2}[0+2\cdot25+2\cdot45+2\cdot60+2\cdot80+2\cdot55+60]$$

$$\frac{1}{4}[50+90+120+160+110+60]$$

$$\frac{1}{4}[590]$$

147.5

5. The train traveled 147.5 miles.

15. Implicit Differentiation

Consider the curve in the xy-plane given by $x^3 + 3x^2 y - 6xy^2 + 2y^3 = 0$.
a) Find $\dfrac{dy}{dx}$.
b) Write an equation for the line tangent to the curve at the point $(1,1)$.

a) 1. Differentiate term by term. Remember that differentiating expressions involving y demands the chain rule.	$x^3 + 3x^2 y - 6xy^2 + 2y^3 = 0$ $3x^2 + \left(3x^2\dfrac{dy}{dx} + 6xy\right) - \left(6x\cdot 2y\dfrac{dy}{dx} + 6y^2\right) + 6y^2\dfrac{dy}{dx} = 0$

2. Move terms involving $\dfrac{dy}{dx}$ to one side, terms without to the other.	$3x^2 + \left(3x^2\dfrac{dy}{dx} + 6xy\right) - \left(6x \cdot 2y\dfrac{dy}{dx} + 6y^2\right) + 6y^2\dfrac{dy}{dx} = 0$ $3x^2 + 3x^2\dfrac{dy}{dx} + 6xy - 12xy\dfrac{dy}{dx} - 6y^2 + 6y^2\dfrac{dy}{dx} = 0$ $3x^2\dfrac{dy}{dx} - 12xy\dfrac{dy}{dx} + 6y^2\dfrac{dy}{dx} = 6y^2 - 6xy - 3x^2$
3. Factor out $\dfrac{dy}{dx}$.	$3x^2\dfrac{dy}{dx} - 12xy\dfrac{dy}{dx} + 6y^2\dfrac{dy}{dx} = 6y^2 - 6xy - 3x^2$ $\dfrac{dy}{dx}\left(3x^2 - 12xy + 6y^2\right) = 6y^2 - 6xy - 3x^2$
4. Solve for $\dfrac{dy}{dx}$.	$\dfrac{dy}{dx}\left(3x^2 - 12xy + 6y^2\right) = 6y^2 - 6xy - 3x^2$ $\dfrac{dy}{dx} = \dfrac{6y^2 - 6xy - 3x^2}{3x^2 - 12xy + 6y^2}$ $\dfrac{dy}{dx} = \dfrac{2y^2 - 2xy - x^2}{x^2 - 4xy + 2y^2}$

16. Average Value

The radius of a circle is changing over time so that the length of the radius, in centimeters, is given by the function $r(t) = 12 - \dfrac{3}{t^2}$ for $t > 0$. Find the average value of the radius over the time interval $1 \le t \le 5$.

The average value over $a \le t \le b$ is $f_{avg} = \dfrac{1}{b-a}\displaystyle\int_a^b f(x)\,dx$.

1. Set up the integral.	$\dfrac{1}{5-1}\displaystyle\int_{1}^{5}\left(12-\dfrac{3}{t^2}\right)dt$
2. Find the antiderivative.	$=\dfrac{1}{4}\left[12t+\dfrac{3}{t}\right]_{1}^{5}$
3. Evaluate.	$=\dfrac{1}{4}\left[60.6-15\right]=11.4$

The average value of the radius is 11.4 cm.

17. Related Rates

The radius r of a sphere is increasing at a constant rate of 0.30 centimeters per second. At the time when the radius of the sphere is 5 centimeters, what is the rate of increase of its volume? $\left(V=\dfrac{4}{3}\pi r^3\right)$

1. Identify changing parameters.	The volume and the radius are changing.
2. Identify known rates of change.	The radius is changing at 0.30 cm/sec.
3. Identify moment of interest.	Time at which $r=5$ cm
4. Write an equation that connects changing quantities.	$V=\dfrac{4}{3}\pi r^3$
5. Differentiate with respect to t.	$\dfrac{dV}{dt}=4\pi r^2\dfrac{dr}{dt}$

6. Freeze motion and plug in all known quantities and rates of change.	$\dfrac{dV}{dt} = 4\pi(5)^2(0.30)$
7. Solve for the remaining unknown.	$\dfrac{dV}{dt} = 30\pi$ At the moment that the radius is 5 cm, the volume is changing at 30π cm³/sec.

18. Taylor Series and Error Bounds

Find the first four nonzero terms in the Taylor series expansion about $x = 0$ for $f(x) = \sqrt{1-x}$. Use the Lagrange error bound to show the error of approximation at $x = 0.05$.

1. Take derivatives.	$f(x) = \sqrt{1-x}$ $f'(x) = -\dfrac{1}{2\sqrt{1-x}}$ $f''(x) = -\dfrac{1}{4(1-x)^{\frac{3}{2}}}$ $f'''(x) = -\dfrac{3}{8(1-x)^{\frac{5}{2}}}$
2. Evaluate at $x = 0$.	$f(0) = 1$ $f'(0) = -\dfrac{1}{2}$ $f''(0) = -\dfrac{1}{4}$ $f'''(0) = -\dfrac{3}{8}$

3. Form the Taylor polynomial.	$f(x) \approx 1 - \dfrac{1}{2}x - \dfrac{\frac{1}{4}}{2!}x^2 - \dfrac{\frac{3}{8}}{3!}x^3$ $f(x) \approx 1 - \dfrac{1}{2}x - \dfrac{1}{8}x^2 - \dfrac{1}{16}x^3$

Find the next derivative.	$f'''(x) = -\dfrac{3}{8(1-x)^{\frac{5}{2}}}$ $f^{(4)} = -\dfrac{15}{16(1-x)^{\frac{7}{2}}}$
$\left\| \dfrac{f^{n+1}(c)(x-a)^{n+1}}{(n+1)!} \right\|$	$\left\| \dfrac{\dfrac{-15}{16(1-c)^{\frac{7}{2}}} \cdot x^4}{24} \right\|$ for some c in the interval $0 \le x \le 0.05$
Evaluate at $x = 0$.	$\left\| \dfrac{\dfrac{-15}{16(1-x)^{\frac{7}{2}}} \cdot x^4}{24} \right\| = \left\| \dfrac{\dfrac{-15}{16(1-0)^{\frac{7}{2}}} \cdot 0^4}{24} \right\| = 0$
Evaluate at $x = 0.05$.	$\left\| \dfrac{\dfrac{-15}{16(1-0.05)^{\frac{7}{2}}} (0.05)^4}{24} \right\| = \left\| \dfrac{\dfrac{-15}{16(0.95)^{\frac{7}{2}}} (0.05)^4}{24} \right\| \approx 2.040 \times 10^{-7}$
Maximum value is the error bound.	The error is less than or equal to 2.040×10^{-7}.

19. Series and Intervals of Convergence

The Maclaurin series for the function f is given by
$2x + \dfrac{2x^3}{3} + \dfrac{2x^5}{5} + \dfrac{2x^7}{7} + ... + \dfrac{2x^{2n-1}}{2n-1} + ...$ on its interval of convergence.

a) Find the interval of convergence of the Maclaurin series for f.

b) Find the first four terms and the general term for the Maclaurin series for f'.

a) 1. Find the ratio of successive terms.	$\dfrac{\dfrac{2x^{2n+1}}{2n+1}}{\dfrac{2x^{2n-1}}{2n-1}} = \dfrac{2x^{2n+1}}{2n+1} \cdot \dfrac{2n-1}{2x^{2n-1}} = \dfrac{(2n-1)x}{2n+1} = \left(\dfrac{2n-1}{2n+1}\right)x$
2. Find the limit as $n \to \infty$. $n \to \infty$.	$\left(\dfrac{2n-1}{2n+1}\right)x \to (1)x = x$
3. The series converges when $|x| < 1$.	$-1 < x < 1$
4. Test the end points.	When $x = -1$, $\dfrac{2(-1)^{2n-1}}{2n-1} = \dfrac{-2}{2n-1} \to 0$ as n becomes large. When $x = 1$, $\dfrac{2(1)^{2n-1}}{2n-1} = \dfrac{2}{2n-1} \to 0$ as n becomes large.

5. Series converges on the closed interval $[-1,1]$.

b) The Maclaurin series for f on the interval $[-1,1]$ is

$2x + \dfrac{2x^3}{3} + \dfrac{2x^5}{5} + \dfrac{2x^7}{7} + ... + \dfrac{2x^{2n-1}}{2n-1} + ...$

1. Differentiate term by term to find the Maclaurin series for f'.	$2x + \dfrac{2x^3}{3} + \dfrac{2x^5}{5} + \dfrac{2x^7}{7} + \ldots + \dfrac{2x^{2n-1}}{2n-1} + \ldots$ $2 + 2x^2 + 2x^4 + 2x^6 + \ldots + 2x^{2n-2} + \ldots$
2. Check the end points.	When $x = -1$, $2x^{2n-2} = 2$ as n becomes large. When $x = 1$, $2x^{2n-2} = 2$ as n becomes large.
3. Series converges on the open interval $(-1,1)$.	

20. Critical Theorems

Let f be a twice-differentiable function such that $f(a) = b+1$ and $f(b) = a+1$. Let g be the function defined by $g(x) = f(f(x)-1)$.

a) Explain why there must be a value c for $a < c < b$ such that $f'(c) = -1$.

b) Show that $g'(a) = g'(b)$. Use this result to explain why there must be a value k for $a < k < b$ such that $g''(k) = 0$.

a) 1. f is differentiable.	Therefore, f is continuous.
2. By the Mean Value Theorem, there is a value c between a and b such that $f'(c) = \dfrac{f(b)-f(a)}{b-a}$.	$f'(c) = \dfrac{f(b)-f(a)}{b-a}$ $= \dfrac{(a+1)-(b+1)}{b-a} = \dfrac{a-b}{b-a} = -1$

b) 1. Use the chain rule.	$g(x) = f(f(x)-1)$ $g'(x) = f'(f(x)-1)\dfrac{d[f(x)-1]}{dx}$ $= f'(f(x)-1) \cdot f'(x).$
2. Evaluate at a.	$g'(a) = f'(f(a)-1) \cdot f'(a) = f'(b) \cdot f'(a)$
3. Evaluate at b.	$g'(b) = f'(f(b)-1) \cdot f'(b) = f'(a) \cdot f'(b).$
4. Therefore, $g'(a) = g'(b).$	
5. Rolle's Theorem says that if $f(x)$ is continuous and $f(a) = f(b)$, then there is a value c between a and b such that $f'(c) = 0$.	$g'(a) = g'(b)$, therefore there is a value k between a and b such that $g''(k) = 0$.

Strategies for Maximizing Your Score

The best strategy for scoring well on the AP Calculus Exam is a simple one: know the math. However, even if you know your math inside and out, you probably won't answer every question correctly. There are simply too many questions and too little time. Here are some strategies for solving the problems you can—and increasing your odds for the problems you can't solve.

First, Answer What You Know

You'll have to attack the multiple choice questions in two sections: first, a group of questions done without a calculator and then another section with a calculator. For each section, plan to scan the test quickly for the questions you immediately know how to answer, and get those done first.

You don't score any bonus for answering a difficult question, and unlike some tests, you're not guaranteed that the most difficult questions, or even the most time-consuming ones, are at the end. If you're a typical calculus student, a tangent line problem will take you a lot less time and effort than a series problem, but both questions earn the same number of points. Move through the section at a steady pace, reading each question and answering the ones you can answer comfortably.

Circle Items for Later

Circle the items you've skipped on the test, so you can quickly come back to them. Make sure you skip the item on your answer sheet too, so that you continue answering the right questions. Keep an eye out for information later in the test that can help you solve the problems you've skipped.

Solve What You Can

After you've racked up all the points you can with the easy problems, start to tackle the more time-consuming ones. Look for ways of keeping the problem simple and avoiding extra work. (For more strategies on how to do this, turn to page 249.)

If All Else Fails, Take a Guess

Starting in 2011, the College Board changed its rules for AP tests. There's no longer any penalty for getting the wrong answer. So it's worthwhile to guess, even if you have no idea of the answer. Of course, you'll greatly increase your odds if you can start eliminating the answer choices you know, or suspect, are wrong. In the next section, you'll learn a few ways of narrowing your choices.

How to Guess

1. Eliminate the Impossible

If you don't know how to do the problem, how to you eliminate answer choices? Details in the question may help.

What are the coordinates of the inflection point on the graph of $y = \arctan x$?

A. $(-1,0)$ B. $(0,0)$ C. $(0,1)$ D. $\left(1,\frac{\pi}{4}\right)$ E. $\left(1,\frac{\pi}{2}\right)$

You knew you should have memorized the derivatives of the inverse trig functions, but it's too late now. You need to guess, so how do you narrow your choices?

The inflection point is "on the graph of $y = \arctan x$," and $y = \arctan x$ is a function. It's not possible that both $(0,0)$ and $(0,1)$ are on the graph, or that both $\left(1, \frac{\pi}{4}\right)$ and $\left(1, \frac{\pi}{2}\right)$ are on the graph, so eliminate C $(0,1)$ because $\arctan(0) = 0$ and E $\left(1, \frac{\pi}{2}\right)$ because $\arctan(1) = \frac{\pi}{4}$. Neither C not E is on the graph of $y = \arctan x$. When you're down to three choices, you could take a guess. If you have an idea what the graph of $y = \arctan x$ looks like, and what "inflection point" means, you should be able to choose B $(0,0)$ as the correct answer. A memory of the graph of a function can help you eliminate the impossible in this question as well.

The equation for a tangent to the graph of $y = \arcsin \dfrac{x}{3}$ at the origin is

A. $x - 3y = 0$ B. $x - y = 0$ C. $x = 0$ D. $y = 0$ E. $\pi x - y = 0$

You should notice that C $(x = 0)$ is a vertical line and D $(y = 0)$ is a horizontal line. A vertical tangent would mean that the function is not differentiable, and a horizontal tangent would indicate a turning point. If you remember the graph of the inverse sine function, you'll realize that both of these can be eliminated. With three choices remaining, you can risk a guess. A further look at the remaining options will show you that they differ only in slope, and the fact that you're looking at $y = \arcsin \dfrac{x}{3}$, which has a derivative of $\dfrac{1}{3}$, should give you the hint that A $(x - 3y = 0)$ is the right choice.

2. Play What-If

The common advice for guessing on standardized tests includes plugging possible answers back into the problem. The danger in that strategy, for any test, is that it can be time-consuming, and on the AP exam, there really aren't many questions where you can just "plug in." There are some, however, where you can make a guess by exploring what would happen under certain assumptions or choices.

If $f(x) = \begin{cases} \dfrac{\sqrt{2x+5} - \sqrt{x+8}}{x-3} & \text{for } x \neq 3 \\ k & \text{for } x = 3 \end{cases}$ and if f is continuous at x = 3,

then k =

A. 0   B. $\dfrac{\sqrt{11}}{22}$ C. $\sqrt{11}$ D. 1   E. $\dfrac{11}{2}$

The question is asking you to plug the hole in the graph of $y = \dfrac{\sqrt{2x+5} - \sqrt{x+8}}{x-3}$. It's about rationalizing the numerator, limits, and the definition of continuity, but it boils down to finding that hole. Look at what happens near $x = 3$. When $x = 2$, $f(2) = \sqrt{10} - \sqrt{9}$. When $x = 4$, $f(4) = \sqrt{13} - \sqrt{12}$. Both of these are small positive values, which suggests that you can eliminate C ($\sqrt{11}$), D (1) and E ($\dfrac{11}{2}$) as too big. If you can estimate the values of $\sqrt{10} - \sqrt{9}$ and $\sqrt{13} - \sqrt{12}$, you'll find that B ($\dfrac{\sqrt{11}}{22}$) looks like the best choice.

Now and then you will find a question for which plugging the answers back in will at least narrow your choices. In the question below, evaluating v for each of the four numerical answer choices will tell you which gives you the lowest velocity. Then you can decide between that value and the no minimum option by thinking about the shape of the graph of v. The correct answer is D.

A point moves on the x-axis in such a way that its velocity at time t $(t > 0)$ is given by $v = t \ln t$. At what value of t does v attain its minimum?

A. 1   B. e^2 C. e D. e^{-1} E. There is no minimum value for v.

3. Set Up the Problem

Some free response questions will say "set up but do not integrate." Some multiple choice questions will ask which expression or equation you would use to solve a problem, rather than asking for the answer. On many other multiple choice questions, however, setting up, and then pausing to consider the consequences of that setup, can save you some work. You can often eliminate several answer choices just by setting up the problem and thinking ahead to the kind of answer it will produce. For example, look at this question:

The volume of the solid formed when the area enclosed by $f(x) = 1 - \dfrac{1}{2}x$ and $g(x) = e^{-2x}$ between $x = 0$ and $x = 1$, is revolved about the x-axis is

A. $2\pi\left(\dfrac{1}{4} + \dfrac{1}{2}e^{-2}\right)$ B. $\pi\left(\dfrac{5}{6} + \dfrac{1}{4}e^{-4}\right)$ C. $\pi\left(-\dfrac{1}{3} - \dfrac{1}{4}e^{-4}\right)$

D. $\pi\left(\dfrac{1}{3} + \dfrac{1}{4}e^{-4}\right)$ E. $\pi\left(\dfrac{1}{12} - \dfrac{1}{4}e^{-4} + \dfrac{1}{4}e^{-2}\right)$

Set up the integral that will produce the volume: $\pi \displaystyle\int_0^1 \left(1 - \dfrac{1}{2}x\right)^2 - (e^{-2x})^2 \, dx$. Then stop and realize that your answer is going to involve $\displaystyle\int_0^1 e^{-4x} \, dx$. Even if you don't have the integral quite right, if you've remembered that $A = \pi r^2$, you're going to have e^{-4x}

to evaluate somewhere in your result. When $x = 1$, $e^{-4x} = e^{-4}$, and when $x = 0$, $e^{-4x} = 1$. That should let you eliminate choices A and E. Why would your answer have an e^{-2}?

Examine the remaining choices, and notice that C is the opposite of D, that is, $\pi\left(-\frac{1}{3} - \frac{1}{4}e^{-4}\right) = (-1)\pi\left(\frac{1}{3} + \frac{1}{4}e^{-4}\right)$. Did you sketch the graph to make sure you've designated inner and outer radii correctly?

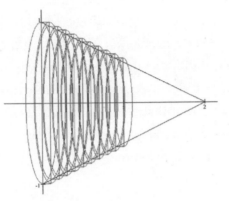

You should be down to two answer choices now, and that sketch can help you make a guess, if you must. The value of $\frac{1}{4}e^{-4}$ is small, so you're basically choosing between $\frac{5}{6}\pi$ and $\frac{1}{3}\pi$. $\pi\int_{0}^{1}\left(1 - \frac{1}{2}x\right)^2 dx$ would give you the volume of the frustum of a cone. That cone would have a volume of $\frac{2}{3}\pi$, so the volume of the frustum will be less than $\frac{2}{3}\pi$, which means definitely less than $\frac{5}{6}\pi$. Only one answer left!

4. Draw a Picture

Sketching a graph of the function in the question can often help you narrow the choices.

If $f(x) = \dfrac{x+1}{x-1}$ for all $x \neq 1$, then $f'(-1) =$

A. -1 B. $-\dfrac{1}{2}$ C. 0   D. $\dfrac{1}{2}$ E. 1

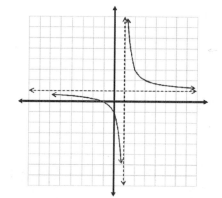

A quick sketch of the graph of $f(x) = \dfrac{x+1}{x-1}$ will allow you to conclude that the function is decreasing everywhere, so the derivative must be negative. That allows you to eliminate choices C, D, and E, and may help you choose between the remaining options. The correct answer is B.

Even a question that doesn't specify a particular function may be easier to answer if you create a sketch.

Suppose that f is an even function; that is, $f(-x) = f(x)$ for all x, and suppose that $f'(a)$ exists. Which of the following must necessarily be equal to $f'(-a)$?

A. $f'(a)$ B. $-f'(a)$ C. $\dfrac{1}{f'(a)}$ D. $\dfrac{-1}{f'(a)}$ E. None of the above

Sketch your favorite even function; $f(x) = x^2$ will work just fine. Use the symmetry of the function to help you realize that slopes of tangents on one side of the y-axis will be positive and those on the other side will be negative. That will eliminate choices A and C. Whatever even function you choose, it will give you a practical way to test the remaining answers, and determine that the correct answer is B.

6. Ask Why

Part of guessing success is learning to think like a test writer, and one way to learn that is to look at a question and ask why similar answer choices were included.

$\ln(x-5) < 0$ if and only if

A. $x < 5$ B. $0 < x < 5$ C. $5 < x < 6$ D. $x > 5$ E. $x < 6$

If you're guessing at this question, you probably won't find the appearance of 5 in the answer choices surprising. The presence of $x-5$ in the stem suggests 5 could be a significant number, even if you don't know exactly why. Five shows up in four answer choices, each a little different. Why are they different? How are those differences significant? And where did 6 come from?

Once you're asking those questions, you can start testing numbers to eliminate some answer choices. Log functions are only defined when the argument is greater than zero, so x must be greater than five. That lets you choose between answer choices C and D. Testing numbers will show you that when $5 < x < 6$, $\ln(x - 5) < 0$.

In the question below, you might ask why some answer choices are so much simpler than others, but even before you get to the choices, you should wonder why the stem involves both a natural log and e to a power. Simplify that expression, and the problem becomes much simpler. $f(x) = \ln e^{3x-1} = 3x - 1$ and $f'(x) = 3$.

If $f(x) = \ln e^{3x-1}$, then $f'(x) =$

A. $\dfrac{1}{e^{3x-1}}$ B. $\dfrac{3}{e^{3x-1}}$ C. $\dfrac{3x-1}{e^{3x-1}}$ D. $3x-1$ E. 3

7. Beware of Absolutes

A quick scan of the answer choices for this question should make you suspicious.

For what values of x does the series $1 + \left(\dfrac{1}{2}\right)^x + \left(\dfrac{1}{3}\right)^x + \left(\dfrac{1}{4}\right)^x + \ldots + \left(\dfrac{1}{n}\right)^x + \ldots$ converge?

A. No values of x B. $x < 1$ C. $x \geq 1$ D. $x > 1$ E. All values of x

"No values of x" and "All values of x" are unusual answer choices, and both of them in the same question should make you examine the question closely. Extreme answers are unlikely to be right, and the presence of two of them in the same question should be a warning. One is saying this series is always convergent and the other that it's always divergent. Even if you don't recognize the series as a p-series that will converse when $x > 1$, your time is best spent exploring the other answer choices.

Now look at the next question. Do the choices "The limit does not exist" and "It cannot be determined from the information given" seem odd?

What is $\displaystyle\lim_{h \to 0} \dfrac{32\left(\dfrac{1}{4} + h\right)^3 - 32\left(\dfrac{1}{4}\right)^3}{h}$?

A. 0   B. $-\dfrac{3}{8}$ C. 6   D. The limit does not exist.

E. It cannot be determined from the information given

Would you write a question that asked for a limit and didn't give enough information to determine if the limit existed? It's unlikely that the test writers would either, so examine the other choices first. When you look at $\lim\limits_{h \to 0}\dfrac{32\left(\frac{1}{4}+h\right)^3-32\left(\frac{1}{4}\right)^3}{h}$, hopefully it suggests $\lim\limits_{h \to 0}\dfrac{f(x+h)-f(x)}{h}$ and you can recognize that you're looking at the derivative of $f(x)=32\left(\frac{1}{x}\right)^3$ at $x=4$. In the worst case, you can simplify $\lim\limits_{h \to 0}\dfrac{32\left(\frac{1}{4}+h\right)^3-32\left(\frac{1}{4}\right)^3}{h}$ and find that the correct answer is C.

How to Show Your Work

Increasingly, the creators of the AP exam are interested in your ability to communicate your knowledge of calculus. It's important that you present what you've done and why you've done it clearly and succinctly. The free response questions are read by teachers who are experienced with the AP curriculum and the AP exam. You don't have to translate the calculus into some other language for them, but you do need to make it clear to them what you think needs to be done to answer the question, and then show them how you did it and what answer you arrived at. A lot of that will be the symbols of calculus and its inherent algebra, but some of it will be clear, concise English sentences.

1. Spell It Out

There's an old adage for teachers planning a lesson: tell them what you're going to tell them, tell them, and tell them what you told them. It's a good structure for your answers. Write a sentence explaining what you're going to do, do it, and then write a sentence telling them what you found out. For example:

The number of passengers in a subway car t minutes after it comes into service is modeled by the function $P(t)$ for $0 \leq t \leq 16$. Values of $P(t)$ are given in the table below.

t	0	1	4	9	16
$P(t)$	1	5	11	1	0

Estimate the rate at which the number of passengers is changing at $t = 3$ minutes. Show the calculations that lead to your answer and indicate units.

Tell them what you're going to do.	The rate of at which the number of passengers is changing is given by the derivative of $P(t)$. This can be estimated by the average rate of change.
Do it.	$P(1) = 5$, $P(4) = 11$ $P'(3) \approx \dfrac{11-5}{4-1} = \dfrac{6}{3} =$
Tell them what you found out.	At $t = 3$ minutes, the number of passengers in the subway car is changing at approximately 2 people per minute.

2. Keep Your House in Order

Hopefully, over the course of your mathematical education you've built the habit of working in a neat, organized fashion. If not, start now. The readers are not required to search all over your paper to see if possibly somewhere there's something they can award points for. Write legibly, and keep your writing to a moderate size.

Free response questions have several sections. Mark your work to show which section of the question it relates to, and try to keep things in order. If you must put some work out of sequence, use boxes and arrows or other clear labels to help the reader follow you.

You can mark up the question sheets—the blue or green inserts containing the questions—in any way you want: circle, underline, make notes. But your solutions must be written in the test booklet. Readers will not look at the question sheet for your work. If there's nothing in the test booklet, or the work in the booklet is incomplete, the readers will assume you left out that question or part of a question.

3. Show *All* Your Work

It's important that you show the process that leads you to any answer. You may have done enough antiderivatives to know immediately that the antiderivative of $3x^2$ is x^3, but you still want to show $\int 3x^2 dx = x^3 + C$. You need to demonstrate that you had a mathematical reason for the x^3 and you didn't just pull it out of the air.

You also want to show your work because you can gain points for the work, even if the answer you arrive at isn't quite right. You might be mistaken about the antiderivative, or you might have gotten the right antiderivative and then made an arithmetic error in the evaluation, but if you've shown the work step by step, you can earn some of the credit for the problem.

If you realize you've done a problem incorrectly, don't immediately grab your eraser. Re-work the problem in a nearby space, and see if you can come up with a better answer. Once you've found what you believe is the correct solution, cross out the incorrect one, but not until you have a better solution. If your second attempt is no more successful, the first one will still be there, and have the possibility of earning some credit. Don't spend a lot of time erasing, either, just cross out and move on. Neatness may count, but solved problems count more.

The different sections of a free response question are often independent, but sometimes one section will build on the one before. Work the sections in order if at all possible, but if you aren't sure how to do one part, don't let that stop you from earning points for the other sections.

If they're independent, that's wonderful. Do the sections you know how to do.

If a latter section depends on the part you don't know how to do, make something up. You need an answer to take into the section you do know how to do. Ideally, it will be the right answer, but you need some answer, even if it's wrong. With an answer to the early part, you can show that you know how to do the later part, and score some points. Without it, you lose all the points for both sections.

4. Don't Do a Brain Dump

On the other hand, don't try to bluff the readers by writing down everything you can think of that might be vaguely related to a problem you don't know how to solve. They're not going to wade through all that. Go ahead and take a guess. There's no penalty for guessing. If it sounds like it might involve a derivative, because you heard words like "rate of change," take a derivative. If you think it's an integral, integrate. Choose your best path, follow it through, and then move on. Don't present the reader with six different "solutions" for the same problem. You will only receive credit for the first solution, and the scorer will ignore the rest.

5. Conserve Your Time

If you're pressed for time during the free response, make smart choices about where to cut corners. If the question says you should justify your answer, don't skip that, but if it just asks for a value, find the value and move on. If you need to do a first derivative test to check for a maximum or minimum, or a second derivative test to check for a point of inflection, don't just draw a number line with a few pluses and minuses and leave it to the reader to understand what that means. It may save you time, but it will cost you points. On the other hand, you don't need to approximate the values for expressions like $\sqrt{17}$ or $\sin(5.7)$. Don't waste time simplifying your answers, either, as you will lose points if you simplify incorrectly.

6. Use Your Calculator Wisely

According to the College Board, there are only four things you must be able to do on your calculator: graph a function, find the zeros of a function, calculate a derivative numerically, and calculate a definite integral numerically. Does that mean you can't use your calculator for anything else? No, but it does mean that you need to show the reader that you know how to do the math the calculator did for you.

You're finding the area enclosed between two curves. The limits of integration are x-values of the points where the two curves intersect. Can you find those intersection points on your calculator? No one's going to stop you, although getting too dependent on the calculator is a time waster, so if the intersection points are 0 and 1, you shouldn't be using the calculator. If you do use the calculator, however, you need to say "...find the point's intersection by solving..." and give the equation that you'd need to solve.

Can you ask your calculator to graph a function and its derivative, or a function and its integral, to check to see if your conclusions are correct? You can, although the integral in particular may be slow to plot, so hopefully you'll do some other work while you're waiting. But you want to use that to check conclusions you've reached by doing the calculus, or to confirm that the approach you're taking to the problem is correct, not as the sole basis for your answers.

If you're asked for relative extrema, you must find the zeros of the derivative, and test for the change from increasing to decreasing. Yes, you can find a max or a min on your calculator, but that's not enough to earn credit. You're taking this exam, not your calculator. The readers already know what your calculator can do. They're interested in what you can do. Show the math and do it in standard calculus notation, not calculator notation. The reader wants to see $\int_1^5 xe^x dx$, not $\text{fnInt}(xe^x, x, 1, 5)$.

7. Finish the Job

Before you move on to the next question, stop a moment and make sure you've taken care of all the details. Have you indicated the correct units? Some questions will specifically instruct you to indicate correct units, but even if it's not mentioned in the question, do it. It shows you are playing attention to the little things and that you are working within the parameters of the problem. Equally important, it can give you a warning flag. If you're not getting the right units, you're not getting the right answer.

If you've given an approximate answer, make sure you've rounded correctly. Three decimal places is standard, but occasionally a question will give other instructions. Again, it's context. Would 3294.736 people at a concert make sense? Would you want to sit next to the .736 of a person? That question would tell you to round to the nearest whole number. Double-check before you move on.

While you're checking, look for instructions to justify or to explain the meaning of your answer. Don't skip over these. They're not just window dressing. This is where you show that you've really learned what calculus is about, rather than just learning to execute a bunch of calculations. You'll only need to write a sentence or two, but take the time to do it. You've had a fine education. Show it. Write in full sentences, watch your spelling and grammar, and use symbols only when absolutely necessary.

A Note about Calculators

The College Board's website includes a long list of calculators that are permitted on the AP exam. Hopefully, you've been using something from that list all year and are familiar with its features and able to use it comfortably. If you're thinking about what calculator to use, however, be aware of what is not permitted.

You may not use any device with:

- a typewriter-style keyboard, whether that keyboard is an actual keypad or an electronic on-screen version.

- a stylus or touch screen

- Internet access, wireless or Bluetooth capabilities

- a camera, still or video

- a cell phone

- audio recording

In addition, you may not use a calculator that needs to be plugged into an electrical outlet, a calculator that makes noise, or any device that prints.

Some of these restrictions are clearly designed to maintain the security of the test and to prevent distractions. The motivation behind others is less clear, but the restrictions stand. So, no, you're not going to use the really cool calculator app on your cell phone during the exam. Get an approved calculator and leave the smart phones at home.

Checklist for Test Day

The quickest and easiest step you can take to maximize your chances for success on the AP exam is to arrive at the test alert, organized, and prepared. Pay attention to these details in the last few hours of your preparation.

Before the Test

- Change the batteries in your calculator. Even if you don't think they're getting low, change them. This is not the day to have your calculator die.

- If you have any programs stored in your calculator that you're in the habit of using, make sure they're loaded in memory, and that they work correctly. You shouldn't need anything, but you want to be able to work the way you're accustomed to working.

- Set the calculator to radian mode. Clear anything unnecessary out of memory.

- Put together a daypack or small bag with everything you'll need for the test. Have it ready the night before so that you can grab it and go, knowing you're properly equipped. Here is what you might put inside:

- Several pencils, a good eraser (test it first to make sure it erases without marking the paper), and your calculator. You may bring a spare calculator if you wish.

- A small, easy to eat snack. Avoid chocolate, which could melt and get all over your hands and your desk. Avoid nuts, which could trigger allergies in other testers. An energy bar, an easy-to-eat piece of fruit, or some crackers would be good choices.

- A bottle of water. Avoid drinks with sugar or caffeine. You may think they'll give you energy, but they're more likely to make you jittery.

- Don't stay up all night studying. Get a good night's sleep so you will be alert and ready for the test.

- Eat a light but satisfying meal before the test. Protein-rich foods like eggs, nuts, and yogurt are a good choice. Don't eat too heavily—you don't want to be sleepy or uncomfortably full. If you must have coffee, don't overdo it.

- Dress in layers. You'll want to be able to adjust if the testing room is too warm or too cool. Wear comfortable clothes.

Test Time

- Bring a photo ID and your school code.

- Wear or bring a watch (not a cell phone, as it will be prohibited). If your watch has any alarms, buzzers, or beepers, turn them off.

- Don't bring anything you don't need. Cell phones, pagers, and anything else that might let you communicate outside the test room will be prohibited.

- Once you get to the testing room, take a few deep breaths, remind yourself that you're well prepared, and try to relax. You may have the jitters. That's normal and may even be helpful. It makes you alert and energetic. When the test begins, set all worries aside—you've done all you can to prepare. Now show off what you've learned and go for that 5.

THE MAIN COURSE: COMPREHENSIVE STRATEGIES AND REVIEW

With three weeks to go before the exam, you have plenty of time to brush up before the big day. Here's a plan of what to do before test day:

- Start by taking the practice test that begins on page 255 to get used to the test and the questions asked. As you go through the answers, take note of areas of weakness.

- Review all the key calculus topics by working your way through the Review portion of this book, which begins on page 51. Pay special attention to topics covered at the beginning of the year, as well as any areas of weakness you identified in the practice test.

- Learn how to attack both multiple choice problems and free response problems on pages 31 and 41. You'll also benefit from the test-taking tips that begin on page 31.

- Take at least one more practice test before test day. You can find another practice test on our Web site at **www.mymaxscore.com/ aptests**.

- The night before the test, go back to the "Last-Minute Study Guide" section and review the materials there.

- Pack you materials for the next day, get a good night's sleep, and you'll be ready to maximize your score.

Topic 1: Limits

The formal $\varepsilon - \delta$ definition of a limit is no longer included in the AP exam, so you only need to understand that when we say $\lim\limits_{x \to a} f(x) = L$, we mean that the function is extremely close to L when x gets close to a. If $f(a)$ exists, it is possible—but not assured—that $f(a) = L$.

If the function is smooth and well-behaved near a, and defined at a, the limit is the value of the function.		
If $f(x) = x^2 - 2$	then $\lim\limits_{x \to 0} f(x) = -2$	As $x \to 0$, the values of $f(x) \to -2$ and $f(0) = -2$.
	$\lim\limits_{x \to 3} f(x) = 7$	As $x \to 3$, the values of $f(x) \to 7$ and $f(3) = 7$.
	$\lim\limits_{x \to -2} f(x) = 2$	As $x \to -2$, the values of $f(x) \to 2$ and $f(-2) = 2$.
"Well-behaved" functions include polynomials, and, where defined, rational functions, basic trigonometric functions, and simple exponential and logarithmic functions.		

If the function is not defined at a, or not smooth in the neighborhood around a, examine the values of the function for values of x close to a, both above and below a.

Piecewise defined functions may be well behaved on portions of the domain, but check carefully at the points where the rule changes.	If $f(x) = \begin{cases} 3x+2, & x<1 \\ x^2+4, & 1\le x\le 3 \\ -x, & x>3 \end{cases}$	$\lim_{x\to 1} f(x) = 5$ $3x+2$ is close to 5 for values of x close to but below 1, and x^2+4 is close to 5 for values of x close to but above 1.
		$\lim_{x\to 3} f(x)$ does not exist. For values below 3, x^2+4 is close to 13, but for values above 3, $-x$ is close to -3.
For $\lim_{x\to a} g(x)$ to exist and equal L, values of $g(x)$ must come close to L as $x\to a$ both from the right and from the left.		$\lim_{x\to -1} g(x) = 0$ $\lim_{x\to 0} g(x)$ DNE

One-Sided Limits

If the values of the function become very close to L as values of x are increasing toward a, then the limit of $f(x)$ as x approaches a from the left is L. We write $\lim_{x\to a^-} f(x) = L$. For example,

$$\lim_{x\to 0^-} \frac{|x|}{x} = -1$$

If the values of the function become very close to L as values of x are decreasing toward a, then the limit of $f(x)$ as x approaches a from the right is L. We write $\lim_{x\to a^+} f(x) = L$. For example,

$$\lim_{x\to 0^+} \frac{|x|}{x} = 1$$

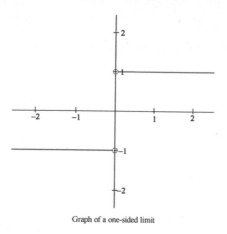

Graph of a one-sided limit

DNE

The limit does not exist if:

- The limit from the left is not equal to the limit from the right.

In Figure 1.02, $\lim_{x \to 0} f(x)$ DNE because $\lim_{x \to 0^-} f(x) = -1$ but $\lim_{x \to 0^+} f(x) = 1$.

- The function oscillates wildly.

$\lim_{x \to 0} \sin\left(\frac{1}{x}\right)$ DNE because as $x \to 0$, $\frac{1}{x} \to \infty$, and $\sin\left(\frac{1}{x}\right)$ oscillates rapidly.

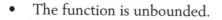

- The function is unbounded.

$\lim_{x \to 0} \frac{1}{x^2}$ DNE because as $x \to 0$, $\frac{1}{x^2} \to \infty$ and does not approach a real number, L.

Properties of Limits

Provided that all of the limits involved exist and are finite:

Limit of constant	$\lim_{x \to a} c = c$	$\lim_{x \to 4} 5 = 5$
Constant multiple	$\lim_{x \to a} cf(x) = c \lim_{x \to a} f(x)$	$\lim_{x \to 3} 5(x-2) = 5 \lim_{x \to 3}(x-2)$ $= 5(1) = 5$
Sum or difference	$\lim_{x \to a}[f(x) \pm g(x)] = \lim_{x \to a} f(x) \pm \lim_{x \to a} g(x)$	$\lim_{x \to 0}(e^x + x^2) = \lim_{x \to 0} e^x + \lim_{x \to 0} x^2$ $= 1 + 0 = 1$
Product	$\lim_{x \to a}[f(x) \cdot g(x)] = \lim_{x \to a} f(x) \cdot \lim_{x \to a} g(x)$	$\lim_{x \to 3}(x^2 \cdot 2^x) = \lim_{x \to 3} x^2 \cdot \lim_{x \to 3} 2^x$ $= 9 \cdot 8 = 72$
Quotient	$\lim_{x \to a} \dfrac{f(x)}{g(x)} = \dfrac{\lim_{x \to a} f(x)}{\lim_{x \to a} g(x)}$	$\lim_{x \to 3} \dfrac{x^2 + 2}{x^2 - 4} = \dfrac{\lim_{x \to 3} x^2 + 2}{\lim_{x \to 3} x^2 - 4}$ $= \dfrac{11}{5}$
Power	$\lim_{x \to a}[f(x)]^n = \left[\lim_{x \to a} f(x)\right]^n$	$\lim_{x \to 1}[2x - 1]^3 = \left[\lim_{x \to 1} 2x - 1\right]^3$ $= [1]^3 = 1$
Root	$\lim_{x \to a} \sqrt[n]{f(x)} = \sqrt[n]{\lim_{x \to a} f(x)}$	$\lim_{x \to 3} \sqrt[3]{x^2 - 1} = \sqrt[3]{\lim_{x \to 3} x^2 - 1}$ $= \sqrt[3]{8} = 2$

Algebraic Techniques for Calculating Limits

When it is difficult or impossible to calculate the limit of an expression directly, changing the form of the expression may solve the problem.

Factor and cancel	$\lim\limits_{x \to 2}\dfrac{x-2}{x^2-4} = \lim\limits_{x \to 2}\dfrac{x-2}{(x-2)(x+2)}$ $= \lim\limits_{x \to 2}\dfrac{1}{(x+2)} = \dfrac{1}{4}$	Factor the numerator and the denominator and cancel to find a function that is identical except at the discontinuity.
Rationalize denominator	$\lim\limits_{x \to 5}\dfrac{x-5}{\sqrt{x-5}} = \lim\limits_{x \to 5}\dfrac{(x-5)\sqrt{x-5}}{\sqrt{x-5}^2}$ $= \lim\limits_{x \to 5}\dfrac{(x-5)\sqrt{x-5}}{x-5}$ $= \lim\limits_{x \to 5}\sqrt{x-5} = 0$	Rationalize the denominator and look for an opportunity to cancel.
Rationalize numerator	$\lim\limits_{x \to 3}\dfrac{\sqrt{x+1}-2}{x-3} = \lim\limits_{x \to 3}\dfrac{(\sqrt{x+1}-2)(\sqrt{x+1}+2)}{(x-3)(\sqrt{x+1}+2)}$ $= \lim\limits_{x \to 3}\dfrac{x+1-4}{(x-3)(\sqrt{x+1}+2)}$ $= \lim\limits_{x \to 3}\dfrac{x-3}{(x-3)(\sqrt{x+1}+2)}$ $= \lim\limits_{x \to 3}\dfrac{1}{\sqrt{x+1}+2} = \dfrac{1}{4}$	Rationalize the numerator and look for an opportunity to cancel.
Trig substitution	$\lim\limits_{x \to \pi/4}\dfrac{\cos x - \sin x}{1 - \tan x} = \lim\limits_{x \to \pi/4}\dfrac{\cos x - \sin x}{1 - \dfrac{\sin x}{\cos x}}$ $= \lim\limits_{x \to \pi/4}\dfrac{(\cos x - \sin x)\cos x}{\cos x - \sin x}$ $= \lim\limits_{x \to \pi/4}\cos x = \dfrac{\sqrt{2}}{2}$	Make substitutions based on trigonometric identities to simplify the expression.

The Squeeze Theorem

If $g(x)$ and $h(x)$ are two functions for which $\lim\limits_{x \to a}g(x) = \lim\limits_{x \to a}h(x)$, and if $g(x) \le f(x) \le h(x)$ on an open interval containing a, except possibly at a, then $\lim\limits_{x \to a}f(x) = \lim\limits_{x \to a}g(x) = \lim\limits_{x \to a}h(x)$.

Memory Work

Two useful limits should be committed to memory.

$$\lim_{x \to 0} \frac{\sin x}{x} = 1 \qquad\qquad \lim_{x \to 0} \frac{1 - \cos x}{x} = 0$$

Limits at Infinity

$\lim_{x \to \infty} f(x)$ describes the end behavior of the function as x becomes a very large positive number. $\lim_{x \to -\infty} f(x)$ describes the end behavior of f as x becomes a very large negative number.

Infinite Limits

$\lim_{x \to a} f(x) = \infty$, while seemingly contradicting the definition of the limit, is used to say that as x approaches a, f increases without bound. In similar fashion, $\lim_{x \to a} f(x) = -\infty$ indicates that for values close to a, f decreases without bound.

Asymptotes

Horizontal asymptote	If the limit of the function as $x \to \infty$ (or as $x \to -\infty$) is a constant, c, then the horizontal asymptote is the line $y = c$.	$\lim_{x \to \infty} f(x) = c$ $\lim_{x \to -\infty} f(x) = c$
	If the limit of the derivative as $x \to \infty$ (or as $x \to -\infty$) is zero, it signals that the tangent line is approaching horizontal, so the graph of f has a horizontal asymptote.	$\lim_{x \to \infty} f'(x) = 0$ $\lim_{x \to -\infty} f'(x) = 0$

Note that the limit of zero indicates a horizontal tangent, but the tangent line may have the form $y = c$ for any constant, c.

Vertical asymptote	If the value of the function increases without bound or decreases without bound as x approaches a from the left or the right, then the function has a vertical asymptote at $x = a$.	$\lim\limits_{x \to a^-} f(x) = \infty$ and $\lim\limits_{x \to a^+} f(x) = -\infty$
		$\lim\limits_{x \to a^-} f(x) = -\infty$ and $\lim\limits_{x \to a^+} f(x) = \infty$
		$\lim\limits_{x \to a^-} f(x) = \infty$ and $\lim\limits_{x \to a^+} f(x) = \infty$
		$\lim\limits_{x \to a^-} f(x) = -\infty$ and $\lim\limits_{x \to a^+} f(x) = -\infty$

Continuity

| A function $f(x)$ is continuous at $x = a$ if $f(a)$ is defined, $\lim\limits_{x \to a} f(x)$ exists, and $\lim\limits_{x \to a} f(x) = f(a)$ | If $f(x) = \begin{cases} x^2 - 3 & x \le 1 \\ 2x - k & x > 1 \end{cases}$ is a continuous function, find the value of k. |
| | If $f(x)$ is continuous at $x = 1$, then $f(1) = -2$ exists, $\lim\limits_{x \to 1^-}(x^2 - 3) = -2$, $\lim\limits_{x \to 1^+}(2x - k)$ must equal -2, so that $\lim\limits_{x \to 1} f(x)$ exists, $2(1) - k = -2$, $2 - k = -2$, and $k = 4$. |

L'Hopital's Rule

On the BC exam, you may be asked to use L'Hopital's Rule on limits that involve indeterminate forms.

If $f(x)$ and $g(x)$ are differentiable on the open interval (a,b) containing c, except possibly at c itself, if $g'(x) \neq 0$ for x in (a,b) except possibly at c itself, and if $\lim\limits_{x \to c}\dfrac{f(x)}{g(x)}$ produces an indeterminate form, then $\lim\limits_{x \to c}\dfrac{f(x)}{g(x)} = \lim\limits_{x \to c}\dfrac{f'(x)}{g'(x)}$.	$\lim\limits_{x \to 0}\dfrac{\sin x}{e^x - 1} = \lim\limits_{x \to 0}\dfrac{\cos x}{e^x} = 1$

Practice

1. $\lim\limits_{x \to -1}\dfrac{1 - e^{x+1}}{x+1} =$

A. –1   B. 0   C. 1   D. 2   E. Does not exist

2. $\lim\limits_{x \to 0}\dfrac{1 - \cos^2 x}{x^2} =$

A. –2   B. 0   C. 1   D. 2   E. 4

3. $\lim\limits_{x \to \infty}\dfrac{5x^3}{x^3 + 1000x^2}$ is

A. 0   B. $\dfrac{1}{200}$ C. 1   D. 5   E. ∞

4. $\lim\limits_{x \to 16}\left(\dfrac{x - 16}{\sqrt{x} - 4}\right) =$

A. –4   B. –1   C. 0   D. 1   E. 8

5. If $f'(x) = 2\sin 2x$ and $g'(x) = 2$ for all x and if $f(0) = g(0) = 0$,

then $\lim\limits_{x \to 0}\dfrac{f(x)}{g(x)} =$

A. –2   B. –1   C. 0   D. 1   E. 2

Free Response Prompt

Note that you are unlikely to find a question on the free response section of the AP exam that deals exclusively, or even primarily, with limits. These questions, while not representative of the exam, are designed to allow you to apply limit concepts.

A piecewise function $f(t)$ is defined on the interval $0 \le x \le 12$ by

$$f(t) = \begin{cases} \frac{2}{3}x + 2 & 0 \le x \le 3 \\ \frac{11 - x}{2} & 3 < x < 5 \\ x - 3 & 5 \le x < 7 \\ 4 & 7 \le x \le 10 \\ -2x + 24 & 10 < x \le 12 \end{cases}$$

a) Find $\lim\limits_{t \to 3} 6f(t) - \dfrac{f(t)}{4}$

b) Find the value of b if $\lim\limits_{t \to b^-} f(t) = f(9) - f(3)$.

c) Is f continuous at $t = 3$? Is f continuous at $t = 5$? Explain your answers.

d) If $g(x) = \displaystyle\int_5^x f(t)\, dt$, find $\lim\limits_{x \to 12} g(x)$.

Answers and Explanations

1. A   2. C   3. D   4. E   5. C

1. $\displaystyle\lim_{x\to-1}\frac{1-e^{x+1}}{x+1} = \lim_{x\to-1}\frac{-e^{x+1}}{1} = -1$

2. $\displaystyle\lim_{x\to0}\frac{1-\cos^2 x}{x^2} = \lim_{x\to0}\frac{\sin^2 x}{x^2} = \lim_{x\to0}\left(\frac{\sin x}{x}\right)^2 = 1$

3. $\displaystyle\lim_{x\to\infty}\frac{5x^3}{x^3+1000x^2} = \lim_{x\to\infty}\frac{5}{1+\dfrac{1000}{x}} = \frac{\displaystyle\lim_{x\to\infty}5}{\displaystyle\lim_{x\to\infty}\left(1+\dfrac{1000}{x}\right)} = \frac{5}{1} = 5$

4. $\displaystyle\lim_{x\to16}\left(\frac{x-16}{\sqrt{x}-4}\right) = \lim_{x\to16}\left(\frac{(x-16)(\sqrt{x}+4)}{x-16}\right) = \lim_{x\to16}\sqrt{x}+4 = 8$

5. If $f'(x) = 2\sin 2x$, then $f(x) = -\cos 2x + C$. Because $f(0) = 0$, $-\cos 0 + C = 0$ and $C = 1$. $f(x) = 1 - \cos 2x$. If $g'(x) = 2$, then $g(x) = 2x + C$ and if $g(0) = 0$, then $2\cdot 0 + C = 0$, $C = 0$, and

$$g(x) = 2x \cdot \lim_{x\to0}\frac{f(x)}{g(x)} = \lim_{x\to0}\frac{1-\cos 2x}{2x} = 0$$

Free Response Prompt

a) Apply properties of limits to rewrite $\displaystyle\lim_{t\to3}6f(t) - \frac{f(t)}{4}$ as

$6\displaystyle\lim_{t\to3}f(t) - \frac{1}{4}\lim_{t\to3}f(t)$. Verify that $\displaystyle\lim_{t\to3^-}f(t) = \lim_{t\to3^+}f(t) = 4$. Then

$\displaystyle\lim_{t\to3}6f(t) - \frac{f(t)}{4} = 6\cdot 4 - \frac{4}{4} = 23$.

b) $\displaystyle\lim_{t\to b^-}f(t) = f(9) - f(3) = 4 - 4 = 0$. $\displaystyle\lim_{t\to b^-}f(t) = 0$ when $b = 12$.

c) The function will be continuous at a point $t = a$ if $f(a)$ exists, $\lim_{x \to a} f(t)$ exists, and $\lim_{x \to a} f(t) = f(a)$. For $t = 3$, $f(3) = \frac{2}{3} \cdot 3 + 2 = 4$, $\lim_{t \to 3^-} f(t) = 4$, and $\lim_{t \to 3^+} f(t) = 4$, so $\lim_{t \to 3} f(t) = 4$. Because $f(3)$ exists, $\lim_{t \to 3} f(t)$ exists, and both equal 4, the function is continuous at $t = 3$. At $t = 5$, however, $f(5) = 5 - 3 = 2$, but $\lim_{t \to 5^-} f(t) = 3$ and $\lim_{t \to 5^+} f(t) = 2$. Because the limit from the left and the limit from the right are not equal, $\lim_{t \to 5} f(t)$ does not exist. Therefore $f(t)$ is not continuous at $t = 5$.

d) If $g(x) = \int_5^x f(t)\,dt$, $\lim_{x \to 12} \int_0^x f(t)\,dt$ can be evaluated by finding the area under the curve $f(t)$ from 5 to 12. $A = \int_5^7 (x - 3)dx + \int_7^{10} 4dx + \int_{10}^{12} (24 - 2x)dx$

$$= \left(\frac{x^2}{2} - 3x\right)\Big|_5^7 + 4x\,\Big|_7^{10} + \left(24x - x^2\right)\Big|_{10}^{12} = 22.$$

Topic 2: Derivatives

You can expect to see a variety of questions about derivatives. Your understanding of the definition of the derivative will probably be evaluated indirectly, and you'll obviously have to find the derivative of a function given to you as an equation. You'll also be asked about the derivative of a function presented as a graph or by a table of values, but we'll look at those in a later chapter. You'll need the product and quotient rules, and you can be certain that you'll be called upon to use the chain rule and implicit differentiation.

Difference Quotient

The heart of the definition of the derivative, the difference quotient, represents the slope of a secant, or the average rate of change.

Formula	What It Means	Example
$\dfrac{f(b)-f(a)}{b-a}$	slope of a secant to the graph through the points $(a, f(a))$ and $(b, f(b))$	Secant to the graph of $y = -\dfrac{1}{2}x^2 + 4$ intersects the graph at $x = -2$ and $x = 1$. The slope of the secant line is $$\dfrac{f(1)-f(-2)}{1-(-2)} = \dfrac{3.5-2}{3} = \dfrac{1.5}{3} = 0.5$$

average rate of change of $f(x)$ on the interval (a,b)	t	1	2	3	4	5
	$f(t)$	3	7	1	8	6

Average rate of change on $(3, 5)$ is

$$\frac{f(b)-f(a)}{b-a} = \frac{6-11}{5-3} = -\frac{5}{2}.$$

Derivative of a Function f at a Point

The derivative at a point represents the slope of a tangent line or the instantaneous rate of change.

$f'(a) = \lim_{h \to 0} \frac{f(a+h)-f(a)}{h}$	slope of the tangent line to the graph at $(a, f(a))$	Tangent line to the graph of $y = \dfrac{1}{x+3}$ at $x = 2$ has a slope of $f'(2) = \lim_{h \to 0} \dfrac{f(2+h)-f(2)}{h}$ $= \lim_{h \to 0} \dfrac{\frac{1}{5+h} - \frac{1}{5}}{h}$ $= \lim_{h \to 0} \dfrac{\frac{-h}{5(5+h)}}{h}$ $= \lim_{h \to 0} \dfrac{-1}{5(5+h)} = -\dfrac{1}{25}$

	instantaneous rate of change at $x = a$	At $t = 3$, $f(t) = e^{t+4}$ is changing at a rate of $$f'(3) = \lim_{h \to 0} \frac{f(3+h) - f(3)}{h}$$ $$= \lim_{h \to 0} \frac{e^{3+h+4} - e^{3+4}}{h}$$ $$= \lim_{h \to 0} \frac{e^7(e^h - 1)}{h} = e^7$$

If $f'(a)$ exists, the function is differentiable at $x = a$.

Derivative Function

$f'(x) = \lim_{h \to 0} \dfrac{f(x+h) - f(x)}{h}$	The derivative of $f(x) = -2x + 7x^3$ is $$f'(x) = \lim_{h \to 0} \frac{-2(x+h) + 7(x+h)^3 - (-2x + 7x^3)}{h}$$ $$f'(x) = \lim_{h \to 0} \frac{-2h + 21x^2h + 21xh^2 + 7h^3}{h}$$ $$f'(x) = \lim_{h \to 0}(-2 + 21x^2 + 21xh + 7h^2) = -2 + 21x^2$$

Differentiability

The derivative does not exist

- at discontinuities

- at cusps (sharp points)

- when the tangent becomes vertical

If the derivative exists at every point in an interval, the function is differentiable on that interval.

If a function is differentiable, then it is continuous, but not every continuous function is differentiable.

Basic Derivatives

Constants	$\dfrac{d}{dx}c = 0$	Given
Powers	$\dfrac{d}{dx}\left(ax^n\right) = nax^{n-1}$	$f(x) = 2x^5 - 3x^4 + 6x^3 - 2x^2 + 5x + 11 + \dfrac{3}{x^4}$ the derivative is
Sums and differences	$\dfrac{d}{dx}(f \pm g) = \dfrac{d}{dx}f \pm \dfrac{d}{dx}g$	$f'(x) = 5 \cdot 2x^{5-1} - 4 \cdot 3x^{4-1} + 3 \cdot 6x^{3-1}$ $\quad - 2 \cdot 2x^{2-1} + 5x^0 + 0 + (-4 \cdot 3x^{-4-1})$ $= 10x^4 - 12x^3 + 18x^2 - 4x + 5 - \dfrac{12}{x^5}$

Memory Work

See the formula glossary and make sure you have committed to memory the derivatives of:

- Trigonometric functions

- Inverse trigonometric functions

- Exponential functions

- Logarithmic functions

Also be sure to memorize the following rules for differentiation:

Product rule	
$\dfrac{d}{dx}(f \cdot g) = fg' + gf'$	The derivative of $f(x) = (x^2 + 4x - 3)(3x - 1)$ is $f'(x) = (x^2 + 4x - 3)(3) + (2x + 4)(3x - 1)$ $= 3x^2 + 12x - 9 + 6x^2 + 10x - 4$ $= 9x^2 + 22x - 13$

The derivative of $y = 2\sin x \cos x$ is

$$y' = 2\sin x(-\sin x) + 2\cos x(\cos x)$$
$$= 2\cos^2 x - 2\sin^2 x$$

Quotient rule	
$\dfrac{d}{dx}\left(\dfrac{f}{g}\right) = \dfrac{gf' - fg'}{g^2}$	The derivative of $f(x) = \dfrac{5x+2}{6x^2 + x - 1}$ is $$f'(x) = \dfrac{(5x+2)(12x+1) - 5(6x^2 + x - 1)}{(6x^2 + x - 1)^2}$$ $$= \dfrac{60x^2 + 29x + 2 - 30x^2 - 5x + 5}{(6x^2 + x - 1)^2}$$ $$= \dfrac{30x^2 + 24x + 7}{(6x^2 + x - 1)^2}$$

Chain rule	
$\dfrac{d}{dx}[f \circ g]$ $= f'(g(x))g'(x)$	$y = \sqrt{\tan(3x)}$ is the composition of $f(x) = \sqrt{x}$, $g(x) = \tan x$, and $h(x) = 3x$. The derivative of $f(g(h(x)))$ is $$y' = \dfrac{1}{2}(\tan(3x))^{-\frac{1}{2}} \cdot \sec^2(3x) \cdot 3$$ $$= \dfrac{3\sec^2(3x)}{2\sqrt{\tan(3x)}}$$

Inverses	
If $f(x)$ and $g(x)$ are inverse functions, $$g'(x) = \frac{1}{f'(g(x))}$$	$f(x) = \sin x$ and $g(x) = \sin^{-1}(x)$ are inverses. $f'(x) = \cos x$, $$f'(g(x)) = \cos(\sin^{-1}(x)) = \sqrt{1 - x^2}$$ and $$g'(x) = \frac{1}{\cos(\sin^{-1}(x))} = \frac{1}{\sqrt{1 - x^2}}$$

Implicit Differentiation

Use implicit differentiation when it is impossible to isolate y.

1. Remember that y is a function of x.	Although it is not possible to isolate y, y does equal an expression in terms of x. $y = (\text{quantity in } x)$
2. Expressions involving y require the chain rule.	$\frac{dy}{dx} = \frac{d}{dx}(\text{quantity in } x)$ so the derivative of $$y^2 = 2y\frac{dy}{dx}$$
3. Differentiate term by term. Consider using $\frac{dy}{dx}$, rather than y', to make the derivatives easier to see.	The derivative of $3xy^2 - 5xy + 8x^2y = 16$ is $$6xy\frac{dy}{dx} + 3y^2 - 5x\frac{dy}{dx} - 5y + 8x^2\frac{dy}{dx} + 16xy = 0$$
Move terms involving $\frac{dy}{dx}$ to one side, terms without to the other.	$$6xy\frac{dy}{dx} - 5x\frac{dy}{dx} + 8x^2\frac{dy}{dx} = 5y - 3y^2 - 16xy$$

Factor out $\dfrac{dy}{dx}$.	$\dfrac{dy}{dx}\left(6xy - 5x + 8x^2\right) = 5y - 3y^2 - 16xy$
Solve for $\dfrac{dy}{dx}$.	$\dfrac{dy}{dx} = \dfrac{5y - 3y^2 - 16xy}{6xy - 5x + 8x^2}$

Higher Order Derivatives

The second derivative, $f''(x)$, of $f(x)$ is the derivative of $f'(x)$.

If $f(x) = 3x^3 + 11x^2 - 13x + 3$, $f'(x) = 9x^2 + 22x - 13$ and $f''(x) = 18x + 22$.

The third derivative is denoted f'''. Here, $f'''(x) = 18$.

Fourth derivatives (and higher) are denoted $f^{(n)}$, as in $f^{(4)}$.

When using the $\dfrac{dy}{dx}$ notation for the derivative, the second derivative is

denoted $\dfrac{d^2y}{dx^2}$. Similarly, the nth derivative is denoted $\dfrac{d^ny}{dy^n}$.

Practice

1. If $f(x) = 3\cos x - \cos 3x$, then $f'(x) =$

A. $3\sin x - \sin 3x$ B. $\sin 3x - 3\sin x$ C. $3\left(\sin 3x - \sin x\right)$

D. $3\sin 2x$ E. $3\sin 3x + \sin x$

2. If $f(x) = \dfrac{5x + 2}{x - 3}$ for all $x \neq 3$, $f'(2) =$

A. -17 B. 17 C. -13 D. 13 E. 5

3. $\dfrac{d}{dx}\left(\arctan 3x\right) =$

A. $\dfrac{1}{1 + 9x^2}$ B. $\dfrac{3}{1 + 9x^2}$ C. $\dfrac{3}{1 + 3x^2}$ D. $\dfrac{3}{\sqrt{1 + 3x^2}}$ E. $\dfrac{3}{\sqrt{1 + 9x^2}}$

4. $\displaystyle\lim_{h\to 0}\frac{1}{h}\ln\left(\frac{3+h}{3}\right)$ is

A. 0   B. $\ln 3$ C. $\dfrac{1}{3}$ D. $\dfrac{\ln 3}{3}$ E. undefined

5. If $\sin(x-2y)=xy$, then $\dfrac{dy}{dx}=$

A. $\dfrac{\cos(x-2y)-y}{x}$ B. $\dfrac{\cos(x-2y)-2\cos(x-2y)-y}{x}$

C. $\dfrac{x+2\cos(x-2y)}{\cos(x-2y)-y}$ D. $\dfrac{\cos(x-2y)-y}{x+2\cos(x-2y)}$ E. $\dfrac{1-y}{x+2}$

Free Response Prompt

A particle moves along the x-axis so that its velocity at time $t\geq 0$ is given by $v(t)=e^{t}\sin t$

a) Find the acceleration of the particle at time $t=\pi$ seconds.

b) Is the speed of the particle increasing or decreasing at time $t=2$ seconds? Give a reason for your answer.

c) Find the time(s) t in the interval $0\leq t\leq 2\pi$ at which the particle changes direction.

Answers and Explanations

1. C   2. A   3. B   4. C   5. D

1. $f'(x)=-3\sin x-(-\sin 3x)\cdot 3=-3\sin x+3\sin 3x=3(\sin 3x-\sin x)$.

2. If $f(x)=\dfrac{5x+2}{x-3}$ for all $x\neq 3$,

$f'(x)=\dfrac{(x-3)(5)-(5x+2)(1)}{(x-3)^2}=\dfrac{5x-15-5x-2}{(x-3)^2}=\dfrac{-17}{(x-3)^2}$. Thus

$f'(2)=\dfrac{-17}{(2-3)^2}=-17$.

3. $\dfrac{d}{dx}(\arctan 3x) = 3\left(\dfrac{1}{1+(3x)^2}\right) = \dfrac{3}{1+9x^2}$

4. $\lim\limits_{h\to 0}\dfrac{1}{h}\ln\left(\dfrac{3+h}{3}\right) = \lim\limits_{h\to 0}\dfrac{[\ln(3+h)-\ln 3]}{h}$ is the derivative of $\ln x$ at

$x = 3$. The derivative of $\ln x$ is $\dfrac{1}{x}$, so $\lim\limits_{h\to 0}\dfrac{1}{h}\ln\left(\dfrac{3+h}{3}\right) = \dfrac{1}{3}$

5. If $\sin(x-2y) = xy$, then

$\cos(x-2y)\cdot\left(1-2\dfrac{dy}{dx}\right) = x\dfrac{dy}{dx} + y$

$\cos(x-2y) - 2\cos(x-2y)\dfrac{dy}{dx} = x\dfrac{dy}{dx} + y$

$\cos(x-2y) - y = x\dfrac{dy}{dx} + 2\cos(x-2y)\dfrac{dy}{dx}$

$\cos(x-2y) - y = \left[x + 2\cos(x-2y)\right]\dfrac{dy}{dx}$

$\dfrac{dy}{dx} = \dfrac{\cos(x-2y) - y}{x + 2\cos(x-2y)}$

Free Response Prompt

a) $a(t) = v'(t) = e^t\cos t + e^t\sin t$
$a(\pi) = e^\pi(\cos\pi + \sin\pi) = -e^\pi$

b) Speed is increasing when acceleration and velocity have the same sign. $v(2) = e^2\sin 2 > 0$ and $a(2) = e^2(\cos 2 + \sin 2) > 0$. The speed of the particle is increasing at $t = 2$ seconds.

c) Particle changes direction when $v(t) = 0$. $v(t) = e^t\sin t = 0$ when $\sin t = 0$, at $t = 0, \pi,$ and 2π seconds.

Topic 3: Applications of the Derivative

Derivatives describe change, whether increase or decrease, and slope. The applications that are based on, or related to, the derivative all focus on these ideas.

Average Rate of Change

The average rate of change of a function on a closed interval is the slope of the secant line joining the endpoints of the interval.

The average rate of change of f on the interval $a \leq x \leq b$ can be evaluated using the formula $\dfrac{f(b) - f(a)}{b - a}$.

Example: If the position of a particle on the y-axis at time t is $y(t) = 2t^3 - t$, what is the average velocity of the particle for $0 \leq t \leq 5$?

Average velocity is the average rate of change in position, so begin by finding the position of the particle at $t = 0$, and at $t = 5$. $y(0) = 0$ and $y(5) = 250 - 5 = 245$. The average value is $\dfrac{245 - 0}{5 - 0} = 49$.

Instantaneous Rate of Change

While the average rate of change is the slope of a secant line, the instantaneous rate of change is the slope of the tangent line, which is the derivative at a point.

Example: What is the instantaneous rate of change at $x = 1$ of the function given by $f(x) = \dfrac{x^2 - 5}{x + 3}$?

The instantaneous rate of change is the value of the derivative at $x = 1$.

$$f'(x) = \frac{(x+3)(2x) - (x^2 - 5)(1)}{(x+3)^2} = \frac{2x^2 + 6x - x^2 + 5}{(x+3)^2} = \frac{x^2 + 6x + 5}{(x+3)^2}$$

$$f'(1) = \frac{1 + 6 + 5}{4^2} = \frac{12}{16} = \frac{3}{4}$$

Tangent Lines

The derivative, evaluated at a point, is the slope of the tangent line to the curve at that point. To find the equation of the tangent line:

- find the derivative

- evaluate the derivative at the point of tangency

- use point-slope form

Example: Find the equation of the tangent line to the curve $x^2 + 2xy = 7$ at the point $(1, 3)$.

Find the derivative.	$x^2 + 2xy = 7$ $2x + 2x\dfrac{dy}{dx} + 2y = 0$ $2x\dfrac{dy}{dx} = -2x - 2y$ $\dfrac{dy}{dx} = \dfrac{-2x - 2y}{2x} = \dfrac{-x - y}{x}$
Evaluate the derivative at $(1, 3)$.	$\dfrac{dy}{dx} = \dfrac{-1 - 3}{1} = -4$. The slope of the tangent line is -4.

Use point-slope form.	The equation of the tangent line is $y - 3 = -4(x - 1)$.

Tangent Line Approximation

It is possible to approximate the value of a function at a value of x near $x = a$ by the value of the tangent line to the curve at $x = a$.

Local linearization	$L(x) = f(a) + f'(a)(x - a)$
Tangent line approximation	$f(x) \approx f(x_0) + f'(x_0)(x - x_0)$
Both are simply variations of the tangent line equation.	

Example: If $f(x) = \sqrt{x - 3}$, find the approximate value of $f(6.9)$, obtained from the tangent line to the graph of $f(x)$ at $x = 7$.

- The derivative of $f(x) = \sqrt{x - 3}$ is $f'(x) = \dfrac{1}{2\sqrt{x - 3}}$.

- The slope of the tangent is $f'(7) = \dfrac{1}{2\sqrt{7 - 3}} = \dfrac{1}{4}$.

- The equation of the tangent line to $f(x)$ at $x = 7$ is $y - 2 = \dfrac{1}{4}(x - 7)$.

- $f(6.9) \approx 2 + \dfrac{1}{4}(6.9 - 7) \approx 1.975$

Local Linearization = First Degree Taylor Polynomial

The local linearization $f(x) \approx f(x_0) + f'(x_0)(x - x_0)$ is the first-degree Taylor polynomial approximation of $f(x)$ about x_0. For more on Taylor polynomials, see the chapter on Infinite Series.

Error of Estimate

The closer x is to the point of tangency $x = a$, the better the approximation. But how good is it, or how bad? The error in approximating $f(x)$ is the difference between the actual value $f(x)$ and the approximation,

$f(a) + f'(a)(x - a)$. The error of estimate in the previous example is

$$\sqrt{6.9 - 3} - \left(2 + \frac{1}{4}(6.9 - 7)\right) \approx 1.974841766 - 1.975 \approx -1.582 \times 10^{-4}.$$

Sign of the Error

You can measure the size of the error of the approximation, but is it an underestimate or an overestimate? That depends on the concavity of the graph.

To check concavity, examine the second derivative. For $f(x) = \sqrt{x - 3}$,

$$f'(x) = \frac{1}{2\sqrt{x - 3}} \text{ and so } f''(x) = -\frac{1}{4\sqrt{(x - 3)^3}} = -\frac{1}{4(x - 3)\sqrt{(x - 3)}}.$$

For $x > 3$, the second derivative is negative, so $f(x)$ is always concave down. Since the graph is concave down, the tangent line will sit above the graph, so the tangent line approximation will be larger than the actual value.

Differentials

Close to the point of tangency, the tangent line is almost indistinguishable from the function. If the value of x can be measured with a possible error of $\pm \Delta x$, then the possible error in the value of the function can be approximated as the change in the y-value of the tangent line. If Δx is small, the differential, $df = f'(x)dx$, gives the variation or error in f.

Example: The diameter of a circular disk is measured as 2.5 cm with an error of ± 0.05 cm. Estimate the error in the area of the disk.

- $d = 2.5$ and $\Delta d = \pm 0.05$.
- The area of the disk is $A = \pi r^2 = \pi \left(\frac{d}{2}\right)^2 = \frac{\pi}{4}d^2$.
- The derivative is $A' = \frac{\pi}{2}d$.
- The possible error in the area is equal to

$$dA = \left(\frac{2.5\pi}{2}\right)(\pm 0.05) = \pm 0.0625.$$

Newton's Method

Newton's Method uses the tangent line approximation to estimate a zero of a differentiable function. The degree of accuracy desired is often indicated by giving a limit for the difference between successive estimates. Make an initial estimate of the zero, close enough to the actual zero to avoid any critical points, and then repeat the steps until the desired accuracy is reached.

			Second iteration	Third iteration
0	Function: $f(x)$ Derivative: $f'(x)$ Initial estimate: x_0 Desired accuracy: $\|x_{n+1} - x_n\| \le k$	$f(x) = x^3 - 5$ $f'(x) = 3x^2$ $x = 2$ $\|x_{n+1} - x_n\| \le 0.01$		
1	Evaluate: $f(x_n)$	$f(2) = 8 - 5 = 3$	$f(1.75)$ $= 0.359375$	$f(1.71089)$ ≈ 0.008022
2	Evaluate: $f'(x_n)$	$f'(2) = 12$	$f'(1.75)$ $= 9.1875$	$f'(1.71089)$ ≈ 8.781374
3	New estimate: $x_{n+1} = x_n - \dfrac{f(x_n)}{f'(x_n)}$	$x_1 = 2 - \dfrac{3}{12}$ $= 1.75$	$x_2 \approx 1.71089$	$x_3 \approx 1.709974$
4	Check: $\|x_{n+1} - x_n\| \le k?$	$\|x_1 - x_0\| =$ 0.25	$\|x_2 - x_1\| =$ 0.039112	$\|x_3 - x_2\| =$ 0.00091644

				Approxi-mate zero is $x_3 \approx 1.709974$
5	Yes: x_{n+1} is the approximate zero.			
	No: Repeat steps 1–5.	Perform another iteration using the new estimate.	Perform another iteration using the new estimate.	

Particle Motion

If the position of a particle is defined as a function of time:

- Velocity is the derivative of position.

    - Positive velocity indicates movement to the right or upward.

    - Negative velocity indicates movement to the left or downward.

    - Zero velocity indicates a change in direction.

- Speed is the absolute value of velocity.

- Acceleration is the derivative of velocity.

    - Speed is increasing when velocity and acceleration have the same sign.

    - Acceleration equal to zero indicates constant speed.

Example: A particle moves along a line so that at time t, where $0 \leq t \leq \dfrac{\pi}{2}$, its position is given by $s(t) = 4 - 4\sin t - t^2$. What is the velocity of the particle when its acceleration is zero?

Position	$s(t) = 4 - 4\sin t - t^2$
Velocity	$v(t) = s'(t) = -4\cos t - 2t$
Acceleration	$a(t) = v'(t) = 4\sin t - 2$

Set acceleration to zero and solve.	$4\sin t - 2 = 0$ $\sin t = \dfrac{1}{2}$ In the given interval, this occurs at $t = \dfrac{\pi}{6}$.
Find velocity at $t = \dfrac{\pi}{6}$.	$v\left(\dfrac{\pi}{6}\right) = -4\cos\left(\dfrac{\pi}{6}\right) - 2\cdot\dfrac{\pi}{6}$ $= -4\left(\dfrac{\sqrt{3}}{2}\right) - \dfrac{\pi}{3} \approx -4.511$

Optimization

To determine maximum or minimum values of a function, look for the points at which the first derivative is zero. To identify whether the point is a maximum or a minimum, check the sign of the derivative on each side and look for a change from positive to negative for a maximum or negative to positive for a minimum. Alternately, find the second derivative and evaluate at the point. If the second derivative is positive, the curve is concave up and you have a minimum. If the second derivative is negative, the curve is concave down and you have a maximum.

In many optimization problems, several variables are involved in the function that must be optimized. Use other information in the problem to re-express it as a function of one variable.

Example: Find the dimensions of the cone of maximum volume if the diameter and height of the cone total 24 cm.

Function to be optimized:	$V = \dfrac{1}{3}\pi r^2 h$
Other information:	$2r + h = 24$ $h = 24 - 2r$

Substitute.	$V = \frac{1}{3}\pi r^2 (24 - 2r) = 8\pi r^2 - \frac{2}{3}\pi r^3$
Differentiate.	$\frac{dV}{dr} = 16\pi r - 2\pi r^2$
Set derivative equal to zero.	$\frac{dV}{dr} = 16\pi r - 2\pi r^2 = 0$
Solve for r.	$16\pi r - 2\pi r^2 = 0$ $2\pi r(8 - r) = 0$ $r = 0 \quad r = 8$
Use 1st or 2nd derivative test.	$V''(r) = 16\pi - 4\pi r$ $V''(0) = 16\pi$ indicates a minimum $V''(8) = 16\pi - 32\pi = -16\pi$ indicates a maximum
Evaluate other variables.	$h = 24 - 2r = 24 - 16 = 8$

Related Rates

Related rates problems involve two quantities are that changing simultaneously and for which the rates of change are interconnected. Each variable is a function of time, and the chain rule is necessary for differentiation.

Example: Air is escaping from a spherical balloon so that the radius of the sphere is decreasing at a rate of 0.1 cm per second. How quickly is the surface area of the balloon changing at the moment when its volume is 288π cm³? (Note: $S = 4\pi r^2$ and $V = \frac{4}{3}\pi r^3$)

Identify changing parameters.	$r(t), S(t),$ and $V(t)$

Identify known rates of change.	$\dfrac{dr}{dt} = -0.1$
Identify moment of interest.	$V(t) = 288\pi$
Write an equation that connects changing quantities.	$S = 4\pi r^2$
Differentiate with respect to t.	$\dfrac{dS}{dt} = 8\pi r \dfrac{dr}{dt}$
Freeze motion.	When $V = \dfrac{4}{3}\pi r^3 = 288\pi$, $r^3 = 216$ and $r = 6$.
Plug in all known quantities and rates of change.	$\dfrac{dS}{dt} = 8\pi r \dfrac{dr}{dt}$ $= 8\pi(6)(-0.1)$
Solve for the remaining unknown.	$\dfrac{dS}{dt} = -4.8\pi$

Normal Line

The normal line is a line perpendicular to the tangent at the point of tangency. To find the equation of the normal line, begin as you would when finding a tangent. Take the derivative and evaluate at the point of tangency. The slope of the normal line is the negative reciprocal of the slope of the tangent.

Example: For what value of k is the line $y = \dfrac{1}{2}x - k$ normal to the curve defined by $y = x^3 - 2x$?

- Find the derivative. $y' = 3x^2 - 2$.

- The normal line has a slope of $\dfrac{1}{2}$, which is the negative reciprocal of the slope of the tangent.

- The slope of the tangent must be –2.

- Set $3x^2 - 2 = -2$ and solve to find that the point of tangency is $(0,0)$.

- The normal passes through the origin, so $k = 0$.

Rolle's Theorem and the Mean Value Theorem

Both theorems require that $f(x)$ is

- continuous on the closed interval $[a,b]$

- differentiable on the open interval (a,b)

Mean value	For some value c between a and b, $f'(c) = \dfrac{f(b) - f(a)}{b - a}$.	Slope of tangent = slope of secant Instantaneous rate of change = average rate of change
Rolle's	If $f(a) = f(b)$, then for some value c between a and b, $f'(c) = 0$	If the endpoints of the interval are level, there is a turning point (max or min) in between.

Example: The Mean Value Theorem guarantees the existence of a special point on the graph of $y = \dfrac{1}{x+3}$ between $\left(0, \dfrac{1}{3}\right)$ and $\left(3, \dfrac{1}{6}\right)$. What are the coordinates of that point?

Check the conditions.	$y = \dfrac{1}{x+3}$ is continuous on $[0,3]$ and differentiable on $(0,3)$.
Find the average value.	$\dfrac{f(3) - f(0)}{3 - 0} = \dfrac{\frac{1}{6} - \frac{1}{3}}{3} = \dfrac{-\frac{1}{6}}{3} = -\dfrac{1}{18}$
Find the derivative.	$y' = \dfrac{-1}{(x+3)^2}$

Equate and solve.	$\dfrac{-1}{(x+3)^2} = \dfrac{-1}{18}$ $(x+3)^2 = 18$ $x+3 = \pm 3\sqrt{2}$ $x = -3 \pm 3\sqrt{2}$
Choose value in the interval.	$0 < -3 + 3\sqrt{2} < 3$
Find the y-coordinate.	$y = \dfrac{1}{-3+3\sqrt{2}+3} = \dfrac{1}{3\sqrt{2}} = \dfrac{\sqrt{2}}{6}$

The point is $\left(-3 + 3\sqrt{2}, \dfrac{\sqrt{2}}{6}\right)$.

Practice

1. For what value of k will $y = x + \dfrac{k}{x}$ have a relative minimum at $x = 3$?

A. 1   B. 3   C. 6   D. 9   E. –1

2. The point on the line $x + 3y = 9$ that is nearest to the point $(2,4)$ occurs where x is

A. 6   B. 3   C. 2   D. 1.33   E. 0.6

3. Let $f(x) = x^3 + 4x - 1$. If the rate of change of f at $x = c$ is 16 times its rate of change at $x = 1$, then $c =$

A. 2   B. 6   C. 7   D. 21   E. 42

4. An equation for the normal to the graph of $y = e^{\frac{x-1}{2}}$ at $x = 3$ is

A. $y - e = \dfrac{e}{2}(x-3)$

B. $y - e = \frac{-2}{e}(x-3)$

C. $y - e = \frac{2}{e}(x-3)$

D. $y = \frac{-2}{e}x - 3$

E. $y = \frac{e}{2}x - 3$

5. The approximate value of $y = \sqrt{4 + \cos x}$ at $x = 1.5$, obtained from the tangent to the graph at $x = \frac{\pi}{2}$ is

A. –0.4823   B. 1.9292   C. 1.9825   D. 2.0175   E. 2.0177

Free Response Prompt

A particle moves along the x-axis so that its velocity at time $t \geq 0$ is given by $v(t) = e^{-t} \cos 2t$

a) Find the acceleration of the particle at time $t = \frac{\pi}{2}$ seconds.

b) Is the speed of the particle increasing or decreasing at time $t = \frac{\pi}{3}$ seconds? Give a reason for your answer.

c) Find the time(s) t in the interval $0 \leq t \leq \pi$ at which the particle changes direction.

Answers and Explanations

1. D   2. E   3. B   4. B   5. E

1. If $y = x + \frac{k}{x}$, then $y' = 1 - \frac{k}{x^2}$. At the relative minimum, the derivative will be zero, so solve $1 - \frac{k}{x^2} = 0$ to find that $x^2 = k$. Since $x = 3$, $k = 9$.

2. The distance between a point (x, y) on the line and the point $(2, 4)$ is $d = \sqrt{(x-1)^2 + (y-4)^2}$. The distance will be a minimum when $d' = 0$.

Find $d' = \dfrac{2(x-1) + 2(y-4)\frac{dy}{dx}}{2\sqrt{(x-1)^2 + (y-4)^2}} = \dfrac{(x-1) + (y-4)\frac{dy}{dx}}{\sqrt{(x-1)^2 + (y-4)^2}}$. Realizing that

$\dfrac{(x-1) + (y-4)\frac{dy}{dx}}{\sqrt{(x-1)^2 + (y-4)^2}} = 0$ when $(x-1) + (y-4)\frac{dy}{dx} = 0$ will simplify the solution.

The given equation, $x + 3y = 9$, or $y = \dfrac{9-x}{3}$ and its slope, $\dfrac{dy}{dx} = -\dfrac{1}{3}$, can be substituted into the numerator of d'.

$(x-1) + \left(\dfrac{9-x}{3} - 4\right)\left(-\dfrac{1}{3}\right) = 0$

$x - 1 + \dfrac{x-9}{9} + \dfrac{4}{3} = 0$

$9x - 9 + x - 9 + 12 = 0$

$10x - 6 = 0$

$x = 0.6$

3. The rate of change is given by the derivative of $f(x)$. If $f(x) = x^3 + 4x - 1$, then $f'(x) = 3x^2 + 4$ and $f'(1) = 3(1)^2 + 4 = 7$. To find the value of c for which the rate of change is 16 times this, set $f'(x) = 3x^2 + 4 = 16 \cdot 7$ Solve $3x^2 = 112 - 4$ to find that $x^2 = \dfrac{108}{3} = 36$ so $x = \pm 6$.

4. If $y = e^{\frac{x-1}{2}}$, then the point $(3, e)$ is on the curve. The derivative $y' = \dfrac{1}{2}e^{\frac{x-1}{2}}$, evaluated at $x = 3$, is $y'(3) = \dfrac{e}{2}$. The slope of the normal line is $-\dfrac{2}{e}$. The equation of the normal line is $y - e = \dfrac{-2}{e}(x - 3)$ or

$2x + ey = 6 + e^2$.

5. If $y = \sqrt{4 + \cos x}$, then at $x = \frac{\pi}{2}$, $y\left(\frac{\pi}{2}\right) = \sqrt{4} = 2$. Differentiate

$y' = \dfrac{-\sin x}{2\sqrt{4 + \cos x}}$ and evaluate at $x = \frac{\pi}{2}$. $y'\left(\frac{\pi}{2}\right) = \dfrac{-1}{2\sqrt{4}} = -\frac{1}{4}$ is the

slope of the tangent. The tangent to the graph of $y = \sqrt{4 + \cos x}$ at

$x = \frac{\pi}{2}$ is $y - 2 = -\frac{1}{4}\left(x - \frac{\pi}{2}\right)$. Use the tangent to approximate the value

of y at $x = 1.5$. $y(1.5) = -\frac{1}{4}\left(1.5 - \frac{\pi}{2}\right) + 2 = -\frac{1}{4}(-0.0708) + 2 = 2.0177$.

At $x = 1.5$, y is approximately 2.0177.

Free Response Prompt

a) The acceleration of the particle is

$a(t) = v'(t) = e^{-t}(-2\sin 2t) + \cos 2t(-e^{-t}) = -e^{-t}(2\sin 2t + \cos 2t)$.

At time $t = \frac{\pi}{2}$ seconds, $a\left(\frac{\pi}{2}\right) = -e^{-\frac{\pi}{2}}(2\sin \pi + \cos \pi) = -e^{-\frac{\pi}{2}}(-1) = e^{-\frac{\pi}{2}}$.

b) At time $t = \frac{\pi}{3}$ seconds, the velocity $v\left(\frac{\pi}{3}\right) = e^{-\frac{\pi}{3}}\cos\frac{2\pi}{3} < 0$ and the

acceleration $a\left(\frac{\pi}{3}\right) = -e^{-\frac{\pi}{3}}\left(2\sin\frac{2\pi}{3} + \cos\frac{2\pi}{3}\right) = -e^{-\frac{\pi}{3}}\left(\sqrt{3} - \frac{1}{2}\right) < 0$.

Since both velocity and acceleration are negative, the speed of the particle is increasing.

c) The particle changes direction when $v(t) = e^{-t}\cos 2t = 0$. Since e^{-t}

is always greater than zero, $v(t) = 0$ when $\cos 2t = 0$, which is when

$2t = \frac{\pi}{2} \pm n\pi$. In the given interval, $t = \frac{\pi}{4}$ and $t = \frac{3\pi}{4}$. The particle

changes direction at $t = \frac{\pi}{4}$ seconds and $t = \frac{3\pi}{4}$ seconds.

Topic 4: Curve Sketching

Before the development of graphing utilities, the information provided by the first and second derivatives was critical to producing a sketch of the graph of a function. Although there are now
other methods of producing the graph, the derivatives still describe the
behavior of the function in important ways. Rather than being given an
equation and asked to sketch a graph, you'll likely be given the graph of
the first derivative and asked to draw conclusions about $f(x)$.

First and Second Derivatives

$f'(x) > 0$	$f(x)$ increasing	
$f'(x) < 0$	$f(x)$ decreasing	

$f'(x) = 0$	$f(x)$ has a critical point	Check the sign of $f'(x)$ to the left and right of the critical point. Positive on the left, negative on the right indicates $f(x)$ has a relative maximum. Negative on the left, positive on the right indicates $f(x)$ has a relative minimum. If the sign of $f'(x)$ is the same on both sides of the critical point, check for an inflection point.

$f''(x) > 0$	$f(x)$ concave up $f'(x)$ is increasing	$f'(x) = 0$ and $f''(x) > 0$ indicates a relative minimum.
$f''(x) < 0$	$f(x)$ concave down $f'(x)$ is decreasing	$f'(x) = 0$ and $f''(x) < 0$ indicates a relative maximum.
$f''(x) = 0$	$f(x)$ has an inflection point $f'(x)$ has a critical point	$f'(x) = 0$ and $f''(x) = 0$ indicates an inflection point.

Absolute Extrema

The critical numbers, those points where the first derivative equals zero, are most often relative extrema. The point that is a relative extremum may also be an absolute extremum, but absolute extrema may also occur at the endpoints of a closed interval. Check the value of the function at each of the endpoints before declaring an absolute maximum or absolute minimum.

Vertical Asymptotes

If $f(x)$ is discontinuous at $x = a$, and the limit of the $f'(x)$ as $x \to a$ from the left or the right goes to infinity or negative infinity, $f(x)$ has a vertical asymptote at $x = a$.

$\lim\limits_{x\to a^-} f'(x) = \infty$		$\lim\limits_{x\to a^-} f'(x) = -\infty$	
$\lim\limits_{x\to a^+} f'(x) = \infty$		$\lim\limits_{x\to a^+} f'(x) = -\infty$	

Cusps

If the limit of the $f'(x)$ as $x \to a$ goes to infinity from one side and negative infinity from the other, but f is continuous at a, $f(x)$ has a cusp at $x = a$.

End Behavior

To determine the end behavior of the graph, examine $\lim\limits_{x\to\infty} f'(x)$ and $\lim\limits_{x\to-\infty} f'(x)$. If $\lim\limits_{x\to\infty} f'(x) = 0$ or $\lim\limits_{x\to-\infty} f'(x) = 0$, the graph of $f(x)$ has a horizontal asymptote. Note that the horizontal asymptote is not necessarily the x-axis. The derivative tells you that the graph approaches a horizontal line, not what line it approaches. If there is no horizontal asymptote, the sign of the first derivative will tell you whether the graph is increasing or decreasing and therefore how the ends behave.

Example: $f(x)$ is a continuous function. The graph of the derivative $f'(x)$ on the closed interval $[-3, 8]$ is shown following.

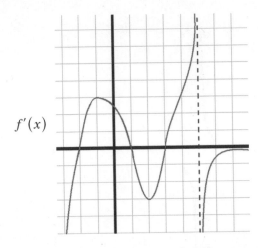

$f'(x)$

a) Find the x-coordinate of each point of inflection of the graph of $y = f(x)$ on the interval $[-3,8]$. Give a reason for your answer.

b) At what values of x does $f(x)$ reach relative maxima or minima on the interval $-3 < x < 3$? Show the analysis that leads to your answer.

c) Describe the behavior of the graph of $y = f(x)$ at the point $x = 5$. Give a reason for your answer.

While the question doesn't ask you to sketch the graph, it does ask many of the questions you'd ask if you had to sketch the graph. Try, as much as possible, to reference the given graph of the derivative in your answers.

a) Inflection points occur when concavity changes. It's common to refer to the second derivative to talk about concavity, but try to keep the focus on the graph of the first derivative. Translate "the second derivative is equal to zero" to "the first derivative changes from increasing to decreasing or from decreasing to increasing." The graph of $f(x)$ has an inflection point at $x = -1$ when the first derivative changes from increasing to decreasing and therefore the graph of $f(x)$ changes from concave up to concave down. There is also an inflection point at $x = 2$, when $f'(x)$ turns from decreasing to increasing and so $f(x)$ changes from concave down to concave up.

b) To find extrema, look first for the zeros of the derivative. The x-intercepts of the graph of $f'(x)$ occur at $x = -2$, $x = 1$, and $x = 3$. Since the question confined your search to the open interval $-3 < x < 3$, the

x-intercept at $x = 3$ should be ignored. Perform a first derivative test in the neighborhood of the other two zeros.

	$x < -2$	$x = -2$	$x > -2$
f'	−	0	+
f	decreasing	MINIMUM	increasing

	$x < 1$	$x = 1$	$x > 1$
f'	+	0	−
f	increasing	MAXIMUM	decreasing

Don't just show your sign charts and leave it at that. Explain what that sign chart told you. There is a relative minimum at $x = -2$, because the first derivative changes from negative to positive and therefore the function changes from decreasing to increasing. There is a relative maximum at $x = 1$, because the first derivative changes from positive to negative and therefore the function changes from increasing to decreasing.

c) The function is not differentiable at $x = 5$, but you were told that $f(x)$ is a continuous function. If $f(5)$ exists, there must be a reason other than discontinuity for the derivative to fail to exist. Since $\lim_{x \to 5^-} f'(x) = \infty$ and $\lim_{x \to 5^+} f'(x) = -\infty$, the graph of $f(x)$ has a cusp at $x = 5$.

Practice

1. The derivative of $f(x) = 2x^2 - e^x$ attains its maximum value at $x =$

A. $\ln\sqrt{2}$ B. $\ln 2$ C. $\ln 4$ D. e^2 E. $\sqrt{e}$

2. The graph of f', the derivative of f, is shown in the figure below. Which of the following could be the graph of f?

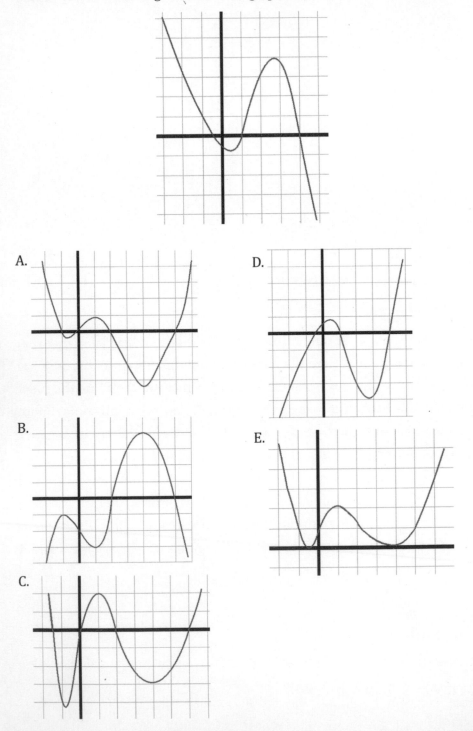

3. The graph of $f'(x)$ is shown in the figure.

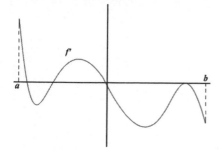

Which of the following describes all relative extrema of f on the interval $a < x < b$?

A. one relative maximum and two relative minima

B. one relative minimum and two relative maxima

C. two relative maxima and two relative minima

D. one relative maximum and one relative minimum

E. one relative maximum and three relative minima

4. The derivative of $f(x)$ is $f'(x) = x^3(x-2)(x+3)^2$. At how many points will the graph of $f(x)$ have a relative maximum?

A. 0   B. 1   C. 2   D. 3   E. 4

5. If the derivative of $f(x)$ is given by $f'(x) = \ln(2x - 3)$ at which of the following values of x does f have a minimum?

A. $x = e$ B. $x = 1$ C. $x = 1.5$ D. $x = 2$ E. $x = 3$

Free Response Prompt

$f(x)$ is a continuous function. The graph of $f'(x)$ on the interval $[0,8]$ is shown.

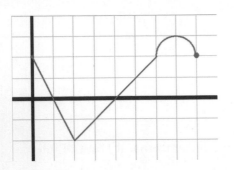

a) For what values of x is $f(x)$ increasing? Give a reason for your answer.

b) Find all the points of inflection of f on the interval $[0,8]$. Explain the reasoning that leads to your answer.

c) For what values of x is the graph of f concave up? Support your answer with the first derivative.

Answers and Explanations

1. C   2. B   3. B   4. B   5. D

1. The derivative attains its maximum when the second derivative changes from positive to negative. Take the derivatives of $f(x) = 2x^2 - e^x$, $f'(x) = 4x - e^x$ and $f''(x) = 4 - e^x$. The second derivative will equal zero when $e^x = 4$ or $x = \ln 4$. Test the sign of the second derivative on either side of $x = \ln 4$ to be certain that the value is a maximum. $f''(\ln 3) = 4 - e^{\ln 3} = 4 - 3 = 1$ and $f''(\ln 5) = 4 - e^{\ln 5} = 4 - 5 = -1$. Because f'' changes from positive to negative, $f'(x)$ changes from increasing to decreasing, so $f'(x)$ has a maximum at $x = \ln 4$.

2. The graph of the derivative has x-intercepts at (approximately) $x = -\frac{1}{2}$, $x = 1$, and $x = 4$, so the relative extrema of f should occur at those points. $x = -\frac{1}{2}$ should be a maximum, since the derivative changes from positive

to negative. By similar reasoning, $x = 1$ should be a minimum and $x = 4$ a maximum. Only B fits that description.

3. The graph of the derivative has four zeros, but only three of them show a change of sign. From left to right, there is a change from positive to negative denoting a maximum, from negative to positive indicating a minimum, and positive to negative from another maximum. The final zero represents a point of inflection.

4. Candidates for the location of the relative maxima are $x = 0$, $x = 2$, and $x = -3$, but you must test the sign of the first derivative, $f'(x) = x^3(x-2)(x+3)^2$.

x	x^3	$(x-2)$	$(x+3)^2$	$f'(x)$
-4	$-$	$-$	$+$	$+$
-1	$-$	$-$	$+$	$+$
1	$+$	$-$	$+$	$-$
3	$+$	$+$	$+$	$+$

The first derivative changes from positive to negative at $x = 0$, so f changes from increasing to decreasing at $x = 0$. $f(x)$ has a relative maximum at $x = 0$.

5. $f(x)$ will have a relative minimum when $f'(x) = \ln(2x-3)$ changes from negative to positive. $f'(x) = \ln(2x-3) = 0$ when $2x - 3 = 1$, so the critical point is $x = 2$. Check that $\ln(2x-3) < 0$ when $\frac{3}{2} < x < 2$ and $\ln(2x-3) > 0$ when $x > 2$.

Free Response Prompt

a) $f(x)$ is increasing when $f'(x) > 0$, which is when $0 \le x < 1$, and $4 < x \le 8$.

b) The points of inflection of f on the interval $[0,8]$ occur when the graph of $f(x)$ changes concavity and, therefore, $f'(x)$ changes from increasing to decreasing or decreasing to increasing. $f'(x)$ changes from decreasing to increasing at $x = 2$, and from increasing to decreasing at $x = 7$. $f(x)$ has two points of inflection at $x = 2$ and $x = 7$.

c) The graph of $f(x)$ is concave up when the second derivative is positive; that is, when the first derivative is increasing. $f(x)$ is concave up when $2 < x < 7$.

Topic 5: Integrals

Just as you associate derivatives with rates of change and slopes, you should associate integrals with accumulation and area. The area under a curve, approximated by a Riemann sum or a trapezoidal approximation, is a fundamental notion.

Riemann Sum

The Riemann sum approximates the area under a curve by the sum of the areas of a collection of rectangles. Each rectangle has its upper right vertex, its upper left vertex, or the midpoint of its upper side on the curve.

Left-hand Riemann sum	Width $= x_{n+1} - x_n$ Height $= f(x_n)$ Area of each rectangle $=$ $(x_{n+1} - x_n)f(x_n)$	
Right-hand Riemann sum	Width $= x_{n+1} - x_n$ Height $= f(x_{n+1})$ Area of each rectangle $=$ $(x_{n+1} - x_n)f(x_{n+1})$	

Midpoint Riemann sum	Width = $x_{n+1} - x_n$ Height = $f\left(\dfrac{x_{n+1} + x_n}{2}\right)$ Area of each rectangle = $\left(x_{n+1} - x_n\right)f\left(\dfrac{x_{n+1} + x_n}{2}\right)$	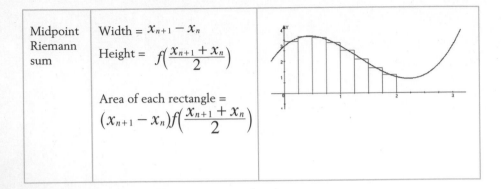

Trapezoidal Rule

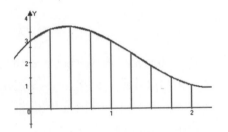

The trapezoidal rule approximates the area under the curve by the sum of the areas of a collection of trapezoids whose parallel sides connect the axis and the curve. The height of the trapezoids is $x_{n+1} - x_n$ and the two parallel bases are $f(x_n)$ and $f(x_{n+1})$. The area of any one trapezoid is

$$A = \frac{1}{2}(x_{n+1} - x_n)(f(x_n) + f(x_{n+1}))$$ If intervals of equal size are used,

then $x_{n+1} - x_n$ is the same for all the trapezoids. The summation has the form

$$A = \frac{1}{2}(x_1 - x_0)(f(x_0) + f(x_1)) + \frac{1}{2}(x_2 - x_1)(f(x_1) + f(x_2)) + \frac{1}{2}(x_3 - x_2)(f(x_2) + f(x_3)) + \dots$$

This sum can be rewritten as

$$A = \frac{1}{2}\Delta x(f(x_0) + f(x_1)) + \frac{1}{2}\Delta x(f(x_1) + f(x_2)) + \frac{1}{2}\Delta x(f(x_2) + f(x_3)) + \dots + \frac{1}{2}\Delta x(f(x_{n-1}) + f(x_n))$$

$$= \frac{1}{2}\Delta x[(f(x_0) + f(x_1)) + (f(x_1) + f(x_2)) + (f(x_2) + f(x_3)) + \dots + (f(x_{n-1}) + f(x_n))]$$

Because the trapezoids share sides, the sum can be simplified to

$$A = \frac{1}{2}\Delta x[f(x_0) + 2f(x_1) + 2f(x_2)... + 2f(x_{n-1}) + f(x_n)]$$

Fundamental Theorem of Calculus

The Fundamental Theorem of Calculus (FTC) ties together the area under the curve and the antiderivative. If f is continuous on $[a, b]$, and F is any antiderivative for f on $[a, b]$, then $\int_a^b f(t)dt = F(b) - F(a)$.

You use the FTC every time you evaluate a definite integral.

$$\int_2^{e^2} 1 - \frac{1}{x}dx = [x - \ln|x|]_2^{e^2} = (e^2 - \ln e^2) - (2 - \ln 2)$$

You'll be expected to find both definite and indefinite integrals. If $F(x)$ is an antiderivative of $f(x)$, and you have limits of integration a and b, as in $\int_a^b f(x)dx$, you can evaluate $F(b) - F(a)$. If you have an antiderivative of $f(x)$ in general form, and you have the value of that antiderivative at $x = a$, you can find the value of the constant and therefore the specific antiderivative. Without specific information, you can only give the general antiderivative, which always includes a constant of integration.

Basic Antiderivatives

Review your list of fundamental antiderivatives. They're your toolkit, and you can't build without tools. Since they are antiderivatives—derivative rules in reverse—most are familiar. Remember to add the constant!

	Expression	Antiderivative	Notes
Constant	-12	$-12x + C$	

Power	x^4	$\dfrac{x^5}{5} + C$	The power rule does not apply to x^{-1}.
	$-7x^{-5}$	$\dfrac{-7x^{-4}}{-4} = \dfrac{7x^{-4}}{4} + C$	
Sum and difference	$5x^4 + \dfrac{2}{x} - \cos x$	$x^5 + 2\ln|x| - \sin x + C$	
Exponential	e^x	$e^x + C$	For base $b \neq e$, $\dfrac{b^x}{\ln b} + C$
Logarithmic	$\dfrac{1}{x}$	$\ln|x| + C$	The antiderivative of $\ln x$ is $x\ln x - x + C$, but that doesn't come up often.
Trigonometric	$\sin x$	$-\cos x + C$	While not the only ones, these are the ones you see most often.
	$\cos x$	$\sin x + C$	
	$\sec^2 x$	$\tan x + C$	
	$\sec x \tan x$	$\sec x + C$	
Inverse trig	$\dfrac{1}{\sqrt{1-x^2}}$	$\arcsin x + C$	The antiderivatives of the inverse trig functions don't generally appear.
	$\dfrac{1}{1+x^2}$	$\arctan x + C$	

If the expression you have to integrate doesn't fit any of the antiderivatives on your list, try a u-substitution.

U-Substitution

Think of u-substitution as the chain rule in reverse. You'll use it to integrate products, if the conditions are right, and the conditions will be right if the product is (or is close to) a derivative the chain rule would have produced.

	Step	Example 1
1.	Decompose. One of your factors is a composite function. Identify the layers, the inner and outer functions.	In $\int_{0}^{\pi/2} \sin^2 x \cos x \, dx$, $\sin^2 x$ is a composite of the sine function (inner) and the squaring function (outer).
2.	Let u = the inner function.	$u = \sin x$
3.	Find $\dfrac{du}{dx}$.	$\dfrac{du}{dx} = \cos x$
4.	Solve for dx.	$du = \cos x \, dx$ so $dx = \dfrac{du}{\cos x}$
5.	Plug in the pieces.	$\int_{0}^{\pi/2} \sin^2 x \cos x \, dx = \int u^2 \, \cos x \, \dfrac{du}{\cos x}$
6.	Simplify.	$\int u^2 \, \cos x \, \dfrac{du}{\cos x} = \int u^2 \, du$
7.	All in terms of u? Yes? Go to step 11. No? Continue with step 8.	Yes! Go to step 11.

8.	Solve u = the inner function for x (or other variable) in terms of u.	
9.	Replace x with the u-expression.	
10.	Simplify.	
11.	Definite integral? Yes? Go to step 12. No? Go to step 13.	Yes! Go to step 12.
12.	Calculate u-limits.	$u = \sin x$ so $x = 0$ becomes $u = \sin 0 = 0$ and $x = \dfrac{\pi}{2}$ becomes $u = \sin\dfrac{\pi}{2} = 1$. $$\int_0^{\pi/2} \sin^2 x \cos x \; dx = \int_0^1 u^2 \, du$$
13.	Find the antiderivative.	$$\int_0^1 u^2 \, du = \frac{1}{3}u^3 \Big|_0^1$$
14.	Definite integral? Yes? Go to step 15. No? Go to step 16.	Yes! Go to step 15.
15.	Evaluate.	$$\frac{1}{3}u^3 \Big|_0^1 = \frac{1}{3} - 0 = \frac{1}{3}$$
16.	Replace u with the quantity it replaced. Simplify. Don't forget + C.	

OK, but they're not all that simple. Let's try a more complicated one.

	Step	Example 2
1.	Decompose. One of your factors is a composite function. Identify the layers, the inner and outer functions.	In $\int (x+1)\sqrt{2-x}\ dx$, $\sqrt{2-x}$ is a composite of the function $u(x) = 2 - x$ (inner) and the square root function (outer).
2.	Let u = the inner function.	$u = 2 - x$
3.	Find $\dfrac{du}{dx}$.	$\dfrac{du}{dx} = -1$
4.	Solve for dx.	$du = -dx$ so $dx = -du$
5.	Plug in the pieces.	$\int (x+1)\sqrt{2-x}\ dx$ $= \int (x+1)\sqrt{u}\ (-du)$
6.	Simplify.	$-\int (x+1)\, u^{\frac{1}{2}}\ du$
7.	All in terms of u? Yes? Go to step 11. No? Continue with step 8.	No! Continue with step 8.
8.	Solve u = the inner function for x (or other variable) in terms of u.	$u = 2 - x$ so $x = 2 - u$
9.	Replace x with the u-expression.	$-\int (x+1)\, u^{\frac{1}{2}}\ du$ $= -\int (2 - u + 1)\, u^{\frac{1}{2}}\ du$
10.	Simplify.	$-\int (3 - u)\, u^{\frac{1}{2}}\ du$ $= -\int (3u^{\frac{1}{2}} - u^{\frac{3}{2}})\ du$

11.	Definite integral? Yes? Go to step 12. No? Go to step 13.	No! Go to step 13.
12.	Calculate u-limits.	
13.	Find the antiderivative.	$-\int \left(3u^{\frac{1}{2}} - u^{\frac{3}{2}}\right)\, du$ $= -\left(\frac{2}{3} \cdot 3u^{\frac{3}{2}} - \frac{2}{5}u^{\frac{5}{2}}\right)$ $= -\left(2u^{\frac{3}{2}} - \frac{2}{5}u^{\frac{5}{2}}\right)$
14.	Definite integral? Yes? Go to step 15. No? Go to step 16.	No! Go to step 16.
15.	Evaluate.	
16.	Replace u with the quantity it replaced. Simplify. Don't forget +C	$-\left(2(2-x)^{\frac{3}{2}} - \frac{2}{5}(2-x)^{\frac{5}{2}}\right) + C$ $= \frac{2}{5}(2-x)^{\frac{5}{2}} - 2(2-x)^{\frac{3}{2}} + C$

Improper Integrals

An improper integral is one in which one or both limits of integration increase without bound. If one of the limits of integration becomes infinite, the improper integral is the limit of a definite integral.

$\displaystyle\int_a^\infty f(x)\,dx = \lim_{b\to\infty}\int_a^b f(x)\,dx$	$\displaystyle\int_2^\infty \frac{1}{x}\,dx = \lim_{b\to\infty}\int_2^b \frac{1}{x}\,dx = \lim_{b\to\infty}\ln|x|\,\big|_2^b = \lim_{b\to\infty}(\ln b - \ln 2) = \infty$
$\displaystyle\int_{-\infty}^b f(x)\,dx = \lim_{a\to-\infty}\int_a^b f(x)\,dx$	$\displaystyle\int_{-\infty}^{-1} e^x\,dx = \lim_{a\to-\infty}\int_a^{-1} e^x\,dx = \lim_{a\to-\infty}e^x\,\big|_a^{-1} = \lim_{a\to-\infty}(e^{-1} - e^a) = \frac{1}{e}$

For integrals from $-\infty$ to ∞, break the integral.

$$\int_{-\infty}^{\infty} f(x)dx = \lim_{a \to -\infty} \int_{a}^{0} f(x)dx + \lim_{b \to \infty} \int_{0}^{b} f(x)dx.$$

Practice

1. $\int_{0}^{1} 6xe^{x^2} - e^{4x-5}dx =$

A. $\dfrac{6e^6 - 6e^5 - e^4 + 1}{e^5}$

B. $6\left(\dfrac{e^2 - 1}{e}\right)$

C. $3 - 3e + \dfrac{e^4 - 1}{4e^5}$

D. $3e - \dfrac{1}{4e}$

E. $3e - 3 + \dfrac{1 - e^4}{4e^5}$

2. $\int \dfrac{\cos 2\theta}{1 - \sin 2\theta}d\theta =$

A. $\ln|1 - 2\sin 2\theta| + C$

B. $\ln|1 - \sin 2\theta| + C$

C. $-\dfrac{1}{2}\ln|1 - \sin 2\theta| + C$

D. $\ln\left|1 - \dfrac{1}{2}\sin 2\theta\right| + C$

E. $2\ln|1 - \sin 2\theta| + C$

3. Which of the following are antiderivatives of $f(x) = -2\sin x \cos x$?

I. $C - \sin^2 x$

II. $\cos^2 x - 1 + C$

III. $\sec^2 x - 1 + C$

A. I and II   B. I and III   C. II and III   D. III only   E. I, II and III

4. If f is the antiderivative of $\dfrac{5}{x+4}$ such that $f(-3) = 3$, then $f(0) \approx$

A. 4.931   B. 14.931   C. 9.93   D. 8.322   E. 7.931

5. Let $F(x)$ be an antiderivative of $\dfrac{\sqrt{e^x}}{2}$. If $F(2) = 0$, then $F(0) =$

A. $\dfrac{1 - e^{\sqrt{2}}}{2}$

B. $1 - e$

C. $\dfrac{1 - e^2}{4}$

D. $\dfrac{1 - e}{2}$

E. $2 - 2e$

Free Response Prompt

The daily temperature outside a fishing cabin at 8 a.m. over a 15-day period is given by

$$F(t) = 20 + 40\sin\pi\left(\frac{t+3}{21}\right), \quad 0 \le t \le 15,$$

where $F(t)$ is measured in degrees Fahrenheit and t is measured in days.

a) Find the average temperature, to the nearest degree, between $t = 4$ and $t = 11$.

b) When the daily temperature fell below 50 degrees, it was necessary to light a fire in a wood stove to heat the cabin. For what values of t was the fire lit?

c) For every degree that the daily temperature falls below 50 degrees, the wood stove burns 2 logs per day. How many logs will be burned over this 15-day period?

Answers and Explanations

1. E   2. C   3. A   4. C   5. B

1. $\int_0^1 (6xe^{x^2} - e^{4x-5})dx = 6\int_0^1 xe^{x^2}dx - \int_0^1 e^{4x-5}dx$. For the first integral, let

$u = x^2$, $du = 2xdx$, and $dx = \dfrac{du}{2x}$, but the limits of integration remain 0

and 1. $\int_0^1 6xe^{x^2}dx = 3\int_0^1 e^u du$. For the second, let $u = 4x - 5$, $du = 4dx$,

and $dx = \dfrac{du}{4}$, and the limits of integration become -5 and -1. Then

$\int_0^1 e^{4x-5}dx = \dfrac{1}{4}\int_{-5}^{-1} e^u du$. Therefore $\int_0^1 (6xe^{x^2} - e^{4x-5})dx = 3\int_0^1 e^u du - \dfrac{1}{4}\int_{-5}^{-1} e^u du$

$= 3(e-1) - \dfrac{1}{4}(e^{-1} - e^{-5}) = 3e - 3 + \dfrac{1 - e^4}{4e^5}$.

2. To find the antiderivative of $f(x) = \dfrac{\cos 2\theta}{1 - \sin 2\theta}$, let $u = 1 - \sin 2\theta$,

$du = -2\cos 2\theta d\theta$, and $d\theta = \dfrac{-du}{2\cos 2\theta}$. Then

$\int \dfrac{\cos 2\theta}{1 - \sin 2\theta}d\theta = \int \dfrac{\cos 2\theta}{u} \cdot \dfrac{-du}{2\cos 2\theta} = \dfrac{-1}{2}\int \dfrac{du}{u} = \dfrac{-1}{2}\ln|1 - \sin 2\theta| + C$.

3. To find the antiderivative of $f(x) = -2\sin x \cos x$, let $u = \sin x$,

$du = \cos xdx$, and $dx = \dfrac{du}{\cos x}$. Then $\int -2\sin x \cos xdx = -2\int u \cos x \dfrac{du}{\cos x}$

$= -2 \int u \, du = C - \sin^2 x$. With the help of trigonometric identities, this can become $C - \sin^2 x = C - (1 - \cos^2 x) = \cos^2 x - 1 + C$.

4. The general antiderivative of $\frac{5}{x+4}$ is $5 \ln|x+4| + C$. If $f(-3) = 3$, then $5 \ln|-3+4| + C = 3$ and $5 \ln 1 + C = 3$, so $C = 3$. Therefore $f(0) = 5 \ln 4 + 3 \approx 9.93$.

5. $F(x) = \int \frac{\sqrt{e^x}}{2} dx = \frac{1}{2} \int e^u \cdot 2 \, du = \int e^u \, du = e^u + C = e^{x/2} + C$.   If $F(2) = e^{2/2} + C = 0$, then $C = -e$ and $F(x) = e^{\frac{x}{2}} - e$, so $F(0) = e^{\frac{0}{2}} - e = 1 - e$.

Free Response Prompt

a) The average temperature between $t = 4$ and $t = 11$ is equal to

$$\frac{1}{11-4} \int_4^{11} \left[20 + 40 \sin \frac{\pi}{21}(t+3) \right] dt = \frac{1}{7} \int_4^{11} 20 \, dt + \frac{40}{7} \int_4^{11} \left[\sin \frac{\pi}{21}(t+3) \right] dt.$$

Let $u = \frac{\pi}{21}(t+3)$ and $du = \frac{\pi}{21} dt$. Then $\frac{1}{7} \int_4^{11} 20 \, dt + \frac{40}{7} \cdot \frac{21}{\pi} \int_{\pi/3}^{2\pi/3} \sin u \, du$

$$= \frac{20t}{7} \Big|_4^{11} - \frac{120}{\pi} \cos u \Big|_{\pi/3}^{2\pi/3} = 20 - \frac{120}{\pi} \left(-\frac{1}{2} - \frac{1}{2} \right) = 20 + \frac{120}{\pi} \approx 58.197.$$ The

average temperature from $t = 4$ and $t = 11$ was approximately 58 degrees.

b) The stove is lit on days when $20 + 40 \sin \pi \left(\frac{t+3}{21} \right) < 50$ or when $\sin \pi \left(\frac{t+3}{21} \right) < \frac{3}{4}$. This occurs when $t < 2.669$ or $t > 12.331$. The stove was lit $0 \leq t < 3$ and $13 \leq t \leq 15$.

c) The number of logs consumed is equal to

$$2\int_0^3 50 - \left[20 + 40\sin\frac{\pi}{21}(t+3)\right] dt + 2\int_{13}^{15} 50 - \left[20 + 40\sin\frac{\pi}{21}(t+3)\right] dt$$

$$2\int_0^3 \left[30 - 40\sin\frac{\pi}{21}(t+3)\right] dt + 2\int_{13}^{15} \left[30 - 40\sin\frac{\pi}{21}(t+3)\right] dt$$

$$u = \frac{\pi}{21}(t+3) \quad u = \frac{\pi}{21}(0+3) = \frac{\pi}{7} \quad \frac{\pi}{21}(13+3) = \frac{16\pi}{21}$$

$$du = \frac{\pi}{21} dt \qquad \frac{\pi}{21}(3+3) = \frac{2\pi}{7} \qquad \frac{\pi}{21}(15+3) = \frac{6\pi}{7}$$

$$2\cdot\frac{21}{\pi}\int_{\pi/7}^{2\pi/7} [30 - 40\sin u] \, du + 2\cdot\frac{21}{\pi}\int_{16\pi/21}^{6\pi/7} [30 - 40\sin u] \, du$$

$$\frac{42}{\pi}[30u + 40\cos u]_{\pi/7}^{2\pi/7} + \frac{42}{\pi}[30u + 40\cos u]_{16\pi/21}^{6\pi/7}$$

$$\frac{42}{\pi}\left[\left(30\cdot\frac{2\pi}{7} + 40\cos\frac{2\pi}{7}\right) - \left(30\cdot\frac{\pi}{7} + 40\cos\frac{\pi}{7}\right)\right] + \frac{42}{\pi}\left[\left(30\cdot\frac{6\pi}{7} + 40\cos\frac{6\pi}{7}\right) - \left(30\cdot\frac{16\pi}{21} + 40\cos\frac{16\pi}{21}\right)\right]$$

$$\frac{42}{\pi}\left[\frac{30\pi}{7} + 40\cos\frac{2\pi}{7} - 40\cos\frac{\pi}{7}\right] + \frac{42}{\pi}\left[\frac{20\pi}{7} + 40\cos\frac{6\pi}{7} - 40\cos\frac{16\pi}{21}\right]$$

$$180 + \frac{42}{\pi}\left(40\cos\frac{2\pi}{7} - 40\cos\frac{\pi}{7}\right) + 120 + \frac{42}{\pi}\left(40\cos\frac{6\pi}{7} - 40\cos\frac{16\pi}{21}\right)$$

$$300 + \frac{42}{\pi}\cdot 40\left(\cos\frac{2\pi}{7} - \cos\frac{\pi}{7} + \cos\frac{6\pi}{7} - \cos\frac{16\pi}{21}\right)$$

$$= 300 + \frac{42}{\pi}\cdot 40(-0.445) = 61.820$$

The stove will burn approximately 62 logs over the 15-day period.

Topic 6: Parts and Partial Fractions

The integration techniques in this section are included only on the BC exam.

Integration by Parts

You've got to integrate a product. You tried a u-substitution, but it didn't work. Now what? Well, if u-substitution is like the chain rule backwards, integration by parts is the product rule backwards.

Integration by parts: $\int u \, dv = uv - \int v \, du$

The LIPET list helps you remember what to choose for u.

LIPET: Logs, Inverse Trig Functions, Polynomials, Exponentials, Tangents

	Step	Example 1
1.	Choose one factor to be u. Remember the LIPET rule.	In $\int_{2}^{4} x \ln x \, dx$, you have a log, so call $u = \ln x$
2.	Find $\dfrac{du}{dx}$.	$\dfrac{du}{dx} = \dfrac{1}{x}$

3.	Make the other factor dv.	$dv = x\,dx$
4.	Find v.	$v = \dfrac{x^2}{2}$
5.	Plug in the pieces and simplify.	$\int u\,dv = uv - \int v\,du$ $= \ln x \cdot \dfrac{x^2}{2} - \int \dfrac{x^2}{2} \cdot \dfrac{1}{x}\,dx$ $= \dfrac{x^2}{2}\ln x - \dfrac{1}{2}\int x\,dx$
6.	Can you find the antiderivative of $\int v\,du$? Yes? Go to step 13. No? Go to step 7 and use parts on $\int v\,du$.	Yes! Go to step 13.
7.	Choose one factor to be u. Remember the LIPET rule.	
8.	Find $\dfrac{du}{dx}$.	
9.	Make the other factor dv.	
10.	Find v.	
11.	Plug in the pieces.	
12.	Can you find the antiderivative of $\int v\,du$? Yes? Go to step 13. No? Use parts on $\int v\,du$.	

13.	Find the antiderivative of $\int v\,du$.	$= \dfrac{x^2}{2}\ln x - \dfrac{1}{2}\int x\,dx$ $= \dfrac{x^2}{2}\ln x - \dfrac{1}{2}\cdot\dfrac{x^2}{2} = \dfrac{x^2}{2}\ln x - \dfrac{x^2}{4}$
14.	Definite integral? No? Go to step 15. Yes? Go to step 16.	Yes! Go to step 16
15.	Don't forget + C.	
16.	Evaluate.	$= \left[\dfrac{x^2}{2}\ln x - \dfrac{x^2}{4}\right]_2^4$ $= \left[\left(\dfrac{16}{2}\ln 4 - \dfrac{16}{4}\right) - \left(\dfrac{4}{2}\ln 2 - \dfrac{4}{4}\right)\right]$ $= 8\ln 4 - 4 - 2\ln 2 + 1$ $= 8(2\ln 2) - 4 - 2\ln 2 + 1$ $= 14\ln 2 - 3$

What if you do all that and it doesn't seem to be getting better? Don't give up.

	Step	Example 2
1.	Choose one factor to be u. Remember the LIPET rule.	In $\int x^2\sin(\pi x)\,dx$, there are no logs or inverse trig functions, so call $u = x^2$.
2.	Find $\dfrac{du}{dx}$.	$\dfrac{du}{dx} = 2x$
3.	Make the other factor dv.	$dv = \sin(\pi x)dx$

4.	Find v.	$v = \dfrac{-\cos(\pi x)}{\pi}$
5.	Plug in the pieces and simplify.	$\int u\,dv = uv - \int v\,du$ $= \dfrac{-x^2\cos(\pi x)}{\pi} - \int \dfrac{-2x\cos(\pi x)}{\pi}\,dx$ $= \dfrac{-x^2\cos(\pi x)}{\pi} + \dfrac{2}{\pi}\int x\cos(\pi x)\,dx$
6.	Can you find the antiderivative of $\int v\,du$? Yes? Go to step 13. No? Go to step 7 and use parts on $\int v\,du$.	No! Go to step 7 and use parts on $\int v\,du$.
7.	Choose one factor to be u. Remember the LIPET rule.	Use parts on $\int x\cos(\pi x)\,dx$. Let $u = x$.
8.	Find $\dfrac{du}{dx}$.	$\dfrac{du}{dx} = 1$, so $du = dx$
9.	Make the other factor dv.	$dv = \cos(\pi x)\,dx$
10.	Find v.	$v = \dfrac{\sin(\pi x)}{\pi}$
11.	Plug in the pieces.	$\int u\,dv = uv - \int v\,du$ $= \dfrac{x\sin(\pi x)}{\pi} - \int \dfrac{\sin(\pi x)}{\pi}\,dx$ $= \dfrac{x\sin(\pi x)}{\pi} - \dfrac{1}{\pi}\int \sin(\pi x)\,dx$

12.	Can you find the antide-rivative of $\int v \, du$? Yes? Go to step 13. No? Use parts on $\int v \, du$.	Yes! Go to step 13.
13.	Find the antiderivative of $\int v \, du$.	$\int \sin(\pi x) \, dx = \dfrac{-\cos(\pi x)}{\pi}$
14.	Put everything together.	$\int x^2 \sin(\pi x) \, dx$ $= \dfrac{-x^2 \cos(\pi x)}{\pi} + \dfrac{2}{\pi} \int x \cos(\pi x) \, dx$ $= \dfrac{-x^2 \cos(\pi x)}{\pi} + \dfrac{2}{\pi} \left[\dfrac{x \sin(\pi x)}{\pi} - \dfrac{1}{\pi} \int \sin(\pi x) \, dx \right]$ $= \dfrac{-x^2 \cos(\pi x)}{\pi} + \dfrac{2}{\pi} \left[\dfrac{x \sin(\pi x)}{\pi} + \dfrac{\cos(\pi x)}{\pi^2} \right]$ $= \dfrac{-x^2 \cos(\pi x)}{\pi} + \dfrac{2x \sin(\pi x)}{\pi^2} + \dfrac{2 \cos(\pi x)}{\pi^3}$
15.	Definite integral? No? Go to step 16. Yes? Go to step 17.	No! Go to step 16.
16.	Don't forget + C.	$= \dfrac{-x^2 \cos(\pi x)}{\pi} + \dfrac{2x \sin(\pi x)}{\pi^2} + \dfrac{2 \cos(\pi x)}{\pi^3} + C$
17.	Evaluate.	

Partial Fraction Decomposition

Finding the antiderivative of a rational expression can be as simple as
$\int \frac{dx}{x} = \ln|x| + C$ or

$$\int \frac{3}{(x-1)^2} \, dx = 3 \int (x-1)^{-2} \, dx = -3(x-1)^{-1} + C = \frac{-3}{x-1} + C. \text{ Other}$$

rational expressions present more of a challenge. Decomposing the expression into a sum of simpler expressions smoothes the way. There are three cases to consider.

Case 1: The denominator can be factored as a product of linear factors without repetition.

	Step	Example 1
1.	Factor the denominator.	$\int_{3}^{4} \frac{1}{x^2 - 1} \, dx = \int_{3}^{4} \frac{1}{(x+1)(x-1)} \, dx$
2.	Express the fraction as a sum. Each factor becomes a denominator with an unknown numerator.	$\frac{1}{(x+1)(x-1)} = \frac{A}{x+1} + \frac{B}{x-1}$
3.	Express each of the individual fractions with the common denominator.	$= \frac{A(x-1)}{(x+1)(x-1)} + \frac{B(x+1)}{(x+1)(x-1)}$
4.	Add the numerators and simplify.	$= \frac{Ax + Bx - A + B}{(x+1)(x-1)}$
5.	Create a system of equations by comparing the current numerator to the numerator of the original expression.	$A + B = 0$ $-A + B = 1$

6.	Solve for the unknown numerators.	$A = -\dfrac{1}{2}$ $B = \dfrac{1}{2}$
7.	Re-express the integral as the sum of simpler integrals.	$\displaystyle\int_3^4 \frac{1}{x^2-1}\,dx = \int_3^4 \frac{-\frac{1}{2}}{x+1}\,dx + \int_3^4 \frac{\frac{1}{2}}{x-1}\,dx$ $= -\dfrac{1}{2}\displaystyle\int_3^4 \frac{dx}{x+1} + \dfrac{1}{2}\int_3^4 \frac{dx}{x-1}$
8.	Take the antiderivative.	$= -\dfrac{1}{2}\ln(|x+1|)\Big|_3^4 + \dfrac{1}{2}\ln(|x-1|)\Big|_3^4$
9.	Evaluate.	$= -\dfrac{1}{2}\ln 5 + \dfrac{1}{2}\ln 4 + \dfrac{1}{2}\ln 3 - \dfrac{1}{2}\ln 2$ $= \dfrac{1}{2}[(\ln 4 + \ln 3) - (\ln 5 + \ln 2)]$ $= \dfrac{1}{2}[(\ln 12) - (\ln 10)]$ $= \dfrac{1}{2}(\ln 1.2) = \ln\sqrt{1.2}$

Case 2: The denominator factors to linear factors, one (or more) of which is repeated.

	Step	Example 2
1.	Factor the denominator.	$\displaystyle\int \frac{x+3}{(x+1)(x-1)^2}\,dx$

2.	Express the fraction as a sum, one fraction for each linear factor and an additional one for the squared factor.	$\dfrac{A}{x+1} + \dfrac{B}{x-1} + \dfrac{C}{(x-1)^2}$
3.	Express each of the individual fractions with the common denominator.	$\dfrac{A(x-1)^2}{(x+1)(x-1)^2} + \dfrac{B(x+1)(x-1)}{(x+1)(x-1)^2} + \dfrac{C(x+1)}{(x+1)(x-1)^2}$
4.	Add the numerators and simplify.	$\dfrac{Ax^2 - 2Ax + A}{(x+1)(x-1)^2} + \dfrac{Bx^2 - B}{(x+1)(x-1)^2} + \dfrac{Cx + C}{(x+1)(x-1)^2}$ $\dfrac{Ax^2 + Bx^2 - 2Ax + Cx + A - B + C}{(x+1)(x-1)^2}$
5.	Create a system of equations by comparing the current numerator to the numerator of the original expression.	$A + B = 0$ $-2A + C = 1$ $A - B + C = 3$
6.	Solve for the unknown numerators.	$A = \dfrac{1}{2},\ B = -\dfrac{1}{2},\ C = 2$
7.	Re-express the integral as the sum of simpler integrals.	$\displaystyle\int \left[\dfrac{\frac{1}{2}}{x+1} - \dfrac{\frac{1}{2}}{x-1} + \dfrac{2}{(x-1)^2} \right] dx$ $= \dfrac{1}{2}\displaystyle\int \dfrac{dx}{x+1} - \dfrac{1}{2}\displaystyle\int \dfrac{dx}{x-1} + 2\displaystyle\int \dfrac{dx}{(x-1)^2}$
8.	Take the antiderivative.	$\dfrac{1}{2}\ln|x+1| - \dfrac{1}{2}\ln|x-1| - \dfrac{2}{x-1} + C$ $= \ln\sqrt{\dfrac{x+1}{x-1}} - \dfrac{2}{x-1} + C$

Case 3: The denominator contains an irreducible quadratic factor.

	Step	Example 3
1.	Factor the denominator.	$\int \dfrac{x^2 - 3x}{(2x - 1)(x^2 + 4)}\,dx$
2.	Express the fraction as a sum, with constants for the numerators of the linear factors and a linear expression for the numerator of the quadratic.	$\dfrac{A}{(2x - 1)} + \dfrac{Bx + C}{(x^2 + 4)}$
3.	Express each of the individual fractions with the common denominator.	$\dfrac{A(x^2 + 4)}{(2x - 1)(x^2 + 4)} + \dfrac{(Bx + C)(2x - 1)}{(x^2 + 4)(2x - 1)}$
4.	Add the numerators and simplify.	$\dfrac{Ax^2 + 4A + 2Bx^2 - Bx + 2Cx - C}{(2x - 1)(x^2 + 4)}$ $\dfrac{Ax^2 + 2Bx^2 - Bx + 2Cx + 4A - C}{(2x - 1)(x^2 + 4)}$
5.	Create a system of equations by comparing the current numerator to the numerator of the original expression.	$A + 2B = 1$ $-B + 2C = -3$ $4A - C = 0$
6.	Solve for the unknown numerators.	$A = -\dfrac{5}{17}$ $B = \dfrac{11}{17}$ $C = -\dfrac{10}{17}$
7.	Re-express the integral as the sum of simpler integrals.	$-\dfrac{5}{17}\int \dfrac{dx}{2x - 1} + \dfrac{4}{17}\int \dfrac{x\,dx}{x^2 + 4} - \dfrac{10}{17}\int \dfrac{dx}{x^2 + 4}$
8.	Take the antiderivative.	$-\dfrac{5}{17} \cdot \dfrac{1}{2}\ln|2x - 1| + \dfrac{11}{17} \cdot \dfrac{1}{2}\ln|x^2 + 4|$ $-\dfrac{10}{17}\arctan\left(\dfrac{x}{2}\right) + C$

Practice

1. $\int_0^1 xe^{2x}\,dx =$

A. $e^2 - 1$ B. $\dfrac{e^2 - 1}{2}$ C. $\dfrac{e^2 + 1}{2}$ D. $\dfrac{e^2 + 1}{4}$ E. $\dfrac{e^2 - 1}{4}$

2. $\int_{-3}^1 x\sqrt{1-x}\,dx =$

A. $\dfrac{368}{15}$ B. $-\dfrac{112}{15}$ C. $\dfrac{218}{15}$ D. $\dfrac{16}{3}$ E. $\dfrac{-128}{15}$

3. $\int x^2 \cos x\,dx =$

A. $x^2 \sin x - 2\cos x + 2\sin x + C$

B. $x^2 \sin x + 2x\cos x - 2\cos x + C$

C. $x^2 \sin x + 2\cos x - 2\sin x + C$

D. $x^2 \sin x + 2x\cos x + C$

E. $x^2 \sin x + 2x\cos x - 2\sin x + C$

4. $\int \dfrac{x+2}{x^2-9}\,dx =$

A. $\dfrac{1}{6}\ln|x+3| + \dfrac{5}{6}\ln|x-3| + C$

B. $\dfrac{5}{6}\ln|x+3| + \dfrac{1}{6}\ln|x-3| + C$

C. $\dfrac{5}{6}\ln|x+3| - \dfrac{5}{6}\ln|x-3| + C$

D. $\dfrac{1}{3}\ln|x+3| + \dfrac{2}{3}\ln|x-3| + C$

E. $\dfrac{2}{3}\ln|x+3| + \dfrac{1}{3}\ln|x-3| + C$

5. $\int_0^1 \dfrac{2x - 3}{(x - 2)(x + 1)^2} dx$

A. 0.630   B. 0.661   C. 0.679   D. –1.232   E. 2.079

Free Response Prompt

An object moving in the xy-plane is at position $(x(t), y(t))$ at time t, where

$$\dfrac{dx}{dt} = 2t\sin(\pi t) \text{ and } \dfrac{dy}{dt} = \dfrac{3}{t(t + 1)}.$$

At time $t = \dfrac{1}{2}$, the position of the object is $\left(\dfrac{1}{\pi}, -3\ln 3\right)$.

a) Find the position of the object at time $t = 2$.

b) Write the equation of the line tangent to the curve at $\left(\dfrac{1}{\pi}, -3\ln 3\right)$.

c) Set up, but do not integrate an expression for the total distance traveled by the object over the time $1 \le t \le 2$.

Answers and Explanations

1. D   2. B   3. E   4. A   5. C

1. Let $u = x$ and $dv = e^{2x}dx$. Then $du = dx$ and $v = \dfrac{1}{2}e^{2x}$. $\int xe^{2x}\,dx$

$= x \cdot \dfrac{1}{2}e^{2x} - \int \dfrac{1}{2}e^{2x}dx = \dfrac{xe^{2x}}{2} - \dfrac{1}{2}\cdot\dfrac{1}{2}e^{2x} = \dfrac{xe^{2x}}{2} - \dfrac{e^{2x}}{4}$. Evaluating from 0

to 1, you get $\left(\dfrac{e^2}{2} - \dfrac{e^2}{4}\right) - \left(0 - \dfrac{1}{4}\right) = \dfrac{e^2 + 1}{4}$.

2. Let $u = x$ and $dv = (1-x)^{\frac{1}{2}}dx$. Then $du = dx$ and $v = -\frac{2}{3}(1-x)^{\frac{3}{2}}$.

$$\int_{-3}^{1} x\sqrt{1-x}\,dx = -\frac{2}{3}x(1-x)^{\frac{3}{2}} + \frac{2}{3}\int(1-x)^{\frac{3}{2}}dx$$

$$= -\frac{2}{3}x(1-x)^{\frac{3}{2}} - \frac{4}{15}(1-x)^{\frac{5}{2}} = -\frac{2}{15}(1-x)^{\frac{3}{2}}(3x+2).\ \text{Evaluating from}$$

-3 to 1, you get $= -\dfrac{112}{15}$

3. Let $u = x^2$ and $dv = \cos x\,dx$. Then $du = 2x\,dx$ and $v = \sin x$. $\int x^2 \cos x\,dx = x^2 \sin x - \int 2x \sin x\,dx$. Use parts again with $u = x$, $du = dx$, $dv = \sin x\,dx$, and $v = -\cos x$. Then the integral $= x^2 \sin x - 2\left[-x\cos x - \int -\cos x\,dx\right] = x^2 \sin x + 2x\cos x - 2\sin x + C$.

4. Factor the denominator and re-express

$\dfrac{A}{x+3} + \dfrac{B}{x-3} = \dfrac{Ax - 3A + Bx + 3B}{(x+3)(x-3)}$. Solve the system $\begin{cases} A+B = 1 \\ -3A + 3B = 2 \end{cases}$ to

find that $A = \dfrac{1}{6}$ and $B = \dfrac{5}{6}$. Then $\int \dfrac{x+2}{x^2-9}dx = \int \dfrac{x+2}{(x+3)(x-3)}dx$

$= \dfrac{1}{6}\int \dfrac{dx}{x+3} + \dfrac{5}{6}\int \dfrac{dx}{x-3} = \dfrac{1}{6}\ln|x+3| + \dfrac{5}{6}\ln|x-3| + C$

5. Decompose the integrand to the sum of three rational expressions:

$\dfrac{A}{x-2} + \dfrac{B}{x+1} + \dfrac{C}{(x+1)^2}$. Combine and simplify.

$$\dfrac{A(x+1)^2}{(x-2)(x+1)^2} + \dfrac{B(x-2)(x+1)}{(x-2)(x+1)^2} + \dfrac{C(x-2)}{(x-2)(x+1)^2}$$

$$= \dfrac{Ax^2 + Bx^2 + 2Ax - Bx + Cx + A - 2B - 2C}{(x-2)(x+1)^2}$$

Solve the system $\begin{cases} A + B = 0 \\ 2A - B + C = 2 \\ A - 2B - 2C = -3 \end{cases}$ to find that $A = \frac{1}{9}$, $B = -\frac{1}{9}$, and

$C = \frac{5}{3}$. Then $\int_0^1 \frac{2x-3}{(x-2)(x+1)^2} dx = \frac{1}{9} \int_0^1 \frac{dx}{x-2} dx - \frac{1}{9} \int_0^1 \frac{dx}{x+1} + \frac{5}{3} \int_0^1 \frac{dx}{(x+1)^2}$

$= \left[\frac{1}{9} \ln|x-2| - \frac{1}{9} \ln|x+1| - \frac{5}{3(x+1)} \right]_0^1$

$= \left[\left(0 - \frac{1}{9} \ln 2 - \frac{5}{6} \right) - \left(\frac{1}{9} \ln 2 - 0 - \frac{5}{3} \right) \right] = -\frac{2}{9} \ln 2 + \frac{5}{6} \approx 0.679$

Free Response Prompt

a) Use integration by parts, with $u = t$, $du = dt$, $dv = \sin(\pi t)dt$, and

$v = \frac{-\cos(\pi t)}{\pi}$ to find $x(t) = \frac{-t\cos(\pi t)}{\pi} + \frac{1}{\pi} \int \cos(\pi t)dt = \frac{\sin(\pi t) - t\cos(\pi t)}{\pi} + C$.

Since $x\left(\frac{1}{2}\right) = \frac{1}{\pi}$, $\frac{\sin\left(\frac{\pi}{2}\right) - \frac{1}{2}\cos\left(\frac{\pi}{2}\right)}{\pi} + C = \frac{1-0}{\pi} + C = \frac{1}{\pi}$ so $C = 0$ and

$x(t) = \frac{\sin(\pi t) - t\cos(\pi t)}{\pi}$.

Use partial fractions to integrate $y(t) = \int \frac{3}{t(t+1)} dt = \int \frac{A}{t} dt + \int \frac{B}{t+1} dt$.

Solve the system $A + B = 0$ and $A = 3$ to find that $A = 3$ and

$B = -3$. Then $y(t) = 3 \int \frac{dt}{t} - 3 \int \frac{dt}{t+1} = 3 \ln t - 3 \ln(t+1) + C$.

Since $y\left(\frac{1}{2}\right) = 3\left(\ln\frac{1}{2} - \ln\left(\frac{3}{2}\right)\right) + C = 3 \ln\frac{1}{3} + C = -3 \ln 3$, $C = 0$, and

$y(t) = 3 \ln t - 3 \ln(t+1)$ or $y(t) = 3 \ln\left(\frac{t}{t+1}\right)$.

The position of the object at time $t = 2$ is $\left(\frac{\sin(\pi t) - t\cos(\pi t)}{\pi}, 3 \ln\left(\frac{t}{t+1}\right) \right)$

$= \left(\frac{\sin(2\pi) - 2\cos(2\pi)}{\pi}, 3 \ln\frac{2}{3} \right) = \left(-\frac{2}{\pi}, 3 \ln\frac{2}{3} \right) \approx (-0.637, -1.216)$.

b) The tangent to the curve at $\left(\frac{1}{\pi}, -3\ln 3\right)$ occurs when $t = \frac{1}{2}$. Evaluate $\frac{dx}{dt} = \frac{1}{2}\sin\left(\frac{\pi}{2}\right) = \frac{1}{2}$ and $\frac{dy}{dt} = \frac{3}{\frac{1}{2}\left(\frac{1}{2}+1\right)} = \frac{3}{\frac{3}{4}} = 4$. Then find

$$\frac{dy}{dx} = \frac{\frac{dy}{dt}}{\frac{dx}{dt}} = \frac{4}{\frac{1}{2}} = 8.$$ The equation of the line is $y + 3\ln 3 = 8\left(x - \frac{1}{\pi}\right)$.

c) The total distance traveled is

$$\int_1^2 \sqrt{x'(t)^2 + y'(t)^2}\, dt = \int_1^2 \sqrt{(t\sin \pi t)^2 + \left(\frac{3}{t(t+1)}\right)^2}\, dt.$$

Topic 7: Applications of the Integral

The integral is an accumulator, a summing up. The integral of a velocity gives a distance traveled. The integral of a rate of flow gives the volume of water that passes through within a time interval. The integral of a function over an interval gives the area under the curve.

Fundamental Theorem of Calculus

The Fundamental Theorem of Calculus (FTC) ties together the area under the curve and the antiderivative. If f is continuous on $[a, b]$, and F is any antiderivative for f on $[a, b]$, then $\int_a^b f(t)\,dt = F(b) - F(a)$.

- You use the FTC every time you evaluate a definite integral.

$$\int_2^{e^2} 1 - \frac{1}{x}\,dx = [x - \ln|x|]_2^{e^2} = (e^2 - \ln e^2) - (2 - \ln 2)$$

- Expect to use FTC for less direct evaluation.

If F and f are differentiable functions such that $F(x) = \int_0^x f(t)\,dt$ and if $F(a) = 3$ and $F(b) = 8$ where $a < b$, find $\int_a^b f(t)\,dt$.

According to FTC, $\int_a^b f(t)\,dt = F(b) - F(a)$, therefore, $\int_a^b f(t)\,dt = 8 - 3 = 5$.

Area Under a Curve

One of the most common applications of the integral is the calculation of the area enclosed between the graph of a function and the x-axis.

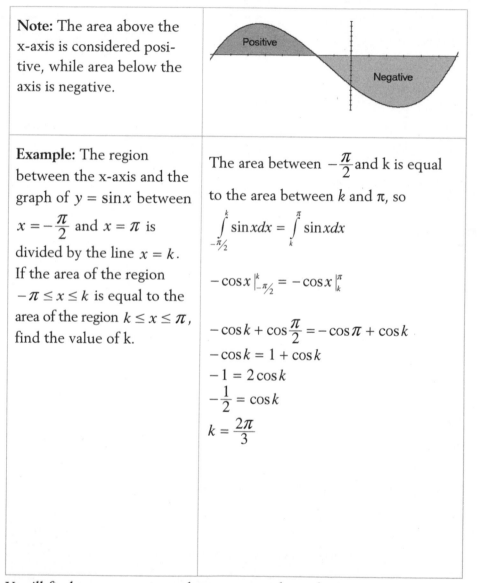

Note: The area above the x-axis is considered positive, while area below the axis is negative.

Example: The region between the x-axis and the graph of $y = \sin x$ between $x = -\dfrac{\pi}{2}$ and $x = \pi$ is divided by the line $x = k$. If the area of the region $-\pi \le x \le k$ is equal to the area of the region $k \le x \le \pi$, find the value of k.

The area between $-\dfrac{\pi}{2}$ and k is equal to the area between k and π, so

$$\int_{-\pi/2}^{k} \sin x\, dx = \int_{k}^{\pi} \sin x\, dx$$

$$-\cos x \Big|_{-\pi/2}^{k} = -\cos x \Big|_{k}^{\pi}$$

$$-\cos k + \cos\frac{\pi}{2} = -\cos\pi + \cos k$$

$$-\cos k = 1 + \cos k$$

$$-1 = 2\cos k$$

$$-\frac{1}{2} = \cos k$$

$$k = \frac{2\pi}{3}$$

You'll find more on area under a curve and area between two curves in the section on area and volume.

Average Value

The average value of a function $f(x)$ over the interval $[a, b]$ is

$$f_{avg} = \frac{1}{b-a} \int_a^b f(x)dx.$$

What is the average value of y for the part of the curve $y = 8 + x^3$ in the second quadrant?	
Determine the values of x for which $y = 8 + x^3$ is in the second quadrant.	Certainly, $x < 0$ gives the upper limit, but the lower limit occurs when $8 + x^3 = 0$ or when $x = -2$.
Find the average by adding up all the values (using an integral)…	$\int_{-2}^{0} (8 + x^3)dx = 8x + \frac{x^4}{4}\Big|_{-2}^{0}$
…and dividing by the number of values, which is the difference $b - a$. Dividing by $b - a$ is equivalent to multiplying by $\frac{1}{b-a}$.	$\frac{1}{2} \int_{-2}^{0} (8 + x^3)dx = \frac{1}{2}\left(8x + \frac{x^4}{4}\right)_{-2}^{0}$ $= \frac{1}{2}\left[0 - \left(-16 + \frac{16}{4}\right)\right] = \frac{1}{2}(12) = 6$

Length of a Curve

If the curve defined by $y = f(x)$ is traced from $x = a$ to $x = b$, the

length of the curve can be found by $L = \int_a^b \sqrt{1 + \left(\frac{dy}{dx}\right)^2}\, dx.$

Example: What is the length of the arc of $y = \sqrt{x}$ from $x = 0$ to $x = 3$?	
Find $\frac{dy}{dx}$.	If $y = \sqrt{x}$, then $\frac{dy}{dx} = \frac{1}{2\sqrt{x}}$

Square $\dfrac{dy}{dx}$.	$\left(\dfrac{dy}{dx}\right)^2 = \left(\dfrac{1}{2\sqrt{x}}\right)^2 = \dfrac{1}{4x}$
Add 1.	$1 + \dfrac{1}{4x} = \dfrac{4x + 1}{4x}$
Take the square root.	$\sqrt{\dfrac{1 + 4x}{4x}} = \dfrac{\sqrt{1 + 4x}}{\sqrt{4x}} = \dfrac{\sqrt{x + 4x^2}}{2x}$
Integrate and evaluate.	$\displaystyle\int_0^3 \dfrac{\sqrt{x + 4x^2}}{2x}\,dx \approx 3.611$

Since the resulting integral is often difficult to evaluate, length of a curve questions will often be "set up but do not integrate" questions, or will be calculator-permitted questions.

Distance Traveled and Displacement

If an object is moving in the xy-plane, you will need length of a curve to find the total distance traveled, but if the particle is moving in only one dimension, then the integral of the velocity will allow you to find the displacement or the total distance traveled.

If the particle does not change direction from time $t = a$ to $t = b$, then $\displaystyle\int_a^b v(t)\,dt$ gives both the displacement and the total distance traveled.	A particle moves along the x-axis so that its velocity at time $t \geq 0$ is $v(t) = 2t + 3$. Since $2t + 3 > 0$ for all $t \geq 0$, the displacement and the total distance traveled for $1 \leq t \leq 5$ is $\displaystyle\int_1^5 (2t + 3)\,dt = t^2 + 3t\,\Big|_1^5$ $= (25 + 15) - (1 + 3) = 36$

If the particle changes direction at time $t = c$, $a < c < b$, then

$$\int_a^b v(t)\,dt$$ gives the displacement,

and

$$\left|\int_a^c v(t)\,dt\right| + \left|\int_c^b v(t)\,dt\right|$$ gives the

total distance traveled.

A particle moves along the x-axis so that its velocity at time t is $v(t) = 3(t-2)(t-4)$. This particle changes direction when $t = 2$ and when $t = 4$. The displacement of the particle over the interval $1 \le t \le 5$ is

$$\int_1^5 3(t-2)(t-4)\,dt$$

$$= 3\int_1^5 (t^2 - 6t + 8)\,dt$$

$$= 3\left[\frac{t^3}{3} - 3t^2 + 8t\right]_1^5 = 4.$$

The total distance traveled is

$$\left|\int_1^2 v(t)\,dt\right| + \left|\int_2^4 v(t)\,dt\right| + \left|\int_4^5 v(t)\,dt\right|$$

$$= 3\left[\left|\int_1^2 (t^2 - 6t + 8)\,dt\right| + \left|\int_2^4 (t^2 - 6t + 8)\,dt\right| + \left|\int_4^5 (t^2 - 6t + 8)\,dt\right|\right]$$

$$= 3\left[\left|\frac{t^3}{3} - 3t^2 + 8t\right|_1^2 + \left|\frac{t^3}{3} - 3t^2 + 8t\right|_2^4 + \left|\frac{t^3}{3} - 3t^2 + 8t\right|_4^5\right]$$

$$= 3\left[\left|\frac{4}{3}\right| + \left|-\frac{4}{3}\right| + \left|\frac{4}{3}\right|\right] = 3\left(\frac{12}{3}\right) = 12$$

The position of the particle at time $t = b$ is the position at time $t = a$ plus the displacement for time $a \le t \le b$, or $s(a) + \int_a^b v(t)\,dt$.

If the particle in the previous example is at $x = 3$ at time $t = 1$, then its position at time $t = 5$ is

$$x = 3 + \int_1^5 3(t-2)(t-4)\,dt = 3 + 4 = 7.$$

Work

If F is a function that represents force, and F is continuous on the closed interval [a, b], *then* the work done in moving a particle from $x = a$ to $x = b$ along a straight line is $$W = \int_a^b F(x)dx.$$	An anchor attached to a rope sits on the bottom of a lake that is 50 feet deep. The force required to lift the anchor x feet off the bottom of the lake is $F(x) = 70 - x$. How much work is done in lifting the anchor back to the surface of the lake?
	$$W(50) = \int_0^{50} (70 - x)dx = 70x - \frac{x^2}{2} \Big|_0^{50}$$ $$= 3500 - \frac{2500}{2} = 2250 \text{ foot pounds.}$$

Practice

1. A force of 5 pounds is required to stretch a spring 3 inches beyond its natural length. Assuming Hooke's Law applies, how much work is done in stretching the spring from its natural length to 9 inches beyond its natural length?

A. 5.4 inch-pounds

B. 15 inch-pounds

C. 27 inch-pounds

D. 45 inch-pounds

E. 67.5 inch-pounds

2. What is the average value of $y = x\sqrt{4-x^2}$ on the interval $[0, 2]$?

A. $\dfrac{4}{3}$ B. 8   C. 16   D. -8 E. -16

A spider crawls on the edge of a desk beginning at time 0. The acceleration, a, in cm/sec², of the spider, at time t, is given by the function $a(t) = 2t - 1$, for $0 \le t \le 5$. At $t = 0$, the spider's velocity is -6 cm/sec.

3. At what time does the spider change direction?

A. $t = 1$ B. $t = 2$ C. $t = 3$ D. $t = 4$ E. $t = 5$

4. What is the total distance the spider traveled?

A. $\dfrac{5}{6}$ cm

B. $9\dfrac{1}{6}$ cm

C. $12\dfrac{2}{3}$ cm

D. $13\dfrac{1}{2}$ cm

E. $26\dfrac{1}{6}$ cm

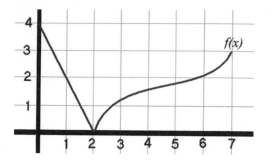

5. The graph of f is shown in the figure above. If $f(x) = F'(x)$ and $\int_{2}^{7} f(x)\,dx = 7.4$, then $F(7) - F(0) =$

A. 3.4   B. 7.4   C. 9.4   D. 11.4   E. 15.4

Free Response Prompt

To determine whether a traffic signal is necessary at an intersection, a town monitors the number of vehicles passing through the intersection. The function

$$F(t) = \begin{cases} 2t + 7 & 0 \le t < 6 \\ 12 + 8\sin\left(\frac{t}{5}\right) & 6 \le t \le 14 \\ 15 + 3\sin\left(\frac{t}{4}\right) & 14 < t \le 24 \end{cases}$$

describes the number of vehicles that pass through the intersection each hour where $F(t)$ is measured in vehicles per hour and t is measured in hours for $0 \le t \le 24$.

a) To the nearest whole number, how many cars pass through the intersection over a 24-hour period?

b) Is the traffic flow increasing or decreasing at $t = 15$? Give a reason for your answer.

c) What is the average value of the traffic flow over the time interval $6 \le t \le 14$? Indicate units of measure.

Answers and Explanations

1. E   2. A   3. C   4. E   5. D

1. Hooke's Law says that the force is proportional to the distance, so $F(x) = kx$ and $5 = k \cdot 3$ means that $k = \frac{5}{3}$. The work required is

$$W = \int_0^9 \frac{5}{3}x\,dx = \frac{5}{6}x^2 \Big|_0^9 = \frac{135}{2} = 67.5 \text{ inch-pounds.}$$

2. $f_{avg} = \frac{1}{2-0}\int_0^2 x\sqrt{4-x^2}\,dx = \frac{1}{2}\int_0^2 x\sqrt{4-x^2}\,dx$. Use a u-substitution with

$u = 4 - x^2$ and $du = -2x\,dx$. Then $\frac{1}{2}\int_0^2 x\sqrt{4-x^2}\,dx = \frac{1}{2}\cdot\frac{1}{-2}\int_4^0 \sqrt{u}\,du$

$= -\frac{1}{4}\int_4^0 \sqrt{u}\,du = -\frac{1}{4}\cdot\frac{2}{3}u^{3/2}\Big|_4^0 = \frac{4}{3}.$

3. The change of direction occurs when velocity is zero. Velocity is the antiderivative of acceleration, so $v(t) = t^2 - t + C$. Since $v(0) = -6$, $v(t) = t^2 - t - 6$. The velocity is equal to zero when $v(t) = t^2 - t - 6 = (t-3)(t+2) = 0$. The particle changes direction at time $t = 3$.

4. The total distance the spider traveled is

$$\left| \int_0^3 (t^2 - t - 6)dt \right| + \left| \int_3^5 (t^2 - t - 6)dt \right| = \left| \frac{t^3}{3} - \frac{t^2}{2} - 6t \right|_0^3 + \left| \frac{t^3}{3} - \frac{t^2}{2} - 6t \right|_3^5$$

$$= \left| -\frac{27}{2} \right| + \left| \frac{38}{3} \right| = \frac{157}{6} = 26\frac{1}{6}.$$

5. You are given $\int_{2}^{7} f(x)dx = F(7) - F(2) = 7.4$, and asked for

$F(7) - F(0)$, which can be thought of as

$\int_{0}^{7} f(x)dx = \int_{0}^{2} f(x)dx + \int_{2}^{7} f(x)dx$. The integral $\int_{0}^{2} f(x)dx$ is the area

under the curve from $x = 0$ to $x = 2$, which is $\frac{1}{2} \cdot 2 \cdot 4 = 4$. Therefore,

$F(7) - F(0) = \int_{0}^{7} f(x)dx = \int_{0}^{2} f(x)dx + \int_{2}^{7} f(x)dx = 4 + 7.4 = 11.4$.

Free Response Prompt

The total number of cars passing through the intersection is

$$\int_{0}^{6} (2t + 7)dt + \int_{6}^{14} 12 + 8\sin\left(\frac{t}{5}\right)dt + \int_{14}^{24} 15 + 3\sin\left(\frac{t}{4}\right)dt$$

$$= t^2 + 7t \big|_{0}^{6} + 12t - 40\cos\left(\frac{t}{5}\right)\Big|_{6}^{14} + 15t - 12\cos\left(\frac{t}{4}\right)\Big|_{14}^{24} \approx 353.424.$$

Approximately 353 vehicles pass through the intersection each day. The sign of the derivative $F'(t)$ will indicate whether the function $F(t)$

is increasing or decreasing. The derivative of $15 + 3\sin\left(\frac{t}{4}\right)$ is $\frac{3}{4}\cos\left(\frac{t}{4}\right)$.

At $t = 15$, $\frac{3}{4}\cos\left(\frac{15}{4}\right) \approx -0.615$. Since the derivative is negative, the

traffic flow is decreasing.

The average value of the traffic flow over the time interval $6 \le t \le 14$ is

$$\frac{1}{14 - 6}\int_{6}^{14}\left(12 + 8\sin\left(\frac{t}{5}\right)\right)dt = \frac{1}{8}\left[12t - 40\cos\left(\frac{t}{5}\right)\right]_{6}^{14} \approx \frac{148.183}{8} \approx 18.523.$$

The average traffic flow is approximately 18.5 vehicles per hour, during the period from $t = 6$ to $t = 14$ hours.

Topic 8: Area and Volume

O ften the first introduction to the integral is the area under a curve, usually approximated by a Riemann sum. More elaborate area problems are still dealt with by integrating the boundary function, or the difference of two boundary functions, from one x-value to another.

Area under a Curve

The area enclosed between the x-axis and the graph of a function f is found by $\int_a^b f(x)dx$.

Note: Area above the x-axis is considered positive and area below the x-axis is negative.	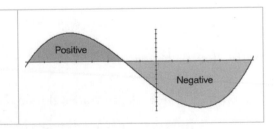

Example 1: The area enclosed between the x-axis and the graph of

$$f(x) = (x+8)(x+2)(x-6)$$

between $x = -8$ and $x = -2$ is

$$\int_{-8}^{-2} (x+8)(x+2)(x-6)dx$$

$$= \int_{-8}^{-2} (x^3 + 4x^2 - 44x - 96)dx$$

$$= \frac{x^4}{4} + \frac{4x^3}{3} - 22x^2 - 96x \Big|_{-8}^{-2}$$

$$= \left(\frac{292}{3}\right) - \left(-298\frac{2}{3}\right) = 396$$

Example 2: The area enclosed between the x-axis and the graph of

$$f(x) = (x+8)(x+2)(x-6)$$

between $x = -2$ and $x = 6$ is

$$\int_{-2}^{6} (x+8)(x+2)(x-6)dx$$

$$= \int_{-2}^{6} (x^3 + 4x^2 - 44x - 96)dx$$

$$= \frac{x^4}{4} + \frac{4x^3}{3} - 22x^2 - 96x \Big|_{-2}^{6}$$

$$= (-756) - \left(\frac{292}{3}\right) = -853\frac{1}{3}$$

The area enclosed by polar functions is covered in the chapter on polar functions.

Area between Two Curves

The area enclosed between two curves, f and g, where $f(x) \geq g(x)$ on the interval $a \leq x \leq b$, is found by $\int_{a}^{b} f(x) - g(x)dx$.

Example: Find the area enclosed between the graphs of $f(x) = x + 2$ and

$g(x) = x^2$.

Sketch a graph to determine whether $f(x) \geq g(x)$ or $g(x) \geq f(x)$.	 $f(x) \geq g(x)$
Find the points of intersection, or determine other limits of integration.	$x^2 = x + 2$ $x^2 - x - 2 = 0$ $(x - 2)(x + 1) = 0$ $x = 2 \quad x = -1$
Set up the integral.	$\int_{-1}^{2} (x + 2 - x^2)dx$
Find the antiderivative.	$\dfrac{x^2}{2} + 2x - \dfrac{x^3}{3} \Big|_{-1}^{2}$
Evaluate.	$\left(\dfrac{4}{2} + 2 \cdot 2 - \dfrac{8}{3}\right) - \left(\dfrac{1}{2} + 2(-1) - \dfrac{(-1)^3}{3}\right)$ $= \dfrac{10}{3} + \dfrac{7}{6} = \dfrac{27}{6} = \dfrac{9}{2}$ square units

Example: Find the area between the graphs of $f(x) = -\cos x$ and $g(x) = \sin \dfrac{x}{2}$ when $0 \leq x \leq 2$.

Sketch a graph to determine whether $f(x) \geq g(x)$ or $g(x) \geq f(x)$	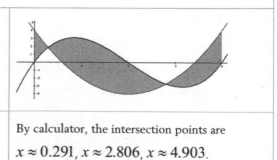 $g(x) > f(x)$
Find the points of intersection, or determine other limits of integration.	Since the curves do not intersect in this interval, the limits of integration are $x = 0$ and $x = 2$.

Calculate the area between the two curves, without regard to what falls above or below the x-axis.	
Set up the integral.	$A = \int_0^2 \left(\sin\frac{x}{2} + \cos x \right) dx$
Find the antiderivative.	$A = -2\cos\frac{x}{2} + \sin x \Big|_0^2$
Evaluate.	$A = (-2\cos 1 + \sin 2) - (-2\cos 0 + \sin 0) \approx 1.829$ square units

Example: Find the area between the graphs of $f(x) = x^3 - 6x^2 + 8x$ and $g(x) = 2x^2 - 8x + 4$ when $0 \leq x \leq 4$.

Sketch a graph to determine whether $f(x) \geq g(x)$ or $g(x) \geq f(x)$.	
Find the points of intersection, or determine other limits of integration.	By calculator, the intersection points are $x \approx 0.291$, $x \approx 2.806$, $x \approx 4.903$.

Since the graphs cross twice in this interval, the area is calculated by the sum of three integrals.	
Set up the integral.	$A = \int_0^{0.291} (2x^2 - 8x + 4) - (x^3 - 6x^2 + 8x)dx$ $+ \int_{0.291}^{2.806} (x^3 - 6x^2 + 8x) - (2x^2 - 8x + 4)dx$ $+ \int_{2.806}^{4} (2x^2 - 8x + 4) - (x^3 - 6x^2 + 8x)dx$
Find the antiderivative.	$A = \left[-\frac{x^4}{4} + \frac{8x^3}{3} - 8x^2 + 4x \right]_0^{0.291}$ $+ \left[\frac{x^4}{4} - \frac{8x^3}{3} + 8x^2 - 4x \right]_{0.291}^{2.806}$ $+ \left[-\frac{x^4}{4} + \frac{8x^3}{3} - 8x^2 + 4x \right]_{2.806}^{4}$
Evaluate.	$A \approx 12.463$ square units

Volume of a Solid of Revolution

If a region in the plane is revolved around a line that serves as an axis, a solid is formed. The outer edge of the solid is defined by the curve that bounds the region.

Method of Discs

Slicing the solid perpendicular to the axis of revolution creates a stack of discs. The volume of the solid can be approached as the summation of the volumes of these cylindrical disks. Remember:

- If the axis of revolution is a horizontal line $y = k$, and $r(x) = k - f(x)$ is the radius, then $V = \pi \int_a^b [r(x)]^2 dx$.
- The volume of a cylinder is $V = \pi r^2 h$.

- The radius, $r(x)$, is the distance between the axis of revolution and the boundary curve, $f(x)$.

- The height is represented by dx.

Example: Find the volume of the solid created when the region under the curve $f(x) = 4 - x^2$ is revolved about the x-axis.

Sketch a graph.	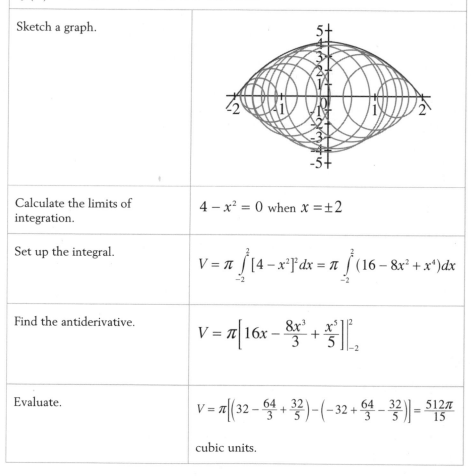
Calculate the limits of integration.	$4 - x^2 = 0$ when $x = \pm 2$
Set up the integral.	$V = \pi \int\limits_{-2}^{2} [4 - x^2]^2 \, dx = \pi \int\limits_{-2}^{2} (16 - 8x^2 + x^4) \, dx$
Find the antiderivative.	$V = \pi \left[16x - \dfrac{8x^3}{3} + \dfrac{x^5}{5} \right]\Big|_{-2}^{2}$
Evaluate.	$V = \pi \left[\left(32 - \dfrac{64}{3} + \dfrac{32}{5} \right) - \left(-32 + \dfrac{64}{3} - \dfrac{32}{5} \right) \right] = \dfrac{512\pi}{15}$ cubic units.

Example: Find the volume of the solid created when the region defined by the graph of $f(x) = \dfrac{3}{x}$, the line $x = 1$, and the line $x = 3$ is revolved about the line $y = -1$.	
Sketch a graph.	
Calculate the limits of integration.	As stated in the problem, the limits of integration are $x = 1$ and $x = 3$
Set up the integral.	$$V = \pi \int_{1}^{3} \left[\frac{1}{x} + 1 \right]^2 dx = \pi \int_{1}^{3} \left(\frac{1}{x^2} + \frac{2}{x} + 1 \right) dx$$
Find the antiderivative.	$$V = -\frac{\pi}{x} + 2\pi \ln x + \pi x \Big|_{1}^{3}$$
Evaluate.	$V = \left(-\frac{\pi}{3} + 2\pi \ln 3 + 3\pi \right) - \left(-\pi + \pi \right) = \frac{8\pi}{3} + 2\pi \ln 3 \approx 15.280$ cubic units

Method of Washers

When a region between two curves is revolved around a line, the result-ing solid has a void, and slicing it perpendicular to the axis of revolution results in washers—disks with holes in their centers—rather than solid disks. Remember:

If the axis of revolution is a horizontal line $y = k$, then

$$V = \pi \int_{a}^{b} [R(x)]^2 - [r(x)]^2 dx, \text{ where } r(x) = k - g(x) \text{ and}$$

$$R(x) = k - f(x).$$

$R(x)$ denotes the outer radius, the distance from the axis of revolution to the farther boundary curve, which forms the outer edge of the solid. $r(x)$ is the inner radius, the radius of the void. It is the distance from the axis of revolution to the nearer boundary curve.

Example: Find the volume of the solid that results when the region between $f(x) = 2x$ and $g(x) = x^2$ is revolved about the line $y = 4$.	
Sketch a graph.	
Identify $R(x)$ and $r(x)$.	The outer radius is the distance from $y = 4$ to $g(x) = x^2$, so $R(x) = 4 - x^2$. The inner radius is the distance from $y = 4$ to $f(x) = 2x$, so $r(x) = 4 - 2x$.
Find the limits of integration.	The boundary graphs intersect at $x = 0$ and $x = 2$.
Set up the integral.	$$V = \pi \int_0^2 [4 - x^2]^2 - [4 - 2x]^2 \, dx$$ $$= \pi \int_0^2 (16 - 8x^2 + x^4) - (16 - 16x + 4x^2) \, dx$$ $$= \pi \int_0^2 (16x - 12x^2 + x^4) \, dx$$
Find the antiderivative.	$$V = \pi \left[8x^2 - 4x^3 + \frac{x^5}{5} \right]_0^2$$

Evaluate.	$V = \pi\left[32 - 32 + \dfrac{32}{5}\right] = 6.4\pi$ cubic units

Example: Find the volume of the solid that results when the region in the first quadrant defined by $f(x) = 5 - e^x$, $g(x) = e^x$ and the y-axis is revolved around the x-axis.

Sketch a graph.	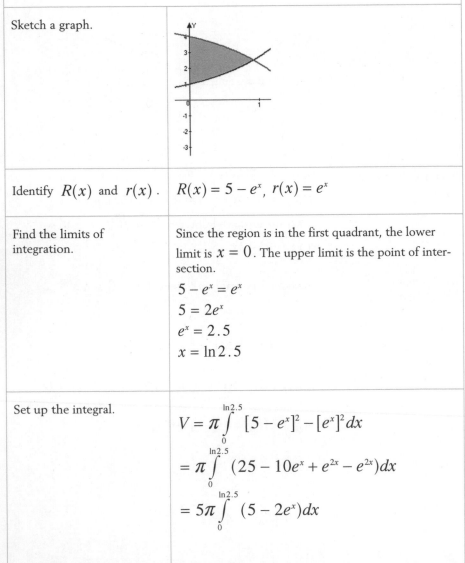
Identify $R(x)$ and $r(x)$.	$R(x) = 5 - e^x$, $r(x) = e^x$
Find the limits of integration.	Since the region is in the first quadrant, the lower limit is $x = 0$. The upper limit is the point of intersection. $5 - e^x = e^x$ $5 = 2e^x$ $e^x = 2.5$ $x = \ln 2.5$
Set up the integral.	$V = \pi \displaystyle\int_{0}^{\ln 2.5} [5 - e^x]^2 - [e^x]^2\, dx$ $= \pi \displaystyle\int_{0}^{\ln 2.5} (25 - 10e^x + e^{2x} - e^{2x})\, dx$ $= 5\pi \displaystyle\int_{0}^{\ln 2.5} (5 - 2e^x)\, dx$

Find the antiderivative.	$V = 5\pi[5x - 2e^x]\Big\|_0^{\ln 2.5}$
Evaluate.	$V = 5\pi[(5\ln 2.5 - 2 \cdot 2.5) - (-2)]$ $= 5\pi[5\ln 2.5 - 3]$ $= 25\pi \ln 2.5 - 15\pi$

If the axis of revolution is a vertical line $x = k$, and $r(y) = k - f(y)$ is the radius, then $V = \pi \displaystyle\int_a^b [r(y)]^2 dy$.

Example: Find the volume of the solid that results when the region in the first quadrant enclosed by $f(x) = 4 - 3x$ and $g(x) = x^2$ is revolved about the y-axis.

Sketch a graph.	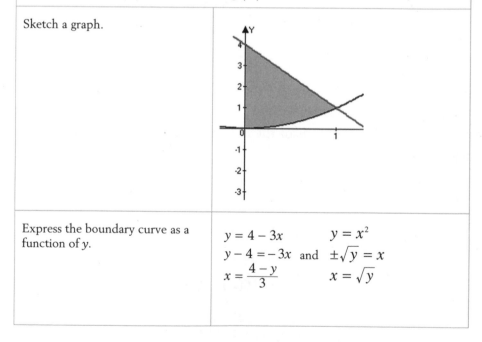
Express the boundary curve as a function of y.	$y = 4 - 3x$ $\qquad$ $y = x^2$ $y - 4 = -3x$ and $\pm\sqrt{y} = x$ $x = \dfrac{4 - y}{3}$ $\qquad$ $x = \sqrt{y}$

Express r (and, if necessary, R) as functions of y.	The radius is determined by $x = \sqrt{y}$ for $0 \le y \le 1$ and by $x = \dfrac{4-y}{3}$ for $1 \le y \le 4$.
Integrate with respect to y. Use limits of integration $y = a$ and $y = b$.	$V = \pi \displaystyle\int_0^1 [\sqrt{y}]^2 \, dy + \pi \int_1^4 \left[\frac{4-y}{3}\right]^2 dy$ $= \pi \displaystyle\int_0^1 y\,dy + \frac{\pi}{9} \int_1^4 (16 - 8y + y^2)\,dy$ $= \dfrac{\pi y^2}{2}\Big|_0^1 + \dfrac{\pi}{9}\left[16y - 4y^2 + \dfrac{y^3}{3}\right]\Big|_1^4$
Evaluate.	$= \dfrac{\pi}{2} + \dfrac{\pi}{9}\left[\dfrac{64}{3} - \left(12 + \dfrac{1}{3}\right)\right] = \dfrac{\pi}{2} + \dfrac{\pi}{9}\left[\dfrac{64}{3} - \dfrac{37}{3}\right]$ $= \dfrac{\pi}{2} + \dfrac{\pi}{9}\left[\dfrac{27}{3}\right] = \dfrac{3\pi}{2}$

Volume of a Solid by Cross Sections

The volume of a solid with known cross sections can be found by summing the areas of the cross sections. The key work is in representing the crucial dimensions in terms of the region in the xy-plane that forms the base of the solid.

Assume the base region is bounded by $f(x)$ and $g(x)$ with $f(x) \ge g(x)$.

Cross section: Square	Area: $A = s^2$	Key dimension: The side of the square: $s = f(x) - g(x)$	Volume: $V = \displaystyle\int_a^b \big(f(x) - g(x)\big)^2 dx$

Example: The base of a solid is the region enclosed between $f(x) = \sin x$ and $g(x) = \cos x$ from $x = \dfrac{\pi}{4}$ to $x = \dfrac{5\pi}{4}$. Find the volume if the cross sections perpendicular to the x-axis are squares.

The side of the square is $\sin x - \cos x$.	$V = \displaystyle\int_{\frac{\pi}{4}}^{\frac{5\pi}{4}} (\sin x - \cos x)^2\, dx$ $= \displaystyle\int_{\frac{\pi}{4}}^{\frac{5\pi}{4}} (\sin^2 x - 2\sin x \cos x + \cos^2 x)\,dx$ $= \displaystyle\int_{\frac{\pi}{4}}^{\frac{5\pi}{4}} (1 - \sin 2x)\,dx$ $= x + \dfrac{1}{2}\cos 2x \,\Big|_{\frac{\pi}{4}}^{\frac{5\pi}{4}}$ $= \dfrac{5\pi}{4} - \dfrac{\pi}{4} = \pi$

Cross section: Equilateral triangle	Area: $A = \dfrac{1}{2}s \cdot \dfrac{1}{2}s\sqrt{3}$ $= \dfrac{1}{4}s^2\sqrt{3}$	Key dimension: The side of the triangle: $s = f(x) - g(x)$	Volume: $V = \dfrac{\sqrt{3}}{4}\displaystyle\int_a^b (f(x) - g(x))^2\,dx$

Example: The base of a solid is the region enclosed between $f(x) = \sin x$ and $g(x) = \cos x$ from $x = \dfrac{\pi}{4}$ to $x = \dfrac{5\pi}{4}$. Find the volume if the cross sections perpendicular to the x-axis are equilateral triangles.

The side of the equilateral triangle is $\sin x - \cos x$.

$$V = \frac{\sqrt{3}}{4} \int_{\frac{\pi}{4}}^{\frac{5\pi}{4}} (\sin x - \cos x)^2 \, dx$$

$$= \frac{\sqrt{3}}{4} \int_{\frac{\pi}{4}}^{\frac{5\pi}{4}} (\sin^2 x - 2\sin x \cos x + \cos^2 x) \, dx$$

$$= \frac{\sqrt{3}}{4} \int_{\frac{\pi}{4}}^{\frac{5\pi}{4}} (1 - \sin 2x) \, dx$$

$$= \frac{\sqrt{3}}{4} \left[x + \frac{1}{2} \cos 2x \right]_{\frac{\pi}{4}}^{\frac{5\pi}{4}}$$

$$= \frac{\sqrt{3}}{4} \left[\frac{5\pi}{4} - \frac{\pi}{4} \right] = \frac{\pi\sqrt{3}}{4}$$

Cross section: Isosceles right triangle, hypotenuse down	Area: $A = \frac{1}{2}\left(\frac{h}{\sqrt{2}}\right)^2$ $= \frac{h^2}{4}$	Key dimension: The hypotenuse of the right triangle: $h = f(x) - g(x)$	Volume: $V = \frac{1}{4}\int_a^b (f(x) - g(x))^2 \, dx$

Example: The base of a solid is the region enclosed between $f(x) = \sin x$ and $g(x) = \cos x$ from $x = \frac{\pi}{4}$ to $x = \frac{5\pi}{4}$. Find the volume if the cross sections perpendicular to the x-axis are isosceles right triangles with hypotenuse on the xy-plane.

The hypotenuse of the triangle is $\sin x - \cos x$.

$$V = \frac{1}{4} \int_{\frac{\pi}{4}}^{\frac{5\pi}{4}} (\sin x - \cos x)^2 dx$$

$$= \frac{1}{4} \int_{\frac{\pi}{4}}^{\frac{5\pi}{4}} (\sin^2 x - 2\sin x \cos x + \cos^2 x) dx$$

$$= \frac{1}{4} \int_{\frac{\pi}{4}}^{\frac{5\pi}{4}} (1 - \sin 2x) dx$$

$$= \frac{1}{4} \left[x + \frac{1}{2} \cos 2x \right] \Big|_{\frac{\pi}{4}}^{\frac{5\pi}{4}}$$

$$= \frac{1}{4} \left[\frac{5\pi}{4} - \frac{\pi}{4} \right] = \frac{\pi}{4}$$

Cross section: Semicircle	Area: $A = \dfrac{\pi r^2}{2}$ $= \dfrac{\pi d^2}{8}$	Key dimension: The diameter of the semicircle: $d = f(x) - g(x)$	Volume: $V = \dfrac{\pi}{8} \int_{a}^{b} (f(x) - g(x))^2 dx$

Example: The base of a solid is the region enclosed between $f(x) = \sin x$ and $g(x) = \cos x$ from $x = \dfrac{\pi}{4}$ to $x = \dfrac{5\pi}{4}$. Find the volume if the cross sections perpendicular to the x-axis are semicircles.

The diameter of the semicircle is $\sin x - \cos x$.	$$V = \frac{\pi}{8} \int_{\frac{\pi}{4}}^{\frac{5\pi}{4}} (\sin x - \cos x)^2 dx$$ $$= \frac{\pi}{8} \int_{\frac{\pi}{4}}^{\frac{5\pi}{4}} (\sin^2 x - 2\sin x \cos x + \cos^2 x) dx$$ $$= \frac{\pi}{8} \int_{\frac{\pi}{4}}^{\frac{5\pi}{4}} (1 - \sin 2x) dx$$ $$= \frac{\pi}{8} \left[x + \frac{1}{2}\cos 2x \right]\Big|_{\frac{\pi}{4}}^{\frac{5\pi}{4}}$$ $$= \frac{\pi}{8} \left[\frac{5\pi}{4} - \frac{\pi}{4} \right] = \frac{\pi^2}{8}$$

Practice

1. The region in the first quadrant bounded by $y = 2\sqrt{\sin x}$, $x = \frac{\pi}{2}$, and the axes is rotated around the x-axis. The volume of the solid generated is

A. 4π B. -4π C. 8π D. 16π E. -16π

2. The base of a solid is the region in the first quadrant enclosed by the graph of $y = 2 - 3x^2, y = x^2 + 1$ and the y-axis. If the cross sections perpendicular to the x-axis are squares, the volume of the solid is approximately

A. 1.509   B. 0.4   C. 0.267   D. 0.384   E. 0.6

3. The volume of the solid that results from rotating the region enclosed by the ellipse $\frac{x^2}{4} + \frac{y^2}{9} = 1$ about the x-axis is

A. 2π B. 4π C. 8π D. 24π E. 32π

4. The region in the first quadrant bounded by $y = \arccos(3x)$ and the axes is rotated around the y-axis. The volume of the solid generated is

A. $\dfrac{2\pi}{9}$ B. $\dfrac{\pi^2}{36}$ C. $\dfrac{\pi}{18}$ D. $\dfrac{\pi^2}{9}$ E. $\dfrac{\pi}{4}$

5. Let R be the region between the graphs of $y = 4 + \sin x$ and $y = \cos x$, between $x = \dfrac{\pi}{6}$ and $x = \dfrac{\pi}{3}$. The volume of the solid that results from rotating region R about the x-axis is approximately

A. 37.163   B. 33.873   C. 26.393   D. 26.319   E. 35.518

Free Response Prompt
Let R be the region enclosed by the graph of $y = 2xe^{x^2}$, the vertical line $x = 1$, and the x-axis.
a) Find the area of R.
b) Find the volume of the solid generated when R is revolved about the horizontal line $y = 6$.
c) The region R is the base of a solid with square cross sections perpendicular to the x-axis. Find the volume of the solid.

Answers and Explanations
1. A   2. C   3. D   4. B   5. E

1. $V = \pi \displaystyle\int_0^{\pi/2} (2\sqrt{\sin x})^2 dx = 4\pi \int_0^{\pi/2} \sin x \, dx = 4\pi[-\cos x]_0^{\pi/2}$

$= 4\pi(0 + 1) = 4\pi$ units³.

2. Determine the point of intersection by solving $2 - 3x^2 = x^2 + 1$. Because $4x^2 = 1$, $x = \dfrac{1}{2}$. Then the volume $V = \displaystyle\int_0^{1/2} (2 - 3x^2 - x^2 - 1)^2 dx$

$= \displaystyle\int_0^{1/2} (1 - 4x^2)^2 dx = \int_0^{1/2} (1 - 8x^2 + 16x^4) dx = x - \dfrac{8x^3}{3} + \dfrac{16x^5}{5} \Big|_0^{1/2} \approx 0.267$ units³.

3. Solve $\dfrac{x^2}{4} + \dfrac{y^2}{9} = 1$ for y. $9x^2 + 4y^2 = 36$, so $y^2 = \dfrac{36 - 9x^2}{4}$ and

$y = \dfrac{3\sqrt{4 - x^2}}{2}$. The region extends from $x = -2$ to $x = 2$. The volume

of the solid that results from rotating this region about the x-axis is

$V = \dfrac{3^2\pi}{2^2} \displaystyle\int_{-2}^{2} (4 - x^2)dx = \dfrac{9\pi}{4}\left[4x - \dfrac{x^3}{3}\right]\Big|_{-2}^{2} = \dfrac{9\pi}{4}\left[\dfrac{32}{3}\right] = 24\pi$ units³.

4. The limits of integration are $y = 0$ and $y = \dfrac{\pi}{2}$. Solve $y = \arccos(3x)$

for x, to get $\dfrac{\cos y}{3} = x$. The volume of the solid is $V = \pi \displaystyle\int_{0}^{\pi/2} \left(\dfrac{\cos y}{3}\right)^2 dy$

$= \dfrac{\pi}{9} \displaystyle\int_{0}^{\pi/2} \cos^2 y\, dy = \dfrac{\pi}{9} \displaystyle\int_{0}^{\pi/2} \dfrac{1}{2}(1 + \cos 2y)dy = \dfrac{\pi}{18}\left[y + \dfrac{1}{2}\sin 2y\right]\Big|_{0}^{\pi/2} = \dfrac{\pi}{18} \cdot \dfrac{\pi}{2} = \dfrac{\pi^2}{36}$.

5. The volume of the solid is $V = \pi \displaystyle\int_{\pi/6}^{\pi/3} [(4 + \sin x)^2 - \cos^2 x]dx$

$= \pi \displaystyle\int_{\pi/6}^{\pi/3} [16 + 8\sin x + \sin^2 x - \cos^2 x]dx \qquad = \pi \displaystyle\int_{\pi/6}^{\pi/3} [16 + 8\sin x - \cos 2x]dx$

$= \pi\left[16x - 8\cos x - \dfrac{1}{2}\sin 2x\right]\Big|_{\pi/6}^{\pi/3} \approx 35.518$.

Free Response Prompt

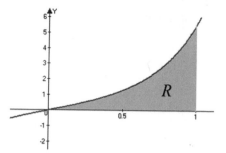

a) The area of R is $A = \int_0^1 2xe^{x^2} dx$. A u-substitution with $u = x^2$ and

$du = 2xdx$ allows you to find the antiderivative. $A = e^{x^2} \big|_0^1 = e - 1$ units^2.

b) The volume of the solid generated when R is revolved about the horizontal line $y = 6$ is

$V = \pi \int_0^1 [(6)^2 - (6 - 2xe^{x^2})^2]dx = \pi \int_0^1 (24xe^{x^2} - 4x^2e^{2x^2})dx$, which, by calculator is approximately $V \approx 48.992$ units^3.

c) The volume of the solid is $V = \int_0^1 (2xe^{x^2})^2 dx = \int_0^1 4x^2e^{2x^2} dx \approx 5.025$ units^3.

Topic 9: Differential Equations

A differential equation is an equation containing a derivative. $y' = 3x - 1$ and $\dfrac{dy}{dx} = \dfrac{2x}{y}$ are examples of differential equations.

Solving a differential equation involves antidifferentiation, but while finding the antiderivative of $y' = 3x - 1$ is simple enough $(y = \dfrac{3x^2}{2} - x + C)$, in order to solve $\dfrac{dy}{dx} = \dfrac{2x}{y}$, you must manipulate the

equation so that there is only one variable on each side of the equation. You will only be expected to solve first order differential equations, or equations that contain the first derivative.

Separable Differential Equations

Differential equations that can be solved by separating the variables, one variable on each side of the equation, are called separable differential equations.

Step	Example 1	Example 2
Manipulate the equation algebraically so that each side of the equation contains only one variable.	$\dfrac{dx}{dt} = \dfrac{t^2 + 1}{2x^2}$ $2x^2\,dx = (t^2 + 1)dt$	$3yy' - 5e^{2x} = 1$ $3y\dfrac{dy}{dx} - 5e^{2x} = 1$ $3y\dfrac{dy}{dx} = (5e^{2x} + 1)$ $3y\,dy = (5e^{2x} + 1)dx$
Integrate each side of the equation.	$\int 2x^2\,dx = \int (t^2 + 1)dt$ $\dfrac{2x^3}{3} = \dfrac{t^3}{3} + t$ $2x^3 = t^3 + 3t$	$\int 3y\,dy = \int (5e^{2x} + 1)dx$ $\dfrac{3y^2}{2} = \dfrac{5}{2}e^{2x} + x$ $3y^2 = 5e^{2x} + 2x$
Add a constant of integration to complete the general equation. (Note that you don't need constants on both sides. They would only be combined to simplify the equation.)	$2x^3 = t^3 + 3t + C$	$3y^2 = 5e^{2x} + 2x + C$

Initial Condition
If one value of the function is provided, you can substitute to find the value of the constant, and find the particular equation.

If an initial condition is given, substitute for each of the variables.	When $t = 2$, $x = 1$ $2x^3 = t^3 + 3t + C$ $2 \cdot 1^3 = 2^3 + 3 \cdot 2 + C$	$y(0) = 2$ $3y^2 = 5e^{2x} + 2x + C$ $3 \cdot 2^2 = 5e^{2 \cdot 0} + 2 \cdot 0 + C$
Solve for C.	$2 = 8 + 6 + C$ $-12 = C$	$12 = 5 + C$ $7 = C$
Write the particular equation.	$2x^3 = t^3 + 3t - 12$	$3y^2 = 5e^{2x} + 2x + 7$

Here is a common differential equation problem related to population growth.

Exponential Growth		
Differential Equation	**Integrates to:**	**Notes:**
$\dfrac{dP}{dt} = kP$	$P = P_0 e^{kt}$	Models unrestricted exponential growth. P_0 represents the population at time $t = 0$.

Example: A certain population is growing at a rate of 5%. If the population at time $t = 0$ is 20,000 individuals, find the particular equation for the population.

The growth rate is 5% of the population, so $\dfrac{dP}{dt} = 0.05P$.

Separate the variables: $\dfrac{dP}{P} = 0.05dt$

Integrate: $\ln|P| = 0.05t + c$ or $P = Ce^{0.05t}$.

Because $P(0) = 20,000$, $P = 20,000e^{0.05t}$

Logistic Growth (BC only)		
Differential Equation	**Integrates to:**	**Notes:**
$\dfrac{dP}{dt} = kP\left(1 - \dfrac{P}{L}\right)$	$P = \dfrac{L}{1 + Ce^{-kt}}$	More common model for population growth, with growth restricted by natural factors. L is the limiting value, or carrying capacity.

Example: A lake, which is estimated to sustain 1000 trout, is initially stocked with 200 trout. If the population of trout grows according to a logistic model with $k = 2.5$, find a particular equation for the population of trout in the lake.

Use the logistic model $\dfrac{dP}{dt} = kP\left(1 - \dfrac{P}{L}\right)$, with $k = 2.5$ and $L = 1000$

$$\frac{dP}{dt} = 2.5P\left(1 - \frac{P}{1000}\right).$$

Separate the variables: $\displaystyle\int \frac{dP}{P\left(1 - P/1000\right)} = \int 2.5dt.$

Integrating requires partial fraction decomposition.

$$\int \frac{dP}{P} + \frac{1}{1000}\int \frac{dP}{1 - P/1000} = \int 2.5dt$$

$$\ln P - \ln\left(1 - P/1000\right) = 2.5t + C$$

$$\ln\frac{1000P}{1000 - P} = 2.5t + C$$

Because $P(0) = 200$, substitute in $\ln\dfrac{1000P}{1000 - P} = 2.5t + C$ and

$C = \ln\dfrac{1000 \cdot 200}{800} = \ln 250$. With this constant, $\ln\dfrac{1000P}{1000 - P} = 2.5t + \ln 250$

becomes $\dfrac{1000P}{250(1000 - P)} = \dfrac{4P}{1000 - P} = e^{2.5t}$ and solving for P gives you

$$P = \frac{1000}{1 + 4e^{-2.5t}}.$$

Euler's Method

Euler's method approximates f by a sequence of line segments.

1. You are given a differential equation involving $f'(x)$ and an initial point. The given initial point is (x_0, y_0).

2. Divide the interval into subintervals of equal size. The x-values that partition the interval are $x_0, x_1, x_2, ..., x_n$ and the width of the interval is Δx.

3. Find $\dfrac{dy}{dx}$ at the current point.

4. Calculate $y_k = y_{k-1} + \dfrac{dy}{dx}\Delta x$

5. Repeat steps 3 and 4 as needed.

6. $y_n \approx f(x)$

Example: Estimate y at $x = 1$, using Euler's Method with four intervals of equal size, if $\dfrac{dy}{dx} + \dfrac{4x}{y} = 2 - x$ and $y(0) = 1$.

The initial point is $(0, 1)$, the x-values that partition the interval are 0, 0.25, 0.5, 0.75, and 1, and the width of the interval is $\Delta x = 0.25$. Each new value y is then plugged into the equation for $\dfrac{dy}{dx}$ until you reach $x = 1$.

x	y	$\frac{dy}{dx} = 2 - x - \frac{4x}{y}$	Δx	$y_{k+1} = y_k + \frac{dy}{dx}\Delta x$
0	1	$2 - 0 - 0 = 2$	0.25	$1 + 2(0.25) = 1.5$
0.1	1.5	$2 - 0.1 - \frac{0.4}{1.5} = 1.633$	0.25	$1.5 + (1.633)(0.25) = 1.908$
0.2	1.908	$2 - 0.2 - \frac{0.8}{1.908} \approx 1.381$	0.25	$1.908 + (1.381)(0.25) \approx 2.253$
0.3	2.253	$2 - 0.3 - \frac{1.2}{2.253} \approx 1.167$	0.25	$2.253 + (1.167)(0.25) \approx 2.544$
0.4	2.544			

$y \approx 2.544$ at $x = 0.4$

Slope Fields

A slope field, or direction field, is a graphical representation of the value

of $\dfrac{dy}{dx}$ at various points in the coordinate plane. The shape of the slope

field for a differential equation can help to determine the general solution of the differential equation.

To produce a slope field for a given differential equation, calculate

the value of $\dfrac{dy}{dx}$ at each point in the plane, and draw a short segment

with that slope through the point.

If $\dfrac{dy}{dx}$ is equal to an expression involving only x, you will see the same

slope repeated along each vertical line. If $\dfrac{dy}{dx}$ is equal to an expression

involving only y, you will see the same slope repeated along each horizontal line. Most differential equations, however, involve both x and y, and you must calculate the slope individually for each point in the field. It may help to organize a chart with values of x as row labels and values of y as column labels, and divide the value of y by the value of x to calculate each slope.

Example: Generate a slope field for the differential equation $\dfrac{dy}{dx} = \dfrac{y}{x}$.

1. Evaluate $\dfrac{dy}{dx}$ for each point in the region.

	y								
	−4	−3	−2	−1	0	1	2	3	4
x −4	1	$3/4$	$1/2$	$1/4$	0	$-1/4$	$-1/2$	$-3/4$	−1
−3	$4/3$	1	$2/3$	$1/3$	0	$-1/3$	$-2/3$	−1	$-4/3$
−2	2	$3/2$	1	$1/2$	0	$-1/2$	−1	$-3/2$	−2
−1	4	3	2	1	0	−1	−2	−3	−4
0	undefined								
1	−4	−3	−2	−1	0	1	2	3	4
2	−2	$-3/2$	−1	$-1/2$	0	$1/2$	1	$3/2$	2
3	$-4/3$	−1	$-2/3$	$-1/3$	0	$1/3$	$2/3$	1	$4/3$
4	−1	$-3/4$	$-1/2$	$-1/4$	0	$1/4$	$1/2$	$3/4$	1

2. Sketch the slopes at each point.

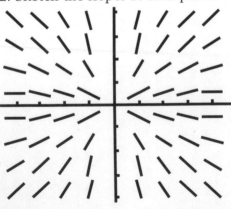

Practice

1. Which of the following is the particular solution of the differential equation $\dfrac{dy}{dx} = \dfrac{3x^2 - 1}{2y}$ where $y(1) = 2$?

A. $y^2 = x^3 - x + 4$

B. $y^2 = x^3 - x - 5$

C. $y^2 = x^3 - x$

D. $\ln|2y| = \ln|3x^2 - 1|$

E. $\dfrac{\ln|2y|}{2} = \dfrac{\ln|6x^2 - 2|}{3}$

2. Which of the following is the slope field for $\dfrac{dy}{dx} = 2 - y$?

A.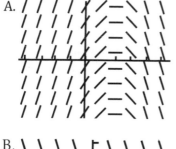

B.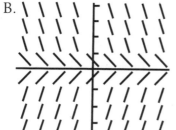

C.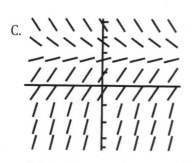

D.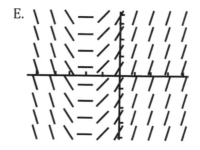

E.

3. The slope field for a certain differential equation is shown. Which of the following could be a general solution of the differential equation?

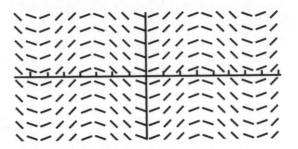

A. $y = \sin x + C$ B. $y = \cos x + C$ C. $y = C - \sin x$

D. $y = C - \cos x$ E. $y = \cos(-x) + C$

4. The general solution of the differential equation $y' = \dfrac{2y}{x+1}$ is $y =$

A. $\dfrac{e^c(x+1)}{2}$ B. $\dfrac{e^c(x+1)^2}{2}$ C. $\sqrt{\dfrac{1}{2}x^2 + x + C}$ D. $\dfrac{2y^2}{x^2+2x} + C$

E. $\ln\left|\dfrac{2y}{x+1}\right| + C$

5. The growth of a population adheres to the model $\dfrac{dP}{dt} = P(100 - P)$, where the initial population $P(0) = 10$ and t is time in years. What is $\lim_{t \to \infty} P(t)$?

A. 0   B. 10   C. 90   D. 100   E. 1000

Free Response Prompt

Consider the differential equation $\dfrac{dy}{dx} = y(x-1)$.

a) On the axes provided, sketch a slope field for the given differential equation at the points indicated.

b) Find the particular solution $y = f(x)$ to the differential equation with the initial condition $f(0) = 3$.

c) For the particular solution, find $\lim\limits_{x \to \infty} f(x)$.

Answers and Explanations

1. A   2. C   3. D   4. B   5. D

1. To solve $\dfrac{dy}{dx} = \dfrac{3x^2 - 1}{2y}$, separate the variables and integrate.

$2y\,dy = (3x^2 - 1)\,dx$

$y^2 = x^3 - x + C$

Use the initial condition $y(1) = 2$ to find that $C = 4$. The particular solution is $y^2 = x^3 - x + 4$.

2. $\dfrac{dy}{dx} = 2 - y$ depends only on the value of y, so the horizontal rows of the slope field should be identical. This eliminates A and E. Upper rows should be negative, eliminating D, and lower ones positive, with the change occurring with a zero slope when $y = 2$. The change from negative to positive slopes occurs at $y = 0$ in B, so C is the correct choice.

3. Let the shape of the slope field tell you that the solution of this differential equation has a minimum value at $x = 0$. Since none of the choices includes a horizontal shift, this suggests an inverted cosine wave, so D is the best choice.

4. To solve $y' = \dfrac{2y}{x+1}$, separate the variables and integrate. Integrating $\dfrac{dy}{2y} = \dfrac{dx}{x+1}$ yields $\dfrac{1}{2}\ln|2y| = \ln|x+1| + C$, and solving for y gives

$y = \dfrac{e^c (x+1)^2}{2}$.

5. If you recognize that $\frac{dP}{dt} = P(100 - P)$ will integrate to a logistic equation, you'll save a great deal of time and effort.

$\frac{dP}{dt} = P(100 - P) = 100P\left(1 - \frac{P}{100}\right)$ and will integrate to $P = \frac{100}{1 + Ce^{-100t}}$.

$\lim_{t \to \infty} P = \lim_{t \to \infty} \frac{100}{1 + Ce^{-100t}} = 100$.

Free Response

a) Evaluate $\frac{dy}{dx} = y(x - 1)$ at each point in the field.

		y						
		-3	-2	-1	0	1	2	3
	-3	12	8	4	0	-4	-8	-12
	-2	9	6	3	0	-3	-6	-9
	-1	6	4	2	0	-2	-4	-6
x	0	3	2	1	0	-1	-2	-3
	1	0	0	0	0	0	0	0
	2	-3	-2	-1	0	1	2	3
	3	-6	-4	-2	0	2	4	6

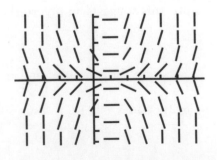

b) $\dfrac{dy}{dx} = y(x - 1)$

Separate the variables: $\dfrac{dy}{y} = (x - 1)dx$

Integrate: $\ln|y| = x^2 - x + C$

Given the initial condition $f(0) = 3$, $\ln 3 = C$ and $\ln|y| = x^2 - x + \ln 3$.
Solve for y: $y = e^{x^2 - x + \ln 3}$

c) $\lim\limits_{x \to \infty} e^{x^2 - x + \ln 3} = \infty$

Topic 10: Graphical and Numerical Presentations

O ver the last decade or so, the AP exams have placed greater emphasis on graphical and numerical presentations of information. Questions will give the graph of a function, the graph of the derivative of a function, or a table summarizing the values of a function at various points. You'll be asked common calculus questions, but rather than analytically finding the derivative or integral of a function presented as an equation, you'll need to demonstrate your understanding of the concepts by estimating derivatives and integrals from the graph or the data.

Task	Solution
Calculate the average rate of change on an interval.	Locate the endpoints of the interval, and calculate the difference quotient.
Estimate derivative at a point.	Find the slopes of secants through points on either side of the given point, and look for a limit.
Determine where f is increasing or decreasing.	f is increasing when f' is positive (above the x-axis) and decreasing when f' is negative (below the x-axis.)

Find relative extrema of f.	**Graph:** Locate the x-intercepts of the graph of f'. Check to see that f' actually changes sign. **Table:** Find values in the table where f' changes from positive to negative or negative to positive. Extrema occur at points of change, but it may not be possible to find the exact point.
Determine concavity of f.	When f' is increasing, f is concave up. When f' is decreasing, f is concave down.
Find inflection points of f.	**Graph:** Locate the relative extrema of f'. **Table:** Examine the table for change from f' increasing to f' decreasing. It may not be possible to find the exact point of change.
Estimate integrals.	**Graph:** Divide the area under the curve into regions for which area can be found geometrically **Table:** Estimate by a Riemann sum or a trapezoidal sum. Use values of f' and width of each interval to calculate areas.

Example 1

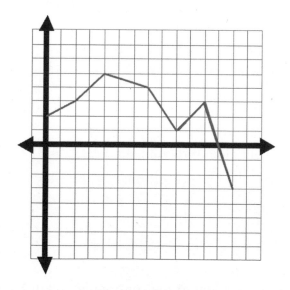

The graph of the first derivative, f', of function f, on the interval $0 \le x \le 13$, is shown here.

a) Find the average rate of change of f' on the interval $2 \leq x \leq 7$.

Average rate of change of $f' = \dfrac{f'(7)-f'(2)}{7-2} = \dfrac{3-4}{5} = -\dfrac{1}{5}$.

b) On what intervals is f decreasing?

f is decreasing when $f' < 0$, which occurs on the interval $12 < x \leq 13$.

c) At what values of x does f have a relative maximum?

Possible relative extrema will occur when $f' = 0$, that is, when $x = 12$. Since f' changes from positive to negative at $x = 12$, f changes from increasing to decreasing, indicating a maximum at $x = 12$.

d) On what interval(s) is f concave down?

f is concave down when f'' is negative, which is when f' is decreasing. f' is decreasing on $4 < x < 9$ and on $11 < x < 13$.

e) Find any inflection points of f.

Inflection points will occur when concavity changes, or when f' changes from increasing to decreasing or decreasing to increasing. f' changes from increasing to decreasing at $x = 4$, from decreasing to increasing at $x = 9$, and from increasing to decreasing at $x = 11$. The inflection points of f occur at $x = 4$, $x = 9$, and $x = 11$.

f) Find $\displaystyle\int_0^9 f'(x)\, dx$.

Divide the interval into four trapezoids at $x = 2$, $x = 4$, $x = 7$ and $x = 9$.

$$\int_0^9 f'(x)\, dx = \frac{1}{2}\cdot 2(2+3) + \frac{1}{2}\cdot 2(3+5) + \frac{1}{2}\cdot 3(5+4) + \frac{1}{2}\cdot 2(4+1)$$
$$= 5 + 8 + 13.5 + 5 = 31.5$$

Example 2

The table below gives values of the continuous and differentiable function $v(t)$.

t	0	2	5	7	10	14	15
v	2	6	-1	-4	2	7	4

a) Find the average rate of change of v on the interval $2 \le x \le 10$.

The average rate of change of $v = \dfrac{v(10)-v(2)}{10-2} = \dfrac{2-6}{10-2} = \dfrac{-4}{8} = -\dfrac{1}{2}$.

b) Estimate $v'(10)$.

You can approximate the value of the derivative by the slope of a secant line: $\dfrac{v(14)-v(7)}{14-7} = \dfrac{7+4}{7} = \dfrac{11}{7} \approx 1.571$. If you have sufficient informa-

tion, you can look for the limit of the slopes of secants. The pattern of slopes suggests that $v'(10) \approx 1.6$, but it is impossible to be certain of the value from the information given.

From	to	Slope	
$t = 0$	$t = 10$	0	
$t = 2$	$t = 10$	-0.5	
$t = 5$	$t = 10$	0.6	
$t = 7$	$t = 10$	2	
Average rate of change from $t = 7$ to $t = 14$		1.571	
$t = 10$	$t = 14$	1.25	
$t = 10$	$t = 15$	0.4	

c) If $d(x) = \displaystyle\int_{x}^{15} v(t)\, dt$, find $d(5)$.

$d(5) = \int\limits_{5}^{15} v(t)\, dt$ can be estimated by a summation. Use four intervals,

dividing the interval from 5 to 15 at $t = 7$, $t = 10$, and $t = 14$.

Interval	Width	Left Riemann	Right Riemann	Trapezoidal
$x = 5$ to $x = 7$	2	$2 \times -1 = -2$	$2 \times -4 = -8$	$\frac{1}{2} \cdot 2(-1 + -4) = -5$
$x = 7$ to $x = 10$	3	$3 \times -4 = -12$	$3 \times 2 = 6$	$\frac{1}{2} \cdot 3(-4 + 2) = -3$
$x = 10$ to $x = 14$	4	$4 \times 2 = 8$	$4 \times 7 = 28$	$\frac{1}{2} \cdot 4(2 + 7) = 18$
$x = 14$ to $x = 15$	1	$1 \times 7 = 7$	$1 \times 4 = 4$	$\frac{1}{2} \cdot 1(7 + 4) = 5.5$
Total		1	30	15.5

Practice

1. Calculate the approximate area of the shaded region by the trapezoidal rule using divisions at $x = -1$, $x = 0$, $x = 1$, and $x = 2$.

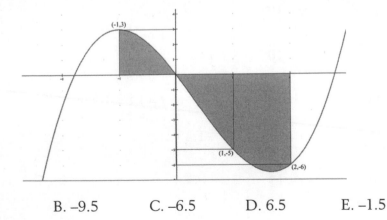

A. 9.5   B. –9.5   C. –6.5   D. 6.5   E. –1.5

2. The graph of the derivative $f'(x)$ is shown. Which of the following could be the graph of $f(x)$?

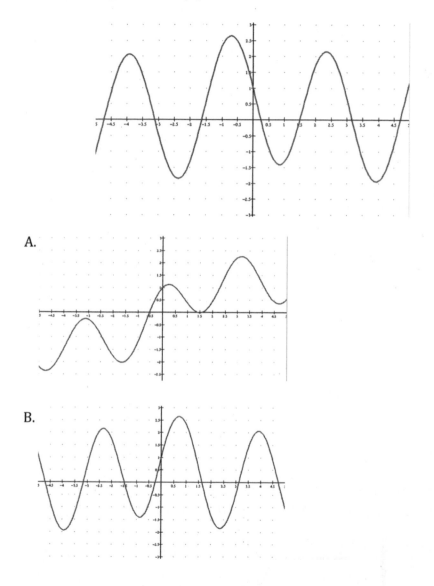

A.

B.

C.

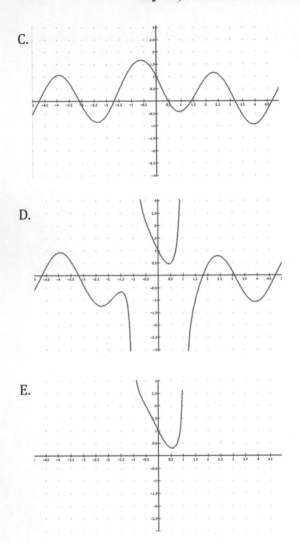

D.

E.

A spider crawls up a waterspout beginning at time $t = 0$. The velocity, v, of the spider, at time t, $0 \le t \le 8$ is given by the function shown in the graph.

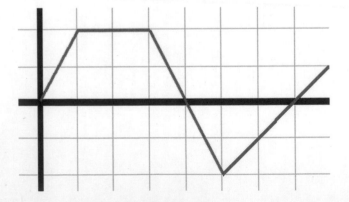

3. At what time does the spider change direction?

A. $t = 1$ B. $t = 3$ C. $t = 4$ D. $t = 5$ E. $t = 6$

4. What is the total distance the spider traveled?

A. 6   B. 3   C. $\dfrac{1}{2}$ D. $9\dfrac{1}{2}$ E. $3\dfrac{1}{2}$

5.

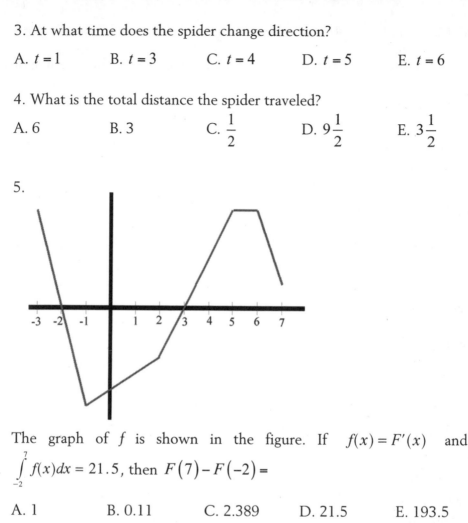

The graph of f is shown in the figure. If $f(x) = F'(x)$ and $\int_{-2}^{7} f(x)\,dx = 21.5$, then $F(7) - F(-2) =$

A. 1   B. 0.11   C. 2.389   D. 21.5   E. 193.5

Free Response Prompt

The rate at which water flows into a tank, in gallons per hour, is given by a differentiable function F of time t, where t is measured in hours. The table shows the rate as measured every 2 hours for a 24-hour period. The tank into which the water flows holds 110 gallons and is empty at $t = 0$.

t	2	4	6	8	10	12	14	16	18	20	22	24
F	1	3	7	8	6	5	4	7	3	1	2	5

a) Use a midpoint Riemann sum with 4 subdivisions of equal length to approximate $\int_0^{24} F(t)\, dt$. Using correct units, explain the meaning of your answer in terms of water flow.

b) Approximate the average rate of water flow during the 24-hour period. Indicate units of measure.

c) The tank into which the water flows has a leak. If water leaks from the tank at a rate of $\dfrac{\int_0^{24} F(t)\, dt}{100}$ gallons per hour, how much water is in the tank at the end of the 24-hour period?

Answers and Explanations

1. C   2. A   3. C   4. D   5. D

1. The approximate area of the shaded region

$$= \frac{1}{2}\cdot 1(3+0) + \frac{1}{2}\cdot 1(0-5) + \frac{1}{2}\cdot 1(-5-6) = \frac{3}{2} - \frac{5}{2} - \frac{11}{2} = \frac{13}{2} = 6.5.$$

2. The graph of the derivative has 7 x-intercepts, four positive and three negative. The graph of f should therefore have 7 relative extrema, at corresponding values of x. Only A meets this description.

3. A change in direction would appear in the velocity graph as a change in the sign of the velocity. There are two t-intercepts, at $t = 4$ and $t = 7$, but only one of those appears as a choice.

4. The total distance the spider traveled is the integral of the velocity from $t = 0$ to $t = 8$. The area $= \frac{1}{2}\cdot 2(2+4) + \frac{1}{2}\cdot 3\cdot 2 + \frac{1}{2}\cdot 1\cdot 1 = 6 + 3 + \frac{1}{2} = 9\frac{1}{2}$.

5. The Fundamental Theorem of Calculus guarantees that

$$\int_{-2}^{7} f(x)\, dx = F(7) - F(-2).$$

Free Response

a) Use four intervals of 6 hours each, and the value of f at the midpoint of each interval.

t	2	4	6	8	10	12	14	16	18	20	22	24
F	1	3	7	8	6	5	4	7	3	1	2	5
$\Delta t \cdot F$	18			36			42			12		
$\int F\, dt$	18			54			96			108		

Over the 24-hour period, a total of 108 gallons of water flows into the tank.

b) The average rate of water flow during the 24-hour period $= \frac{1}{24} \cdot 108 = 4.5$ gallons per hour.

c) Extend the calculation from part a) to include $\dfrac{\int F\, dt}{100}$, the rate at which the tank was leaking, $\Delta t \cdot \dfrac{\int F\, dt}{100}$, the amount of water that leaked over each 6-hour interval, and their difference $\Delta t \cdot F - \Delta t \cdot \dfrac{\int F\, dt}{100}$, the net amount that accumulated in the tank during that interval.

t	2	4	6	8	10	12	14	16	18	20	22	24
F		1	3	7	8	6	5	4	7	3	1	2	5
$\Delta t \cdot F$			18			36			42			12	
$\int F\, dt$			18			54			96			108	
$\dfrac{\int F\, dt}{100}$			.18			.54			.96			1.08	

$\Delta t \cdot \dfrac{\int F\,dt}{100}$	1.08	3.24	5.76	6.48
$\Delta t \cdot F - \Delta t \cdot \dfrac{\int F\,dt}{100}$	16.92	32.76	36.24	5.52
Total in tank	16.92	49.68	85.92	91.44

At the end of the 24-hour period, there was a total of 91.44 gallons in the tank.

Topic 11: Infinite Series

Series Facts

Remember the following facts related to infinite series.

Series Fact	Example
An infinite series is an expression of the form $a_1 + a_2 + a_3 + \ldots + a_n + \ldots = \displaystyle\sum_{k=1}^{\infty} a_k$	$1 + \dfrac{1}{2} + \dfrac{1}{4} + \dfrac{1}{8} + \ldots + \dfrac{1}{2^{n-1}} + \ldots = \displaystyle\sum_{k=1}^{n} \dfrac{1}{2^{k-1}}$
The partial sums of the series $a_1 + a_2 + a_3 + \ldots + a_n + \ldots = \displaystyle\sum_{k=1}^{\infty} a_k$ are $S_1 = a_1,$ $S_2 = a_1 + a_2,$ $S_3 = a_1 + a_2 + a_3, \ldots$ $S_n = \displaystyle\sum_{k=1}^{n} a_k$	$S_1 = 1$ $S_2 = 1 + \dfrac{1}{2} = \dfrac{3}{2}$ $S_3 = 1 + \dfrac{1}{2} + \dfrac{1}{4} = \dfrac{7}{4} \ldots$ $S_n = 1 + \dfrac{1}{2} + \dfrac{1}{4} + \dfrac{1}{8} + \ldots + \dfrac{1}{2^{n-1}}$

If a limit, S, of the sequence of partial sums $\{S_1, S_2, S_3, ..., S_n, ...\}$ exists, the series converges to S.	The sequence of partial sums for $\sum_{k=1}^{n} \frac{1}{2^{k-1}}$ is $$\left\{1, \frac{3}{2}, \frac{7}{4}, \frac{15}{8}, \frac{31}{16}, ..., \frac{2^n - 1}{2^{n-1}}, ...\right\}.$$ The limit of the sequence of partial sums is 2. The series $$1 + \frac{1}{2} + \frac{1}{4} + \frac{1}{8} + ... + \frac{1}{2^{n-1}} + ... = \sum_{k=1}^{n} \frac{1}{2^{k-1}}$$ converges to 2.
If a series converges, then the limit of the terms of the series is 0. $$\lim_{k \to \infty} a_k = 0.$$	The terms of the series get smaller as k increases. $1 + \frac{1}{2} + \frac{1}{4} + \frac{1}{8} + ... + \frac{1}{2^{n-1}} + ...$ $$\lim_{k \to \infty} \frac{1}{2^{k-1}} = 0.$$

Does the Series Converge?

- Is $\lim a_n = 0$? If this is clearly not the case, the series diverges, but $\lim a_n = 0$ alone does not prove the series converges. $\sum_{n=0}^{\infty} 2^n$ diverges, since $\lim_{n \to \infty} 2^n \neq 0$.

- Is the series geometric? If it is, it converges if $|r| < 1$ and diverges otherwise. $\sum_{n=0}^{\infty} 4\left(-\frac{3}{4}\right)^n$ converges because $\left|-\frac{3}{4}\right| < 1$.

- If it's not geometric, is it a *p*-series? A *p*-series will converge if $p > 1$ and diverge otherwise. $\sum_{n=1}^{\infty} \frac{1}{n^3}$ converges, but $\sum_{n=1}^{\infty} \frac{1}{\sqrt{n}}$ diverges.

- Does it converge absolutely, that is, does $\sum_{n=0}^{\infty} |a_n|$ converge? Apply integral test, ratio test, or comparison test to $\sum_{n=0}^{\infty} |a_n|$. If $\sum_{n=0}^{\infty} |a_n|$ converges, $\sum_{n=0}^{\infty} a_n$ converges.

- Is it an alternating series? If so, is there a point beyond which the $|a_n|$

are strictly decreasing? If they approach zero as $n \to \infty$, the original series converges.

	IF	THEN
Integral test	f is positive, continuous, and decreasing for $x \geq 1$ $f(n) = a_n$	$\sum\limits_{n=1}^{\infty} a_n$ and $\int\limits_{1}^{\infty} f(x)dx$ either both converge or both diverge.

Example

$\sum\limits_{n=1}^{\infty} \dfrac{n}{e^n}$ can be shown to converge, because for $x \geq 1$,

$f(x) = \dfrac{x}{e^x}$ is positive, continuous, and decreasing, and

$$\int\limits_{1}^{\infty} \dfrac{x}{e^x}dx = \lim_{k \to \infty} \int\limits_{1}^{k} \dfrac{x}{e^x}dx = \lim_{k \to \infty} \dfrac{-(1+x)}{e^x}\bigg|_{1}^{k} = \lim_{k \to \infty}\left(\dfrac{-1-k}{e^k} + \dfrac{2}{e}\right) = \dfrac{2}{e}$$

	IF	THEN
	all terms are positive AND $\lim\limits_{n \to \infty}\dfrac{a_{n+1}}{a_n} < 1$	$\sum\limits_{n=0}^{\infty} a_n$ converges.
Ratio test	all terms are positive AND $\lim\limits_{n \to \infty}\dfrac{a_{n+1}}{a_n} > 1$	$\sum\limits_{n=0}^{\infty} a_n$ diverges.
	all terms are positive AND $\lim\limits_{n \to \infty}\dfrac{a_{n+1}}{a_n} = 1$	the test is inconclusive.

Examples

$\displaystyle\sum_{n=1}^{\infty} \frac{n+1}{3^n}$ can be shown to converge because $\dfrac{n+2}{3^{n+1}} \div \dfrac{n+1}{3^n} = \dfrac{n+2}{3(n+1)}$ and

$\displaystyle\lim_{n\to\infty} \frac{n+2}{3n+3} < 1$.

$\displaystyle\sum_{n=0}^{\infty} \frac{n!}{3^n}$ diverges since $\dfrac{(n+1)!}{3^{n+1}} \div \dfrac{n!}{3^n} = \dfrac{n+1}{3}$ and $\displaystyle\lim_{n\to\infty}\frac{n+1}{3} = \infty$.

	IF	THEN
Comparison test	$0 \le a_n \le b_n$ for all n AND $\displaystyle\sum_{n=0}^{\infty} b_n$ converges	$\displaystyle\sum_{n=0}^{\infty} a_n$ converges.
	$0 \le a_n \le b_n$ for all n AND $\displaystyle\sum_{n=0}^{\infty} a_n$ diverges	$\displaystyle\sum_{n=0}^{\infty} b_n$ diverges.

Examples

$\displaystyle\sum_{n=0}^{\infty} \frac{1}{n^2+1}$ can be compared to the p-series $\displaystyle\sum_{n=1}^{\infty} \frac{1}{n^2}$. Because $0 \le \dfrac{1}{n^2+1} \le \dfrac{1}{n^2}$ and

$\displaystyle\sum_{n=1}^{\infty} \frac{1}{n^2}$ is known to converge because $p > 1$, $\displaystyle\sum_{n=0}^{\infty} \frac{1}{n^2+1}$ converges.

$\displaystyle\sum_{n=1}^{\infty} \frac{n^2+1}{n^3}$ can be compared to the harmonic series, which is known to diverge.

Because $0 \le \dfrac{1}{n} \le \dfrac{n^2+1}{n^3}$, $\displaystyle\sum_{n=1}^{\infty} \frac{n^2+1}{n^3}$ diverges.

Series to Remember

Knowing the following series can help you conduct the comparison test.

P-series	
$$\sum_{n=1}^{\infty} \frac{1}{n^p} = 1 + \frac{1}{2^p} + \frac{1}{3^p} + \frac{1}{4^p} + \dots + \frac{1}{n^p} + \dots$$	Converges if $p > 1$, diverges if $p \leq 1$

Harmonic series	
$$\sum_{n=1}^{\infty} \frac{1}{n} = 1 + \frac{1}{2} + \frac{1}{3} + \frac{1}{4} + \frac{1}{5} + \dots + \frac{1}{n} + \dots$$	P-series with $p = 1$. The harmonic series does not converge.

Geometric series	Example
If each term of a series is a constant multiple of the previous term, the series is a geometric series.	$2 + \frac{2}{3} + \frac{2}{9} + \frac{2}{27} + \dots + \frac{2}{3^k} + \dots$ is a geometric series because each term is $\frac{1}{3}$ of the previous term.
The infinite geometric series $\sum_{n=1}^{\infty} ar^{n-1}$ converges to $\frac{a}{1-r}$ if $\lvert r \rvert < 1$, but diverges if $\lvert r \rvert \geq 1$.	$2 + \frac{2}{3} + \frac{2}{9} + \frac{2}{27} + \dots + \frac{2}{3^k} + \dots = \sum_{n=1}^{\infty} 2\left(\frac{1}{3}\right)^{n-1}$ converges to $\frac{2}{1 - \frac{1}{3}} = \frac{2}{\frac{2}{3}} = 3$ because $r = \frac{1}{3} < 1$

Power series	Example
A power series centered at $x = a$ is a series of the form $\sum_{n=0}^{\infty} c_n(x - a)^n$.	$1 + 2(x - 2) + 3(x - 2)^2 + 4(x - 2)^3 + \dots + (n + 1)(x - 2)^n + \dots$

If the series is centered at $x = 0$, this becomes $$\sum_{n=0}^{\infty} c_n x^n.$$	$1 + 2x + 3x^2 + 4x^3 + \dots + (n+1)x^n + \dots$

Radius and Interval of Convergence

A power series centered at $x = a$ may converge

- Only at $x = a$

- Everywhere

- On an interval of radius r centered at $x = a$

1. Find the radius.	The series will converge when $$\lim_{n \to \infty} \left| \frac{a_{n+1}}{a_n} \right| < 1. \ \sum_{n=0}^{\infty} x^n \text{ converges}$$ when $\left| \frac{x^{n+1}}{x^n} \right| = |x| < 1$, so the radius of convergence is 1. This means the series converges at least on $-1 < x < 1$.	$\sum_{n=1}^{\infty} (-1)^{n-1} \frac{x^n}{n}$ converges when $$\lim_{n \to \infty} \left| \frac{\frac{x^{n+1}}{n+1}}{\frac{x^n}{n}} \right| = \lim_{n \to \infty} \left| \frac{nx}{n+1} \right| < 1$$ or $|x| < 1$. The series converges at least on $-1 < x < 1$.

| 2. Check the endpoints. | When $x = 1$, $\sum\limits_{n=0}^{\infty} x^n = \sum\limits_{n=0}^{\infty} 1^n$

 $= 1 + 1 + 1 + 1 + \dots$ does not converge since the sequence of partial sums increases without bound.

 When $x = -1$,

 $\sum\limits_{n=0}^{\infty} x^n = \sum\limits_{n=0}^{\infty} (-1)^n$

 $= 1 - 1 + 1 - 1 + \dots$ does not converge since the limit of partial sums does not exist. The interval of convergence is

 $(-1, 1)$. | When $x = -1$,

 $\sum\limits_{n=1}^{\infty} (-1)^{n-1} \dfrac{x^n}{n} = \sum\limits_{n=1}^{\infty} \dfrac{-1}{n}$

 $= -\sum\limits_{n=1}^{\infty} \dfrac{1}{n}$. The harmonic series diverges.

 When $x = 1$, $\sum\limits_{n=1}^{\infty} (-1)^{n-1} \dfrac{x^n}{n}$

 $= \sum\limits_{n=1}^{\infty} \dfrac{(-1)^{n-1}}{n}$. The alternating harmonic series converges. The interval of convergence is

 $(-1, 1]$. |

Deriving Power Series from a Known Series

If a power series converges to a function on an interval, you can derive power series for other related functions, but you must consider how the interval of convergence changes.

Known series	Interval of convergence
$\dfrac{1}{1-x} = 1 + x + x^2 + x^3 + \dots + x^n + \dots = \sum\limits_{n=0}^{\infty} x^n$	$-1 < x < 1$
Derive the power series for $\dfrac{1}{1+x}$ by substituting $-x$ for x.	

$\frac{1}{1-(-x)} = 1 + (-x) + (-x)^2 + (-x)^3 + \ldots + (-x)^n + \ldots = \sum\limits_{n=0}^{\infty} (-x)^n$ $= 1 - x + x^2 - x^3 + \ldots + (-1)^n x^n + \ldots = \sum\limits_{n=0}^{\infty} (-1)^n x^n$	Converges when $-x$ is between -1 and 1. $-1 < -x < 1$ $1 > x > -1$
Derive the power series for $\frac{1}{1-2x}$ by substituting $2x$ for x.	
$\frac{1}{1-2x} = 1 + 2x + (2x)^2 + (2x)^3 + \ldots + (2x)^n + \ldots = \sum\limits_{n=0}^{\infty} (2x)^n$ $= 1 + 2x + 4x^2 + 8x^3 + \ldots + 2^n x^n + \ldots = \sum\limits_{n=0}^{\infty} 2^n x^n$	Converges when $2x$ is between -1 and 1. $-1 < 2x < 1$ $-\frac{1}{2} < x < \frac{1}{2}$

Deriving Series by Differentiation and Integration

The radius of convergence for the derivative or integral is the same as the radius for the original series but check the endpoints of the interval of convergence.

Known series	Converges to function	On the interval
$\sum\limits_{n=0}^{\infty} (-1)^n (x-1)^n$ $= 1 - (x-1) + (x-1)^2 - (x-1)^3 + \ldots + (-1)^n (x-1)^n + \ldots$	$\dfrac{1}{x}$	$(0,2)$
Differentiate the known series.		
$\sum\limits_{n=0}^{\infty} (-1)^{n+1} n(x-1)^{n-1}$ $= -1 + 2(x-1) - 3(x-1)^2 + 4(x-1)^3 + \ldots + (-1)^{n+1}(n+1)(x-1)^n + \ldots$	$-\dfrac{1}{x^2}$	$(0,2)$
Integrate the known series.		

$C + \sum_{n=0}^{\infty} (-1)^n \frac{(x-1)^{n+1}}{n+1}$ $= C + (x-1) - \frac{(x-1)^2}{2} + \frac{(x-1)^3}{3} + \ldots + (-1)^n \frac{(x-1)^{n+1}}{n+1} + \ldots$	$\ln x$	$(0, 2)$

Taylor Polynomial Approximations

- Taylor polynomials approximate $f(x)$ near $x = a$.

- Near $x = a$,

$$f(x) \approx f(a) + f'(a)(x-a) + \frac{f''(a)}{2!}(x-a)^2 + \frac{f'''(a)}{3!}(x-a)^3 + \ldots$$

Example			
$f(x) = \ln x$	$f(1) = \ln 1 = 0$		
Derivatives	at $x = 1$		**Polynomial approximation**
$f'(x) = \frac{1}{x}$	$f'(1) = \frac{1}{1} = 1$	1st degree	$\ln x \approx 0 + 1(x-1) \approx x - 1$
$f''(x) = \frac{-1}{x^2}$	$f''(1) = \frac{-1}{1^2} = -1$	2nd degree	$\ln x \approx (x-1) - \frac{1}{2}(x-1)^2$
$f'''(x) = \frac{2}{x^3}$	$f'''(1) = \frac{2}{1^3} = 2$	3rd degree	$\ln x \approx (x-1) - \frac{1}{2}(x-1)^2 + \frac{1}{3}(x-1)^3$
$f^{(4)}(x) = \frac{-6}{x^4}$	$f^{(4)}(1) = -6$	4th degree	$\ln x \approx (x-1) - \frac{1}{2}(x-1)^2 + \frac{1}{3}(x-1)^3 - \frac{1}{4}(x-1)^4$

Error of Approximation

A polynomial approximation to a function at $x = a$ matches the function at $x = a$, but the farther you move away from $x = a$, the greater the error of the approximation. The more terms in the polynomial, the farther from $x = a$ you can move without significant error. For a decreasing alternating series, the error of approximation in the neighborhood of $x = a$ can be bounded by the absolute value of the next term of the series.

At $x = 1.1$			
Polynomial approximation	Actual error	Next term	Bound of $|error|$
$x - 1 = 0.1$	0.0046	$\dfrac{f''(1)}{2!}(0.1)^2$ $= -0.005$	≤ 0.005
$(x-1)-\frac{1}{2}(x-1)^2 = 0.095$	-0.00031017	$\dfrac{f'''(1)}{3!}(0.1)^3$ $= 0.000\overline{3}$	$\leq 0.000\overline{3}$
$(x-1)-\frac{1}{2}(x-1)^2+\frac{1}{3}(x-1)^3$ $\approx 0.095\overline{3}$	0.000023153	$\dfrac{f^{(4)}(1)}{4!}(0.1)^4$ $= -0.000025$	≤ 0.000025
$(x-1)-\frac{(x-1)^2}{2}+\frac{(x-1)^3}{3}-\frac{(x-1)^4}{4}$ ≈ 0.0953083	-0.000001846471	$\dfrac{f^{(5)}(1)}{5!}(0.1)^5$ $= 0.000002$	≤ 0.000002

Lagrange Error Bound

The Lagrange error bound for a polynomial approximation centered about $x = a$ is a modified version of the next term of the Taylor polynomial. If $P(x)$ is the nth degree Taylor polynomial approximation for $f(x)$, centered at $x = a$, and $x = c$ is near $x = a$, then the actual error is the difference between $P(c)$ and $f(c)$. The Lagrange error bound is $\left|\dfrac{f^{n+1}(c)(x-a)^{n+1}}{(n+1)!}\right|$ where c is the value on the interval from a to x that gives the maximum value of f^{n+1}. Usually, it will happen that either $c = a$ or $c = x$, so generally the error bound is

$$\max\left(\left|\frac{f^{n+1}(a)(c-a)^{n+1}}{(n+1)!}\right|, \left|\frac{f^{n+1}(c)(c-a)^{n+1}}{(n+1)!}\right|\right).$$

Example: The 3rd degree Taylor polynomial for $f(x) = \dfrac{1}{x+1}$ about $x = 0$ is $P(x) = 1 - x + x^2 - x^3$. If the Taylor polynomial is used to estimate $f(0.2)$, the approximate value will be

$P(0.2) = 1 - 0.2 + 0.04 - 0.008 = 0.832$, while the actual value is

$$\frac{1}{0.2+1} = 0.8\overline{3}.$$

To find the Lagrange error bound,
1. Find the 4th derivative $f^{(4)}(x) = -24(x+1)^{-5}$

2. Evaluate $\left|\dfrac{f^{n+1}(a)(c-a)^{n+1}}{(n+1)!}\right|$

$$\left|\frac{f^{(4)}(0)\cdot(0.2-0)^4}{4!}\right| = \left|\frac{-24\cdot 0.0016}{24}\right| = 0.0016$$

3. Evaluate $\left|\dfrac{f^{n+1}(c)(c-a)^{n+1}}{(n+1)!}\right|$

$$\left|\frac{f^{(4)}(0.2)(0.2-0)^4}{4!}\right| = \left|\frac{-9.645\cdot 0.0016}{24}\right| = 0.000643$$

The larger of these results, 0.0016, is the Lagrange error bound.

Practice

1. A series expansion of $f(x) = e^{x^2}$ is

A. $1 + x + \frac{x^2}{2!} + \ldots + \frac{x^n}{n!} + \ldots = \sum_{n=0}^{\infty} \frac{x^n}{n!}$

B. $1 + x^2 + \frac{x^4}{2!} + \ldots + \frac{x^{2n}}{n!} + \ldots = \sum_{n=0}^{\infty} \frac{x^{2n}}{n!}$

C. $1 - x + \frac{x^2}{2!} - \ldots + \frac{(-x)^n}{n!} + \ldots = \sum_{n=0}^{\infty} \frac{(-x)^n}{n!}$

D. $1 - x^2 + \frac{x^4}{2!} - \ldots + \frac{(-1)^n x^{2n}}{n!} + \ldots = \sum_{n=0}^{\infty} \frac{(-1)^n x^{2n}}{n!}$

E. $1 + \frac{x^2}{2!} + \frac{x^4}{4!} \ldots + \frac{x^{2n}}{(2n)!} + \ldots = \sum_{n=0}^{\infty} \frac{x^{2n}}{(2n)!}$

2. Which of the following series converge?

I. $\sum_{n=1}^{\infty} \frac{2^n}{n^3}$ II. $\sum_{n=1}^{\infty} \frac{3}{2n}$ III. $\sum_{n=0}^{\infty} \left(\frac{1}{2^n} - \frac{1}{3^n} \right)$

A. I only   B. II only   C. III only   D. I and II   E. I, II, and III

3. What are all the values of x for which the series $\sum_{n=0}^{\infty} \frac{(-1)^n (x-1)^n}{(n+1)^2}$ converges?

A. $(-1, 1)$ B. $(0, 2)$ C. $[-1, 1)$ D. $(0, 2]$ E. $[0, 2]$

4. The coefficient of the cubic term in the Taylor series for $f(x) = \sin x$ about $x = 0$ is

A. $-\frac{1}{6}$ B. $\frac{1}{6}$ C. $-\frac{1}{3}$ D. $\frac{1}{3}$ E. 1

5. The sum of the infinite geometric series $\sum\limits_{n=0}^{\infty} \frac{5^n}{7^{n+1}}$ is

A. 0   B. 1   C. $\frac{5}{7}$ D. $\frac{1}{2}$ E. $\frac{1}{7}$

Free Response Prompt

The function $f(x) = \dfrac{e^{(x+1)^2} - 1}{(x+1)^2}$ is continuous for $x \neq -1$ and has deriva-

tives of all orders at $x = 0$.

a) Write the first four non-zero terms and the general term of the Maclaurin series for $e^{(x+1)^2}$.

b) Use the Maclaurin series for f to determine whether the graph of f has any points of inflection.

Answers and Explanations

1. B   2. C   3. E   4. A   5. D

1. The Maclaurin series expansion for $f(x) = e^x$ is

$1 + x + \dfrac{x^2}{2!} + \ldots + \dfrac{x^n}{n!} + \ldots = \sum\limits_{n=0}^{\infty} \dfrac{x^n}{n!}$. Substituting x^2 for x,

$f(x) = e^{x^2} = 1 + x^2 + \dfrac{x^4}{2!} + \ldots + \dfrac{x^{2n}}{n!} + \ldots = \sum\limits_{n=0}^{\infty} \dfrac{x^{2n}}{n!}$

2. Series I. $\sum\limits_{n=1}^{\infty} \dfrac{2^n}{n^3} = 2 + \dfrac{1}{2} + \dfrac{8}{27} + \dfrac{1}{4} + \dfrac{32}{125} + \dfrac{8}{27} + \dfrac{128}{343} + \ldots$ While the first

four terms decrease, after $n = 4$, the terms increase. $\lim\limits_{n \to \infty} \dfrac{2^n}{n^3} = \infty$ so the series diverges.

Series II. $\sum\limits_{n=1}^{\infty} \dfrac{3}{2n} = \dfrac{3}{2} \sum\limits_{n=1}^{\infty} \dfrac{1}{n}$. Since the harmonic series diverges, this multiple

also diverges.

Series III. $\sum_{n=0}^{\infty} \left(\frac{1}{2^n} - \frac{1}{3^n} \right) = \sum_{n=0}^{\infty} \frac{1}{2^n} - \sum_{n=0}^{\infty} \frac{1}{3^n}$. Each of these are geometric

series, with ratios of $\frac{1}{2}$ and $\frac{1}{3}$, respectively. Since both these ratios are less

than 1, both series converge. Therefore Series III converges.

3. For $\sum_{n=0}^{\infty} \frac{(-1)^n (x-1)^n}{(n+1)^2}$, consider that

$$\lim_{n \to \infty} \left| \frac{(x-1)^{n+1} \Big/ (n+2)^2}{(x-1)^n \Big/ (n+1)^2} \right| = \lim_{n \to \infty} \left| \frac{(n+1)^2 (x-1)}{(n+2)^2} \right| < 1 \text{ when } |x-1| < 1 \text{, so}$$

the series converges on the open interval $0 < x < 2$. Then check the

endpoints. When $x = 0$, $\sum_{n=0}^{\infty} \frac{(-1)^{2n}}{(n+1)^2} = \sum_{n=0}^{\infty} \frac{1}{(n+1)^2}$. Because

$0 < \frac{1}{(n+1)^2} < \frac{1}{n^2}$, and the p-series converges when $p = 2$, the series

converges at $x = 0$. When $x = 2$, $\sum_{n=0}^{\infty} \frac{(-1)^n}{(n+1)^2}$ is an alternating series, and

$\sum_{n=0}^{\infty} \left| \frac{(-1)^n}{(n+1)^2} \right| = \sum_{n=0}^{\infty} \frac{1}{(n+1)^2}$, which converges. Therefore

$\sum_{n=0}^{\infty} \frac{(-1)^n (x-1)^n}{(n+1)^2}$ converges at $0 \le x \le 2$.

4. The Maclaurin series for

$$f(x) = \sin x = x - \frac{x^3}{3!} + \frac{x^5}{5!} - \dots + (-1)^n \frac{x^{2n+1}}{(2n+1)!} + \dots \text{ so the coefficient of}$$

the cubic term is $-\dfrac{1}{3!} = -\dfrac{1}{6}$.

5. $\displaystyle\sum_{n=1}^{\infty} \frac{5^n}{7^{n+1}} = \sum_{n=1}^{\infty} \frac{1}{7} \cdot \frac{5^n}{7^n} = \sum_{n=1}^{\infty} \frac{1}{7}\left(\frac{5}{7}\right)^n$ is a geometric series with $a = \dfrac{1}{7}$ and

$r = \dfrac{5}{7}$ so the sum of the series is $\dfrac{a}{1-r} = \dfrac{\frac{1}{7}}{1-\frac{5}{7}} = \dfrac{\frac{1}{7}}{\frac{2}{7}} = \dfrac{1}{2}$.

Free Response

a) $e^{(x+1)^2} = 1 + (x+1)^2 + \dfrac{(x+1)^4}{2} + \dfrac{(x+1)^6}{6} + \dots + \dfrac{(x+1)^{2n}}{n!} + \dots$

b) f has no point of inflection
Start by finding the Maclaurin series, $\displaystyle\sum_{n=0}^{\infty} \frac{f^{(n)}}{n!}x^n$, for e^x, which requires

that you find and evaluate the derivatives of e^x at $x = 0$. Since all of
these are $e^0 = 1$, the Maclaurin series for e^x is

$$e^x = 1 + x + \frac{x^2}{2} + \frac{x^3}{6} + \dots + \frac{x^n}{n!} + \dots$$

Then find the Maclaurin series for f.

$$e^{(x+1)^2} - 1 = (x+1)^2 + \frac{(x+1)^4}{2} + \frac{(x+1)^6}{6} + \frac{(x+1)^8}{24} + \dots + \frac{(x+1)^{2n}}{n!} + \dots$$

and

$$\frac{e^{(x+1)^2} - 1}{(x+1)^2} = \frac{(x+1)^2 + \dfrac{(x+1)^4}{2} + \dfrac{(x+1)^6}{6} + \dfrac{(x+1)^8}{24} + \dots + \dfrac{(x+1)^{2n}}{n!} + \dots}{(x+1)^2},$$

so

$$f(x) = 1 + \frac{(x+1)^2}{2} + \frac{(x+1)^4}{6} + \frac{(x+1)^6}{24} + \dots + \frac{(x+1)^{2n-2}}{n!} + \dots$$

To determine whether f has any points of inflection, find f''.

$$f'(x) = 2\frac{x+1}{2} + 4\frac{(x+1)^3}{6} + 6\frac{(x+1)^5}{24} + \ldots + (2n-2)\frac{(x+1)^{2n-3}}{n!} + \ldots$$

$$f''(x) = 1 + \frac{3 \cdot 4}{6}(x+1)^2 + \frac{5 \cdot 6}{24}(x+1)^4 + \cdots + \frac{(2n-3)(2n-2)(x+1)^{2n-4}}{n!}$$

Inflection points occur when $f'' = 0$. For all $x \neq -1$, $f'' > 0$, so f has no point of inflection.

Topic 12: Parametric Equations and Vector Functions

T he information about parametric equations needed for the AP exam parallels the material included on vector functions. While each subject area encompasses a wide range of concepts, the information required for the AP exam is more limited.

Parametric Equations

Rather than expressing the relationship between variables x and y directly, with y as a function of x, a parametric equation gives both x and y as functions of a parameter, t. The parameter t is often considered to be time.

If the parametric function defines $x(t) = \cos t$ and $y(t) = \sin t$, for $0 \le t \le 2\pi$, the set of points $(x(t), y(t))$ describes a unit circle centered at the origin. The parametric equation introduces a notion of directionality not present in the corresponding $x^2 + y^2 = 1$. As t increases, the circle is traced out counterclockwise, starting from the positive x-axis at $(1,0)$. The same circle is traced by $x(t) = \cos t$ and $y(t) = \sin t$, for $\frac{\pi}{2} \le t \le \frac{5\pi}{2}$, but the trace begins at $(0,1)$.

Vector Functions

A function of the form $r(t) = \langle x(t), y(t) \rangle$ is a vector-valued function. Since $x(t)$ and $y(t)$ are functions of the parameter t, the vector-valued function can be viewed as a parametric function $r(t) = \langle x(t), y(t) \rangle$.

Eliminating the Parameter

To convert a parametric equation or vector-valued function to an equivalent function of x:

Express vector function as $x(t)$ and $y(t)$.	$r(t) = \left\langle \dfrac{t+5}{t}, \dfrac{t^2}{2} \right\rangle$ $x(t) = \dfrac{t+5}{t}$ $y(t) = \dfrac{t^2}{2}$
Solve $x(t)$ for t.	$x = \dfrac{t+5}{t}$ $xt = t+5$ $xt - t = 5$ $t(x-1) = 5$ $t = \dfrac{5}{x-1}$
Substitute for t in $y(t)$.	$y = \dfrac{t^2}{2}$ $y = \dfrac{\left(\dfrac{5}{x-1}\right)^2}{2}$

Simplify.	$$y = \frac{25}{2(x-1)^2}$$

Magnitude of a Vector

The magnitude of a vector is akin to the length of a segment or the distance a particle travels. The formula is a variant of the distance formula.

The magnitude of $r(t) = \langle x(t), y(t) \rangle$ is $$\|r(t)\| = \sqrt{[x(t)]^2 + [y(t)]^2}$$	$$r(t) = \left\langle 3t^2, \frac{1}{t} \right\rangle$$ $$\|r(t)\| = \sqrt{[3t^2]^2 + \left[\frac{1}{t}\right]^2}$$ $$\|r(t)\| = \sqrt{9t^4 + \frac{1}{t^2}} = \frac{\sqrt{9t^6 + 1}}{t}$$
If $r(t) = \left\langle 3t^2, \frac{1}{t} \right\rangle$, the magnitude of $r(1) = \langle 3,1 \rangle$ is	$$\|r(1)\| = \frac{\sqrt{10}}{1} = \sqrt{10}$$

Differentiation

To find the derivative of a parametric equation or a vector function, first differentiate $x(t)$ and $y(t)$ with respect to t.

For the curve defined by $x(t)$ and $y(t)$, the derivative $\dfrac{dy}{dx} = \dfrac{y'(t)}{x'(t)}$.	If $x(t) = \arcsin(t)$ and $y(t) = t^2 + 3$, $x'(t) = \dfrac{1}{\sqrt{1-t^2}}$, and $y'(t) = 2t$ so $\dfrac{dy}{dx} = 2t\sqrt{1-t^2}$.

The derivative of the vector function $r(t) = \langle x(t), y(t) \rangle$ is usually given as a vector function $r'(t) = \langle x'(t), y'(t) \rangle$.	If $r(t) = \left\langle 3t^2, \dfrac{1}{t} \right\rangle$, then $r'(t) = \left\langle 6t, \dfrac{-1}{t^2} \right\rangle$.

Tangent Lines

If asked to find the tangent to a curve defined by a parametric equation or a vector function, follow these steps.

	Parametric equation	Vector function
	Find the equation of the tangent line to the curve defined by $x(t) = 4t^2 - 3t$, $y(t) = \dfrac{5}{t^3}$ when $t = 1$	Find the equation of the tangent line to $r(t) = \left\langle \sin^2 t, \cos 2t \right\rangle$ at $t = \dfrac{\pi}{4}$.
Find the x- and y-coordinates of the point of tangency.	$x(1) = 4 - 3 = 1$, $y(1) = \dfrac{5}{1} = 5$ $(1,5)$	$r\left(\dfrac{\pi}{4}\right) = \left\langle \dfrac{1}{2}, 0 \right\rangle$
Find $\dfrac{dx}{dt}$ and $\dfrac{dy}{dt}$.	$x'(t) = 8t - 3$ $y'(t) = -\dfrac{15}{t^4}$ $x'(1) = 5$ $y'(1) = -15$	$r'(t) = \langle 2\sin t \cos t, -2\sin 2t \rangle$ $r'\left(\dfrac{\pi}{4}\right) = \langle 1, -2 \rangle$

Evaluate the slope of the tangent $\dfrac{dy}{dx} = \dfrac{dy/dt}{dx/dt}$	$\dfrac{dy}{dx} = \dfrac{-15}{5} = -3$	$\dfrac{dy}{dx} = \dfrac{-2}{1} = -2$
Write the equation of the tangent line in point-slope form.	$y - 5 = -3(x - 1)$ $y = -3x + 8$	$y - 0 = -2\left(x - \dfrac{1}{2}\right)$ $y = -2x + 1$

Applications of the Derivative

Parametric equations and vector functions are often used to describe particle motion. Common questions involve position, velocity, speed, and acceleration.

		Parametric equation	Vector function
Position $s(t)$	$x(t), y(t)$ or $\langle x(t), y(t) \rangle$	$x(t) = 3t^2$ $y(t) = e^{2t}$	$\langle \sin t, t^2 \rangle$
Velocity $v(t) = s'(t)$	$x'(t), y'(t)$ or $\langle x'(t), y'(t) \rangle$	$x'(t) = 6t$ $y'(t) = 2e^{2t}$	$\langle \cos t, 2t \rangle$
Speed $\|v(t)\|$	$\sqrt{[x'(t)]^2 + [y'(t)]^2}$	$\sqrt{36t^2 + 4e^{4t}}$	$\sqrt{\cos^2 t + 4t^2}$
Acceleration $a(t) = v'(t) = s''(t)$	$x''(t), y''(t)$ or $\langle x''(t), y''(t) \rangle$	$x''(t) = 6$ $y''(t) = 4e^{2t}$	$\langle -\sin t, 2 \rangle$

Integration

Integrating a parametric equation or a vector function begins by integrating $x(t)$ and $y(t)$ with respect to t.

Parametric equation	$\int x(t)\,dt$ and $\int y(t)\,dt$	If $x(t) = te^{t^2}$, and $y(t) = \dfrac{3}{t}$, then $\int x(t)\,dt = \dfrac{1}{2}e^{t^2} + c_1$ and $\int y(t)\,dt = 3\ln\lvert t \rvert + c_2$
Vector function	$\int_a^b r(t)\,dt = \left\langle \int_a^b x(t)\,dt, \int_a^b y(t)\,dt \right\rangle$	If $r(t) = \langle \cos 2t, \sin t \rangle$, then $\int_0^{\pi/2} r(t)\,dt$ $= \left\langle \int_0^{\pi/2} \cos 2t\,dt, \int_0^{\pi/2} \sin t\,dt \right\rangle$ $= \left\langle \dfrac{1}{2}\sin 2t \,\Big|_0^{\pi/2}, -\cos t \,\Big|_0^{\pi/2} \right\rangle$ $= \langle 0, 1 \rangle$

Applications of the Integral

Questions about particle motion may ask for total distance traveled or the location of the particle at a particular moment.

- Total distance traveled over the time interval $a \le t \le b$ is the integral from a to b of the speed of the vector.

- The length of the curve is the total distance traveled if the curve does not retrace itself. $L = \int_a^b \sqrt{1 + \left(\dfrac{dy}{dx}\right)^2}\,dx$ or $L = \int_a^b \sqrt{[x'(t)]^2 + [y'(t)]^2}\,dt$

- If the curve doubles back on itself, choose c and d, with $a \leq c < d \leq b$ so that for $c \leq t \leq d$, the full length of the curve is traced without duplication. Then the length of the curve is the integral from c to d.

- The x-coordinate of particle's position at the end of the time interval

$$a \leq t \leq b \text{ is } x(a) + \int_a^b x'(t)\, dt.$$

- The y-coordinate of particle's position at the end of the time interval

$$a \leq t \leq b \text{ is } y(a) + \int_a^b y'(t)\, dt.$$

Area under a Curve

To calculate the area under the curve defined by $x(t)$ and $y(t)$, the integrals of $x(t)$ and $y(t)$ are not enough. We need to bring them together, just as we had to bring together $\dfrac{dx}{dt}$ and $\dfrac{dy}{dt}$ to find $\dfrac{dy}{dx}$. In the case of the area under the curve, remember that we approximate that area by summing the areas of rectangles with height equal to y and base equal to Δx.

- The area under the curve defined by the parametric equations $x(t)$ and $y(t)$, or by the vector function $\langle x(t), y(t) \rangle$, is equal to

$$\int_a^b y(t)x'(t)\,dt.$$

- Take care in choosing the limits of integration, since parametric functions may retrace themselves.

- Choose values for a and b that will trace the entire curve without duplication.

Parametric equation	Find the area under the curve defined by $x(t) = t^2$ and $y(t) = \sin t$ over the interval $0 \le t \le 2\pi$.	$x'(t) = 2t$ so $A = 2\int_0^{2\pi} t\sin t\, dt$. Use integration by parts. $A = 2(-t\cos t + \sin t)\big|_0^{2\pi}$ $= 2[(-2\pi) - 0] = -4\pi$
Vector function	Find the area under the curve defined by the vector function $r(t) = \langle \sin t, \sin 2t \rangle$ on the interval $0 \le t \le \dfrac{\pi}{2}$.	$\dfrac{d\sin t}{dt} = \cos t$ so $A = \int_0^{\pi/2} \cos t \sin 2t\, dt$ $= 2\int_0^{\pi/2} \cos t \sin t \cos t\, dt$ Use integration by parts repeatedly. $A = -\dfrac{1}{3}[\sin t \sin 2t + 2\cos t \cos 2t]_0^{\pi/2}$ $= \dfrac{2}{3}$

Practice

1. A curve in the plane is defined parametrically by the equations $x = \sin 2t$ and $y = 2t - 5$. An equation of the line tangent to the curve at $t = \dfrac{\pi}{2}$ is

A. $y = -2x + \pi - 5$

D. $y = \dfrac{\pi}{2}x + \pi - 5$

B. $y = -\dfrac{\pi}{2}x + \pi - 5$

E. $y = \pi - 5$

C. $y = -x + \pi - 5$

2. The length of the curve defined by the parametric equations $x = 3t^2$ and $y = e^{2t}$ for $0 \le t \le 2\pi$, is given by

A. $\displaystyle\int_0^{2\pi} \sqrt{6t^2 + e^{4t}}\, dt$

B. $\displaystyle\int_0^{2\pi} \sqrt{36t^2 + e^{4t}}\, dt$

C. $\displaystyle\int_0^{2\pi} \sqrt{9t^4 + e^{4t}}\, dt$

D. $\displaystyle\int_0^{2\pi} \sqrt{36t^2 + 4e^{4t}}\, dt$

E. $\displaystyle\int_0^{2\pi} (6t + 2e^{2t})\, dt$

3. The set of all points $(\sqrt{t}, t + 3)$ is the graph of $y =$

A. $y = x^2 - 3$

B. $y = x^2 + 3$

C. $y = \sqrt{x + 3}$

D. $y = \sqrt{x - 3}$

E. $y = \sqrt{x} + 3$

If a particle moves in the xy-plane so that at time $t \ge 0$, its position vector is $\langle \ln t, t^2 - t \rangle$, then at time $t = 1$, the acceleration vector is

A. $\langle 0, 0 \rangle$ B. $\langle 1, 1 \rangle$ C. $\langle -1, 0 \rangle$ D. $\langle -1, 2 \rangle$ E. $\langle 1, 2 \rangle$

5. A particle moves in the xy-plane so that at time $t \geq 0$, its velocity vector is $\langle 2t - 1, 4t \rangle$. If it begins at the origin at time $t = 0$, then at time $t = 3$, its x-coordinate is

A. 5   B. 6   C. 7   D. 8   E. 9

Free Response Prompt

An object moving along a curve in the xy-plane is at position $\left(x(t), y(t)\right)$ at time t. For $0 \leq t < 1$, $\dfrac{dx}{dt} = \dfrac{1}{3-t}$ and $\dfrac{dy}{dt} = \dfrac{1}{\sqrt{1-t^2}}$. At time $t = 0$, the object is at the point $\left(-\ln 3, 0\right)$.

a) Find the speed and the acceleration of the object at time $t = 0$.

b) Find the position of the object at time $t = \dfrac{1}{2}$.

c) Find the equation of the line tangent to the curve at time $t = \dfrac{1}{2}$.

d) Find the total distance traveled by the object over the time interval $0 \leq t \leq \dfrac{1}{2}$.

Answers and Explanations

1. C   2. D   3. B   4. D   5. B

1. At $t = \dfrac{\pi}{2}$, $x = 0$ and $y = \pi - 5$. Because $\dfrac{dx}{dt} = 2\cos 2t \big|_{t=\frac{\pi}{2}} = -2$ and

$\dfrac{dy}{dt} = 2$, $\dfrac{dy}{dx} = -1$. The equation of the tangent is $y - \pi + 5 = -1(x - 0)$ or $y = -x + \pi - 5$.

2. $\dfrac{dx}{dt} = 6t$ and $\dfrac{dy}{dt} = 2e^{2t}$. The length of the curve is $\displaystyle\int_0^{2\pi} \sqrt{(6t)^2 + (2e^{2t})^2}\, dt$

$= \displaystyle\int_0^{2\pi} \sqrt{36t^2 + 4e^{4t}}\, dt$.

3. Solve $x = \sqrt{t}$ for $t = x^2$ and substitute into $y = t + 3$. The parametric equation defines the graph of $y = x^2 + 3$.

4. The acceleration vector is the second derivative of the position vector. If the position vector is $\langle \ln t, t^2 - t \rangle$, then the velocity vector is $\langle \frac{1}{t}, 2t - 1 \rangle$, and the acceleration vector is $\langle \frac{-1}{t^2}, 2 \rangle$. At $t = 1$, the acceleration is $\langle -1, 2 \rangle$.

5. The x-coordinate at $t = 3$ is $0 + \int_0^3 (2t - 1) \, dt = t^2 - t \Big|_0^3 = 6$.

Free Response

a) The speed of the object is $\sqrt{[x'(t)]^2 + [y'(t)]^2} =$

$\sqrt{\left(\frac{1}{3}\right)^2 + 1^2} = \sqrt{\frac{10}{9}} = \frac{\sqrt{10}}{3}$. Acceleration is the derivative of velocity,

so if $\frac{dx}{dt} = \frac{1}{3-t}$, then $\frac{d^2x}{dt^2} = \frac{1}{(3-t)^2}$ and if $\frac{dy}{dt} = \frac{1}{\sqrt{1-t^2}}$,

$\frac{d^2y}{dt^2} = \frac{t}{\left(1-t^2\right)^{3/2}}$. At $t = 0$, the acceleration vector is $\langle \frac{1}{9}, 0 \rangle$.

b) Position is the antiderivative of velocity, so if $\frac{dx}{dt} = \frac{1}{3-t}$, then

$x(t) = -\ln|3 - t| + C$, and if $\frac{dy}{dt} = \frac{1}{\sqrt{1-t^2}}$, $y(t) = \arcsin t + C$. Be-

cause the initial position of the object is $(-\ln 3, 0)$, we can conclude

that $x(t) = -\ln|3 - t|$ and $y(t) = \arcsin t$. At $t = \frac{1}{2}$, $x\left(\frac{1}{2}\right) = -\ln \frac{5}{2}$ and

$y\left(\dfrac{1}{2}\right) = \arcsin\dfrac{1}{2} = \dfrac{\pi}{6}$. The position of the object is $\left(-\ln\dfrac{5}{2},\dfrac{\pi}{6}\right)$ or approximately $(-0.916, 0.524)$.

c) At $t = \dfrac{1}{2}$, the position of the object is $\left(-\ln\dfrac{5}{2},\dfrac{\pi}{6}\right)$ or approximately $(-0.916, 0.524)$. The values of $\dfrac{dx}{dt} = \dfrac{1}{3-\frac{1}{2}} = \dfrac{2}{5}$

and $\dfrac{dy}{dt} = \dfrac{1}{\sqrt{1-\left(\frac{1}{2}\right)^2}} = \dfrac{2}{\sqrt{3}}$, so the slope of the tangent line is

$\dfrac{dy}{dx} = \dfrac{\frac{2}{\sqrt{3}}}{\frac{2}{5}} = \dfrac{5}{\sqrt{3}} = \dfrac{5\sqrt{3}}{3}$. The equation of the tangent line to the curve

at $t = \dfrac{1}{2}$ is $y - \dfrac{\pi}{6} = \dfrac{5\sqrt{3}}{3}(x + \ln 2.5)$.

d) The total distance traveled by the object over the time interval

$0 \le t \le \dfrac{1}{2}$ is $\displaystyle\int_0^{\frac{1}{2}} \sqrt{\left(\dfrac{1}{3-t}\right)^2 + \left(\dfrac{1}{\sqrt{1-t^2}}\right)^2}\, dt = \int_0^{\frac{1}{2}} \sqrt{\dfrac{1}{(3-t)^2} + \dfrac{1}{1-t^2}}\, dt \approx 0.554$

by calculator.

Topic 13: Polar Curves

T he graphs produced by polar equations are interesting and often beautiful tracings. It is highly unlikely that an AP question will ask you to graph a polar curve. You will find questions that ask you to find a tangent to a polar curve, the area enclosed by a curve, or between two curves, or the length of a curve.

Basics

The polar coordinate system locates each point in the plane by a coordinate pair (r, θ), where r is the radius, or distance of the point from a fixed point called the pole, and θ is the angle between the positive horizontal axis and the radius.

Conversion

Rectangular to Polar $(x, y) \rightarrow (r, \theta)$	
$r = \sqrt{x^2 + y^2}$ $\theta = \tan^{-1}\left(\dfrac{y}{x}\right)$ (Add π for QII or QIII)	$\left(-3, 3\sqrt{3}\right) \rightarrow (r, \theta)$ $r = \sqrt{(-3)^2 + \left(3\sqrt{3}\right)^2} = 6$ $\theta = \tan^{-1}\left(\dfrac{3\sqrt{3}}{-3}\right) = \tan^{-1}(-\sqrt{3}) = -\dfrac{\pi}{3} + \pi = \dfrac{2\pi}{3}$ $\left(-3, 3\sqrt{3}\right) \rightarrow \left(6, \dfrac{2\pi}{3}\right)$
For $x = 0$, $\theta = \dfrac{\pi}{2}$ or $\theta = \dfrac{3\pi}{2}$	
Polar to Rectangular $(r, \theta) \rightarrow (x, y)$	
$x = r\cos\theta$ $y = r\sin\theta$	$\left(8, \dfrac{5\pi}{4}\right) \rightarrow (x, y)$ $x = 8\cos\dfrac{5\pi}{4} = 8\left(-\dfrac{\sqrt{2}}{2}\right) = -4\sqrt{2}$ $y = 8\sin\dfrac{5\pi}{4} = 8\left(-\dfrac{\sqrt{2}}{2}\right) = -4\sqrt{2}$ $\left(8, \dfrac{5\pi}{4}\right) \rightarrow \left(-4\sqrt{2}, -4\sqrt{2}\right)$

Converting Equations

Rectangular to Polar	
Substitute $x = r\cos\theta$ and $y = r\sin\theta$.	$9x^2 + 4y^2 = 36$ $9(r\cos\theta)^2 + 4(r\sin\theta)^2 = 36$
Simplify.	$9r^2\cos^2\theta + 4r^2\sin^2\theta = 36$
Use trig identities where appropriate.	$5r^2\cos^2\theta + 4r^2(\cos^2\theta + \sin^2\theta) = 36$ $5r^2\cos^2\theta + 4r^2 = 36$
Isolate r or r^2.	$r^2(5\cos^2\theta + 4) = 36$ $r^2 = \dfrac{36}{5\cos^2\theta + 4}$
Polar to Rectangular	
Simplify.	$r = \dfrac{4}{\cos\theta - 2\sin\theta}$ $r(\cos\theta - 2\sin\theta) = 4$ $r\cos\theta - 2r\sin\theta = 4$
Substitute $x = r\cos\theta$, $y = r\sin\theta$, $r = \sqrt{x^2 + y^2}$, and $\theta = \tan^{-1}\left(\dfrac{y}{x}\right)$.	$r\cos\theta - 2r\sin\theta = 4$ $x - 2y = 4$

To make conversion easier, you can apply algebraic techniques to the equation first. Possibilities include multiplying both sides by r or a power of r, squaring both sides, or taking the tangent of both sides.

Polar Equations and Their Graphs

Lines	$\theta = c$	Passes through the origin. $y = (\tan c)x$
	$r = \dfrac{c}{a\cos\theta + b\sin\theta}$	$y = -\dfrac{a}{b}x + \dfrac{c}{b}$
Spirals		
	$r = a\theta$	Archimedean spiral
	$r = e^{a\theta}$	Logarithmic spiral
Circles		
	$r = a\cos\theta$	Circle symmetric about x-axis, diameter a
	$r = a\sin\theta$	Circle symmetric about y-axis, diameter a
	$r = a\cos\theta + b\sin\theta$	Circle through the pole
Conics		
	$r = \dfrac{ed}{1 - e\cos\theta}$	Conic, eccentricity e, directrix –d $\quad e > 1$ hyperbola, $e < 1$ ellipse, $e = 1$ parabola
Roses		
	$r = a\cos n\theta$	Roses with petals of length a
	$r = a\sin n\theta$	n petals if n is odd or $2n$ petals if n is even

Limaçons		
	$r = a + b\cos\theta$	Inner loop: $b - a$, outer loop: $b + a$
	$r = a + b\sin\theta$	Cosine is symmetric about x-axis, sine about y-axis.
Cardioids		
	$r = a + a\cos\theta$	Symmetric about x-axis
	$r = a + a\sin\theta$	Symmetric about y-axis

Tangents

To find the tangent to any curve, first find the slope of the tangent line by finding and evaluating the derivative at the point of tangency.

$x = r\cos\theta$	$y = r\sin\theta$
$\dfrac{dx}{d\theta} = -r\sin\theta + \cos\theta\dfrac{dr}{d\theta}$	$\dfrac{dy}{d\theta} = r\cos\theta + \sin\theta\dfrac{dr}{d\theta}$
Divide to find that $\dfrac{dy}{dx} = \dfrac{\dfrac{dr}{d\theta}\sin\theta + r\cos\theta}{\dfrac{dr}{d\theta}\cos\theta - r\sin\theta}$.	
The equation of the tangent line is $y - y_1 = \dfrac{dy}{dx}(x - x_1)$.	

Example: Find the equation of the tangent to the curve $r = 3 - 5\cos\theta$ at $\left(\dfrac{11}{2}, \dfrac{2\pi}{3}\right)$.

Find $\dfrac{dr}{d\theta}$.	$\dfrac{dr}{d\theta} = 5\sin\theta$
Find $\dfrac{dx}{d\theta}$.	$\begin{aligned}\dfrac{dx}{d\theta} &= -r\sin\theta + \cos\theta\,\dfrac{dr}{d\theta}\\ &= -(3 - 5\cos\theta)\sin\theta + \cos\theta(5\sin\theta)\\ &= -3\sin\theta + 10\sin\theta\cos\theta\\ &= -3\sin\dfrac{2\pi}{3} + 10\sin\dfrac{2\pi}{3}\cos\dfrac{2\pi}{3}\\ &= -3\left(\dfrac{\sqrt{3}}{2}\right) + 10\left(\dfrac{\sqrt{3}}{2}\right)\left(-\dfrac{1}{2}\right) = -\dfrac{3\sqrt{3}}{2} - \dfrac{5\sqrt{3}}{2} = -4\sqrt{3}\end{aligned}$
Find $\dfrac{dy}{d\theta}$.	$\begin{aligned}\dfrac{dy}{d\theta} &= r\cos\theta + \sin\theta\,\dfrac{dr}{d\theta}\\ &= (3 - 5\cos\theta)\cos\theta + \sin\theta(5\sin\theta)\\ &= 3\cos\theta - 5\cos^2\theta + 5\sin^2\theta\\ &= 3\left(-\dfrac{1}{2}\right) - 5\left(-\dfrac{1}{2}\right)^2 + 5\left(\dfrac{\sqrt{3}}{2}\right)^2\\ &= -\dfrac{3}{2} - \dfrac{5}{4} + \dfrac{15}{4} = -\dfrac{6}{4} - \dfrac{5}{4} + \dfrac{15}{4} = 1\end{aligned}$
Find $\dfrac{dy}{dx}$.	$\dfrac{dy}{dx} = \dfrac{\dfrac{dr}{d\theta}\sin\theta + r\cos\theta}{\dfrac{dr}{d\theta}\cos\theta - r\sin\theta} = \dfrac{-4\sqrt{3}}{1} = -4\sqrt{3}$
Convert the point $\left(\dfrac{11}{2}, \dfrac{2\pi}{3}\right)$ to rectangular coordinates.	$\begin{aligned}x &= (3 - 5\cos\theta)\cos\theta\\ &= \left(3 - 5\cos\dfrac{2\pi}{3}\right)\cos\dfrac{2\pi}{3}\\ &= \left(3 + \dfrac{5}{2}\right)\left(-\dfrac{1}{2}\right) = -\dfrac{11}{4}\end{aligned}$ $\begin{aligned}y &= (3 - 5\cos\theta)\sin\theta\\ &= \left(3 - 5\cos\dfrac{2\pi}{3}\right)\sin\left(\dfrac{2\pi}{3}\right)\\ &= \left(\dfrac{11}{2}\right)\left(\dfrac{\sqrt{3}}{2}\right) = \dfrac{11\sqrt{3}}{4}\end{aligned}$

Find the equation of the tangent line.	$y - \dfrac{11\sqrt{3}}{4} = -4\sqrt{3}\left(x + \dfrac{11}{4}\right)$
	$y - \dfrac{11\sqrt{3}}{4} = -4\sqrt{3}\,x - 11\sqrt{3}$
	$y = -4\sqrt{3}\,x - 11\sqrt{3}$

Area

The area enclosed by a single polar curve, r, is equal to $A = \dfrac{1}{2}\displaystyle\int_{\alpha}^{\beta} r^2\, d\theta$.

Example: Find the area of the region bounded by the graph of $r = 4 - 4\cos\theta$.

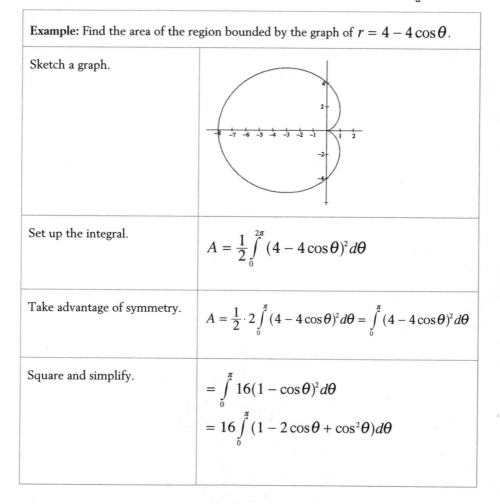

Sketch a graph.	
Set up the integral.	$A = \dfrac{1}{2}\displaystyle\int_{0}^{2\pi} (4 - 4\cos\theta)^2\, d\theta$
Take advantage of symmetry.	$A = \dfrac{1}{2} \cdot 2\displaystyle\int_{0}^{\pi} (4 - 4\cos\theta)^2\, d\theta = \int_{0}^{\pi} (4 - 4\cos\theta)^2\, d\theta$
Square and simplify.	$= \displaystyle\int_{0}^{\pi} 16(1 - \cos\theta)^2\, d\theta$
	$= 16\displaystyle\int_{0}^{\pi} (1 - 2\cos\theta + \cos^2\theta)\, d\theta$

Make a trig substitution if necessary for easier integration.	$= 16 \int_0^\pi \left(1 - 2\cos\theta + \frac{1}{2}(\cos 2\theta + 1)\right) d\theta$ $= 16 \int_0^\pi \left(\frac{3}{2} - 2\cos\theta + \frac{1}{2}\cos 2\theta\right) d\theta$
Integrate and evaluate.	$= 16\left[\frac{3}{2}\theta - 2\sin\theta + \frac{1}{4}\sin 2\theta\right]_0^\pi$ $= 16\left[\frac{3\pi}{2}\right]$ $= 24\pi$

The area enclosed by $r = 4 - 4\cos\theta$ is 24π square units.

If the area is enclosed between two curves, r_1 and r_2, with $0 \le r_1 \le r_2$, the area is $A = \frac{1}{2}\int_\alpha^\beta (r_2^2 - r_1^2) d\theta$.

Example: Find the area of the region inside the graph of $r = 4 + 4\sin\theta$ but outside the graph of $r = 2$.	
Sketch a graph.	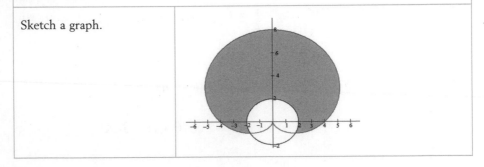

Find the points of intersection.	$4 + 4\sin\theta = 2$ $4\sin\theta = -2$ $\sin\theta = -\dfrac{1}{2}$ $\theta = \dfrac{7\pi}{6} \qquad \theta = -\dfrac{\pi}{6}$
Set up the integral.	$A = \dfrac{1}{2}\displaystyle\int_{\alpha}^{\beta}(r_2^2 - r_1^2)d\theta$ $A = \dfrac{1}{2}\displaystyle\int_{-\pi/6}^{7\pi/6}((4 + 4\sin\theta)^2 - (2)^2)d\theta$
Square and simplify.	$A = \dfrac{1}{2}\displaystyle\int_{-\pi/6}^{7\pi/6}(16 + 32\sin\theta + 16\sin^2\theta - 4)d\theta$ $A = 2\displaystyle\int_{-\pi/6}^{7\pi/6}(3 + 8\sin\theta + 4\sin^2\theta)d\theta$
Make a trig substitution.	$A = 2\displaystyle\int_{-\pi/6}^{7\pi/6}\left(3 + 8\sin\theta + 4\left(\dfrac{1 - \cos 2\theta}{2}\right)\right)d\theta$ $A = 2\displaystyle\int_{-\pi/6}^{7\pi/6}(3 + 8\sin\theta + 2 - 2\cos 2\theta)d\theta$ $A = 2\displaystyle\int_{-\pi/6}^{7\pi/6}(5 + 8\sin\theta - 2\cos 2\theta)d\theta$
Integrate and evaluate.	$A = 2[5\theta - 8\cos\theta - \sin 2\theta]_{-\pi/6}^{7\pi/6}$ $= 2\left[\dfrac{40\pi}{6} + 8\sqrt{3} - \sqrt{3}\right] = \dfrac{40\pi}{3} + 14\sqrt{3} \approx 66.137$

If neither rule fits perfectly, try dividing the region.

Example: Find the area enclosed between $r = 4\cos\theta$ and $r = 4\sin\theta$.	
Sketch a graph.	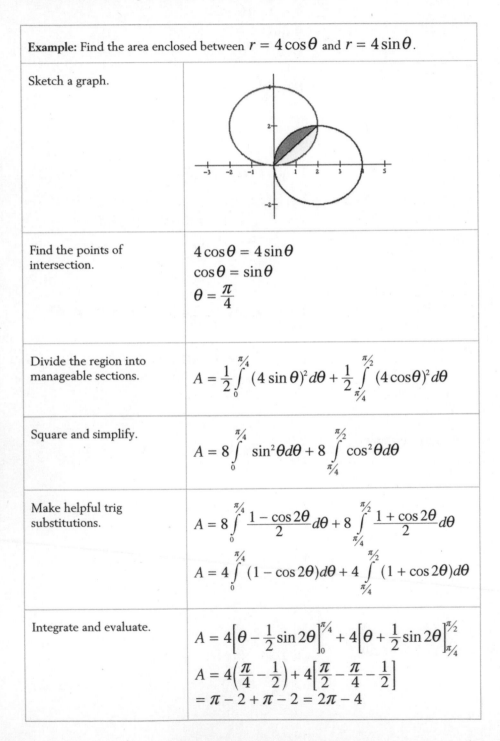
Find the points of intersection.	$4\cos\theta = 4\sin\theta$ $\cos\theta = \sin\theta$ $\theta = \dfrac{\pi}{4}$
Divide the region into manageable sections.	$A = \dfrac{1}{2}\displaystyle\int_{0}^{\pi/4} (4\sin\theta)^2\,d\theta + \dfrac{1}{2}\int_{\pi/4}^{\pi/2} (4\cos\theta)^2\,d\theta$
Square and simplify.	$A = 8\displaystyle\int_{0}^{\pi/4} \sin^2\theta\,d\theta + 8\int_{\pi/4}^{\pi/2} \cos^2\theta\,d\theta$
Make helpful trig substitutions.	$A = 8\displaystyle\int_{0}^{\pi/4} \dfrac{1 - \cos 2\theta}{2}\,d\theta + 8\int_{\pi/4}^{\pi/2} \dfrac{1 + \cos 2\theta}{2}\,d\theta$ $A = 4\displaystyle\int_{0}^{\pi/4} (1 - \cos 2\theta)\,d\theta + 4\int_{\pi/4}^{\pi/2} (1 + \cos 2\theta)\,d\theta$
Integrate and evaluate.	$A = 4\left[\theta - \dfrac{1}{2}\sin 2\theta\right]_{0}^{\pi/4} + 4\left[\theta + \dfrac{1}{2}\sin 2\theta\right]_{\pi/4}^{\pi/2}$ $A = 4\left(\dfrac{\pi}{4} - \dfrac{1}{2}\right) + 4\left[\dfrac{\pi}{2} - \dfrac{\pi}{4} - \dfrac{1}{2}\right]$ $= \pi - 2 + \pi - 2 = 2\pi - 4$

Arc Length

The length of an arc, or section of the curve, of a polar curve is

$$L = \int \sqrt{r^2 + \left(\frac{dr}{d\theta}\right)^2}\, d\theta.$$

Example: Find the length of one petal of the graph of $r = 4\sin 3\theta$.	
Square r.	$r = 4\sin 3\theta$ $r^2 = 16\sin^2(3\theta)$
Find $\dfrac{dr}{d\theta}$ and square it.	$r = 4\sin 3\theta$ $\dfrac{dr}{d\theta} = 12\cos 3\theta$ $\left(\dfrac{dr}{d\theta}\right)^2 = (12\cos 3\theta)^2 = 144\cos^2(3\theta)$
Add $r^2 + \left(\dfrac{dr}{d\theta}\right)^2$.	$r^2 + \left(\dfrac{dr}{d\theta}\right)^2 = 16\sin^2(3\theta) + 144\cos^2(3\theta)$ $= 16[\sin^2(3\theta) + 9\cos^2(3\theta)]$ $= 16[\sin^2(3\theta) + 8\cos^2(3\theta) + \cos^2(3\theta)]$ $= 16[5 + 4\cos(6\theta)]$
Introduce the square root and simplify.	$\sqrt{r^2 + \left(\dfrac{dr}{d\theta}\right)^2} = \sqrt{16(5 + 4\cos(6\theta))}$ $= 4\sqrt{5 + 4\cos 6\theta}$
Integrate.	$L = 4\int_0^{\pi/3} \sqrt{5 + 4\cos(6\theta)}\, d\theta \approx 8.909$ (by calculator)

Practice

1. Which of the following is equal to the area inside the polar curve $r = 5\cos\theta$ but outside the polar curve $r = 2 + 2\cos\theta$?

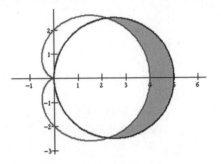

A. $\displaystyle\int_{-0.841}^{0.841} [(5\cos\theta)^2 - (2 + 2\cos\theta)^2]d\theta$

B. $\dfrac{1}{2}\displaystyle\int_{-0.841}^{0.841} [(5\cos\theta)^2 - (2 + 2\cos\theta)^2]d\theta$

C. $\dfrac{1}{2}\displaystyle\int_{-0.841}^{0.841} [(5\cos\theta) - (2 + 2\cos\theta)]d\theta$

D. $\dfrac{1}{2}\displaystyle\int_{-0.841}^{0.841} [(3\cos\theta - 2)^2]d\theta$

E. $\dfrac{1}{2}\displaystyle\int_{-0.785}^{0.785} [(5\cos\theta)^2 - (2 + 2\cos\theta)^2]d\theta$

2. Which of the following gives the area of the region enclosed by the loop of the graph of the polar curve $r = 1 + 2\sin\theta$ shown in the figure?

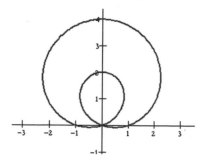

A. $\dfrac{1}{2}\displaystyle\int_{7\pi/6}^{11\pi/6} (1 + 2\sin\theta)^2 \, d\theta$

B. $\dfrac{1}{3}\displaystyle\int_{7\pi/6}^{11\pi/6} (1 + 2\sin\theta)^2 \, d\theta$

C. $\dfrac{1}{2}\displaystyle\int_{7\pi/6}^{11\pi/6} (1 + 2\sin\theta) \, d\theta$

D. $\dfrac{1}{2}\displaystyle\int_{-\pi/6}^{7\pi/6} (1 + 2\sin\theta)^2 \, d\theta$

E. $\displaystyle\int_{7\pi/6}^{11\pi/6} (1 + 2\sin\theta)^2 \, d\theta$

3. Which of the following represents the graph of the polar curve $r = 3\sin 4\theta$?

A.

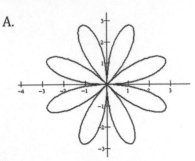

D.

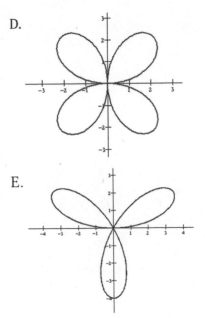

E.

B.

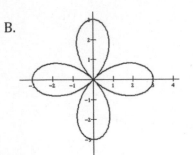

C.

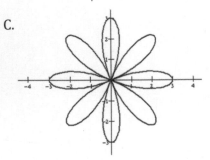

4. The area of the region enclosed by the polar curve $r = 2 - 3\cos\theta$ for $0 \le \theta \le 2\pi$ is

A. 8π B. 4π C. $\dfrac{17\pi}{4}$ D. 17π E. $\dfrac{17\pi}{2}$

5. The area of the region enclosed by one petal of the polar curve $r = 4\cos 3\theta$ is

A. $\dfrac{8\pi}{3}$ B. $\dfrac{2\pi}{3}$ C. π D. $\dfrac{4\pi}{3}$ E. $\dfrac{\pi}{3}$

Free Response Prompt

The graphs of the polar curves $r = 2$ and $r = 4 + 4\cos\theta$ are shown in the figure.

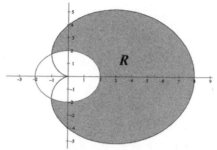

a) Let R be the region that is inside the graph of $r = 4 + 4\cos\theta$ but outside the graph of $r = 2$, as shaded in the figure. Find the area of R.

b) A particle moving with nonzero velocity along the polar curve given by $r = 4 + 4\cos\theta$ has position $(x(t), y(t))$ at time t, with $\theta = -\dfrac{\pi}{2}$ when $t = 0$. This particle moves along the curve so that $\dfrac{dr}{dt} = \dfrac{dr}{d\theta}$. Find the value of $\dfrac{dr}{dt}$ at $\theta = \dfrac{\pi}{4}$ and interpret your answer in terms of the motion of the particle.

c) For the particle described in part (b), $\dfrac{dy}{dt} = \dfrac{dy}{d\theta}$. Find the value of $\dfrac{dy}{dt}$ at $\theta = \dfrac{\pi}{4}$ and interpret your answer in terms of the motion of the particle.

Answers and Explanations

1. B   2. B   3. A   4. E   5. D

1.   The   curves $r = 5\cos\theta$ and $r = 2 + 2\cos\theta$ intersect   at $\theta = \pm\cos^{-1}\left(\dfrac{2}{3}\right) \approx \pm 0841$. The circle $r = 5\cos\theta$ is the outer curve, and the cardioid $r = 2 + 2\cos\theta$ is the inner curve. The area enclosed between them is given by $\dfrac{1}{2}\displaystyle\int_{-0.841}^{0.841} [(5\cos\theta)^2 - (2 + 2\cos\theta)^2]d\theta$.

2. Find the zeros by solving $1 + 2\sin\theta = 0$. $\sin\theta = \frac{1}{2}$, so $\theta = \frac{7\pi}{6}$ or $\theta = \frac{11\pi}{6}$. The area of the inner loop is equal to $\frac{1}{2}\int_{7\pi/6}^{11\pi/6}(1 + 2\sin\theta)d\theta$.

3. $r = 3\sin 4\theta$ is a polar rose with 8 petals, each 3 units long, and the graph is symmetric about the y-axis.

4. The area enclosed by $r = 2 - 3\cos\theta$ is $\frac{1}{2}\int_{0}^{2\pi}(2 - 3\cos\theta)^2 d\theta$

$$= \frac{1}{2}\int_{0}^{2\pi}(4 - 12\cos\theta + 9\cos^2\theta)\theta d\theta = \frac{1}{2}\int_{0}^{2\pi}\left(4 - 12\cos\theta + 9\cdot\frac{1 + \cos 2\theta}{2}\right)\theta d\theta$$

$= 2\theta + 6\sin\theta + \frac{9}{4}\left(\theta - \frac{1}{2}\sin 2\theta\right)$. Evaluating gives you $4\pi + \frac{9}{2}\pi = \frac{17\pi}{2}$.

5. Since the 3 petals of $r = 4\cos 3\theta$ will have identical areas, choose the one most convenient to integrate. The area of one petal is

$$= \frac{1}{2}\int_{\pi/6}^{\pi/2}(4\cos 3\theta)^2 d\theta = 8\int_{\pi/6}^{\pi/2}\frac{1 + \cos 6\theta}{2}d\theta = 4\int_{\pi/6}^{\pi/2}(1 + \cos 6\theta)d\theta.$$ Integrating

and evaluating gives you $4\left[\theta - \frac{1}{6}\sin 6\theta\right]_{\pi/6}^{\pi/2} = 4\left(\frac{\pi}{2} - \frac{\pi}{6}\right) = \frac{4\pi}{3}$.

Free Response

a) The area of

$$R = \frac{1}{2}\int_{-\pi/6}^{7\pi/6}(4 + 4\cos\theta)^2 - (2)^2 d\theta = \frac{1}{2}\int_{-\pi/6}^{7\pi/6}[16(1 + 2\cos\theta + \cos^2\theta) - 4]d\theta$$

$$= 2\int_{-\pi/6}^{7\pi/6}[3 + 8\cos\theta + 4\cos^2\theta]d\theta = 2\int_{-\pi/6}^{7\pi/6}\left[3 + 8\cos\theta + 4\left(\frac{1 + \cos 2\theta}{2}\right)\right]d\theta$$

$$= 2\int_{-\pi/6}^{7\pi/6}[3 + 8\cos\theta + 2(1 + \cos 2\theta)]d\theta = 2\int_{-\pi/6}^{7\pi/6}[5 + 8\cos\theta + 2\cos 2\theta]d\theta$$

$$= 2[5\theta + 8\cos\theta + \sin\theta]_{-\pi/6}^{7\pi/6} = \frac{40\pi}{3} + 2\sqrt{3} \approx 45.352 \text{ square units.}$$

b) $\dfrac{dr}{dt} = \dfrac{dr}{d\theta} = -4\sin\theta$. Evaluated at $\theta = \dfrac{\pi}{4}, \dfrac{dr}{dt} = \dfrac{dr}{d\theta} = -4\left(\dfrac{\sqrt{2}}{2}\right) = -2\sqrt{2}$ units per second. The particle is moving toward the pole at $2\sqrt{2}$ units per second since $r > 0$ and $\dfrac{dr}{dt} < 0$.

c) Since $y(t) = r\sin\theta = (4 + 4\cos\theta)\sin\theta = 4\sin\theta + 2\cos 2\theta$,

$\dfrac{dy}{dt} = \dfrac{dy}{d\theta} = 4\cos\theta - 4\sin 2\theta$. Evaluating for $\theta = \dfrac{\pi}{4}$,

$\dfrac{dy}{dt} = \dfrac{dy}{d\theta} = 4\cos\dfrac{\pi}{4} - 4\sin\dfrac{\pi}{2} = 4\left(\dfrac{\sqrt{2}}{2}\right) - 4(1)2\sqrt{2} - 4 \approx -1.172$ units per second. The particle is moving downward at 1.172 units per second since $\dfrac{dy}{dt} < 0$ and $y > 0$ at $\theta = \dfrac{\pi}{4}$.

Formula Glossary

Trigonometry

Identities learned in trigonometry continue to be important for simplifying expressions. While any of those identities can be used in simplifying, the identities used most often are listed below.

The Pythagorean identities

$\sin^2\theta + \cos^2\theta = 1$

$\tan^2\theta + 1 = \sec^2\theta$

$1 + \cot^2\theta = \csc^2\theta$

Double angle identities

$\sin 2\theta = 2\sin\theta\cos\theta$

$\cos 2\theta = \cos^2\theta - \sin^2\theta$

$\qquad\ = 1 - 2\sin^2\theta$

$\qquad\ = 2\cos^2\theta - 1$

The $\cos 2\theta$ identity, because of its multiple forms, is particularly useful.

Limits

These two limits are frequently used in problems involving properties of limits or the squeeze theorem.

$$\lim_{x \to 0} \frac{\sin x}{x} = 1$$

$$\lim_{x \to 0} \frac{1 - \cos x}{x} = 0$$

L'Hôpital's Rule

If $f(x)$ and $g(x)$ are differentiable on the open interval (a,b) containing c, except possibly at c itself, $g'(x) \neq 0$ for x in (a,b) except possibly at c itself, $\lim_{x \to c} \frac{f(x)}{g(x)}$ produces an indeterminate form, then

$$\lim_{x \to c} \frac{f(x)}{g(x)} = \lim_{x \to c} \frac{f'(x)}{g'(x)} \; .$$

Derivatives and Antiderivatives

Definition of the Derivative

$$f'(a) = \lim_{h \to 0} \frac{f(a+h) - f(a)}{h}$$

Common Derivatives and Antiderivatives

Derivatives	Antiderivatives
$\frac{d}{dx}[c] = 0$	$\int du = u + C$
$\frac{d}{dx}[x] = 1$	
$\frac{d}{dx}[cu] = cu'$	$\int cf(u)du = c \int f(u)du$

$\frac{d}{dx}[u \pm v] = u' \pm v'$	$\int [f(u) \pm g(u)]du = \int f(u)du \pm \int g(u)du$
$\frac{d}{dx}[u^n] = nu^{n-1} \cdot u'$	$\int u^n du = \frac{u^{n+1}}{n+1} + C, n \neq -1$
$\frac{d}{dx}[uv] = uv' + vu'$	
$\frac{d}{dx}\left[\frac{u}{v}\right] = \frac{vu' - uv'}{v^2}$	

Exponential and Logarithmic

$\frac{d}{dx}[e^u] = e^u \cdot u'$	$\int e^u du = e^u + C$
$\frac{d}{dx}[\ln u] = \frac{u'}{u}$	$\int \frac{du}{u} = \ln|u| + C$

Trigonometric

$\frac{d}{dx}[\sin u] = \cos u \cdot u'$	$\int \sin u\, du = -\cos u + C$
$\frac{d}{dx}[\cos u] = -\sin u \cdot u'$	$\int \cos u\, du = \sin u + C$
$\frac{d}{dx}[\tan u] = \sec^2 u \cdot u'$	$\int \sec^2 u\, du = \tan u + C$
$\frac{d}{dx}[\csc u] = -\csc u \cot u \cdot u'$	$\int \csc u \cot u\, du = -\csc u + C$

$\frac{d}{dx}[\sec u] = \sec u \tan u \cdot u'$	$\int \sec u \tan u \, du = \sec u + C$
$\frac{d}{dx}[\cot u] = -\csc^2 u \cdot u'$	$\int \csc^2 u \, du = -\cot u + C$

Inverse Trig

$\frac{d}{dx}[\arcsin u] = \frac{u'}{\sqrt{1-u^2}}$	$\int \frac{du}{\sqrt{a^2-u^2}} = \arcsin \frac{u}{a} + C$
$\frac{d}{dx}[\arctan u] = \frac{u'}{1+u^2}$	$\int \frac{du}{a^2+u^2} = \frac{1}{a}\arctan \frac{u}{a} + C$

Chain Rule

$$\frac{d}{dx} f \circ g = f'\big(g(x)\big)g'(x)$$

Inverses

$$g'(x) = \frac{1}{f'(g(x))} \text{ where } g(x) = f^{-1}(x)$$

Integration by Parts

$$\int u \, dv = uv - \int v \, du$$

Riemann Sum

$$\sum_{k=1}^{n} f(x_k^*)\Delta x_k = f(x_1^*)\Delta x_1 + f(x_2^*)\Delta x_2 + f(x_3^*)\Delta x_3 + \ldots + f(x_n^*)\Delta x_n$$

where Δx_k is the width of an interval and $f\left(x_k^*\right)$ is a specified value from that interval.

Trapezoidal Rule

$$A = \frac{1}{2}\Delta x[f(x_0) + 2f(x_1) + 2f(x_2)... + 2f(x_{n-1}) + f(x_n)]$$

Applications of the Derivative and the Integral

Linear Approximation

$$L(x) = f(a) + f'(a)(x - a)$$

Position

$$s(t) = \int v(t)dt$$

Velocity

$$v(t) = s'(t)$$

$$v(t) = \int a(t)dt$$

Acceleration

$$a(t) = v'(t)$$

$$a(t) = s''(t)$$

Average Value

$$f_{avg} = \frac{1}{b-a}\int_a^b f(x)dx$$

Length of a Curve

$$L = \int_a^b \sqrt{1 + \left(\frac{dy}{dx}\right)^2}\, dx$$

Area under a Curve

$$A = \int_a^b f(x)dx$$

Area between Two Curves

$$A = \int_a^b f(x) - g(x)dx$$

Volume of Revolution—Method of Discs

about a horizontal line $V = \pi \int_a^b [r(x)]^2 dx$

about a vertical line $V = \pi \int_{y=c}^{y=d} [r(y)]^2 dy$

Volume of revolution—Method of Washers

about a horizontal line $V = \pi \int_a^b [R(x)]^2 - [r(x)]^2 dx$

about a vertical line $V = \pi \int_{y=c}^{y=d} [R(y)]^2 - [r(y)]^2 dy$

Volume by Cross Sections

Squares: $V = \int_a^b (f(x) - g(x))^2 dx$

Equilateral Triangles: $V = \dfrac{\sqrt{3}}{4} \int_a^b (f(x) - g(x))^2 dx$

Right Triangles: $V = \dfrac{1}{4} \int_a^b (f(x) - g(x))^2 dx$

Semicircles: $V = \dfrac{\pi}{8} \int_a^b (f(x) - g(x))^2 dx$

Differential Equations

Growth proportional to the population: $\dfrac{dP}{dt} = kP$

Integrates to $P = P_0 e^{kt}$ where P_0 is the initial population.

Logistic growth: $\dfrac{dP}{dt} = kP\left(1 - \dfrac{P}{L}\right)$

Integrates to $P = \dfrac{L}{1 + Ce^{-kt}}$ where L is the carrying capacity.

Euler's Method

Estimate the solution of a differential equation by successive approximations of the form $y_k = y_{k-1} + \dfrac{dy}{dx}\Delta x$, where y_k is the current approximation, y_{k-1} is the previous approximation, $\dfrac{dy}{dx}$ is the given differential and Δx is the width of each interval.

Series

The infinite geometric series $\sum\limits_{n=1}^{\infty} ar^{n-1}$ converges to $\dfrac{a}{1-r}$ if $|r| < 1$, but diverges if $|r| \geq 1$.

Integral Test

If f is positive, continuous, and decreasing for $x \geq 1$, and $f(n) = a_n$, then

$\sum\limits_{n=1}^{\infty} a_n$ and $\int\limits_{1}^{\infty} f(x)\,dx$ either both converge or both diverge.

Ratio Test

If all terms are positive and

$\lim\limits_{n \to \infty} \dfrac{a_{n+1}}{a_n} < 1$ $\sum\limits_{n=0}^{\infty} a_n$ converges

$\lim\limits_{n \to \infty} \dfrac{a_{n+1}}{a_n} > 1$ $\sum\limits_{n=0}^{\infty} a_n$ diverges

$\lim\limits_{n \to \infty} \dfrac{a_{n+1}}{a_n} = 1$ test is inconclusive

Comparison Test

If $0 \leq a_n \leq b_n$ for all n and $\displaystyle\sum_{n=0}^{\infty} b_n$ converges, then $\displaystyle\sum_{n=0}^{\infty} a_n$ converges.

If $0 \leq a_n \leq b_n$ for all n and $\displaystyle\sum_{n=0}^{\infty} a_n$ diverges, then $\displaystyle\sum_{n=0}^{\infty} b_n$ diverges.

P-series

$$\sum_{n=1}^{\infty} \frac{1}{n^p} = 1 + \frac{1}{2^p} + \frac{1}{3^p} + \frac{1}{4^p} + \ldots + \frac{1}{n^p} + \ldots$$ Converges if $p > 1$, diverges if

$p < 1$

Harmonic Series

$$\sum_{n=1}^{\infty} \frac{1}{n} = 1 + \frac{1}{2} + \frac{1}{3} + \frac{1}{4} + \frac{1}{5} + \ldots + \frac{1}{n} + \ldots$$ The harmonic series is a p-series

with $p = 1$. The harmonic series does **not** converge.

Power Series

A power series is an infinite series of the form $\displaystyle\sum_{n=0}^{\infty} a_n x^n$.

Taylor Series

about $x = a$: $\displaystyle\sum_{n=0}^{\infty} \frac{f^{(n)}(a)}{n!}(x-a)^n$

Maclaurin Series (Taylor Series about $x = 0$)

$$\sum_{n=0}^{\infty} \frac{f^{(n)}(0)}{n!}(x)^n$$

Common Maclaurin Series

$$\frac{1}{1-x} = 1 + x + x^2 + x^3 + \ldots + x^n + \ldots \text{ for } -1 < x < 1$$

$$\sin x = x - \frac{x^3}{6} + \frac{x^5}{120} - \frac{x^7}{5040} + \ldots + (-1)^n \frac{x^{2n+1}}{(2n+1)!} + \ldots \text{ for all } x$$

$$\cos x = 1 - \frac{x^2}{2} + \frac{x^4}{24} - \frac{x^6}{720} + \ldots (-1)^n \frac{x^{2n}}{(2n)!} + \ldots \text{ for all } x$$

$$\tan^{-1} x = x - \frac{x^3}{3} + \frac{x^5}{5} - \frac{x^7}{7} + \ldots + (-1)^n \frac{x^{2n+1}}{2n+1} + \ldots \text{ for } -1 \le x \le 1$$

$$e^x = 1 + x + \frac{x^2}{2} + \frac{x^3}{6} + \ldots + \frac{x^n}{n!} + \ldots \text{ for all } x$$

$$\ln(1+x) = x - \frac{x^2}{2} + \frac{x^3}{3} - \frac{x^4}{4} + \ldots + (-1)^{n-1} \frac{x^n}{n} + \ldots \text{ for } -1 < x \le 1$$

Lagrange Error Bound

If an nth degree Taylor series centered at $x = a$, $\sum\limits_{k=0}^{n} \frac{f^{(k)}(a)}{k!}(x-a)^k$, is

used to approximate the value of a function, $f(x)$, at $x = c$, for c close

to a, the error of approximation is bounded by the maximum of

$$\left| \frac{f^{n+1}(a)(c-a)^{n+1}}{(n+1)!} \right| \text{ and } \left| \frac{f^{n+1}(c)(c-a)^{n+1}}{(n+1)!} \right|.$$

Vectors and Parametrics

Magnitude of a Vector

The magnitude of $r(t) = \langle x(t), y(t) \rangle$ is $\| r(t) \| = \sqrt{[x(t)]^2 + [y(t)]^2}$

Length of an Arc

$$L = \int_{a}^{b} \sqrt{[x'(t)]^2 + [y'(t)]^2}\, dt$$

Rectangular-Polar Conversion

$$r = \sqrt{x^2 + y^2}$$

$$\theta = \tan^{-1}\left(\frac{y}{x}\right)$$

$$x = r\cos\theta$$
$$y = r\sin\theta$$

Slope of the Tangent Line

$$\frac{dy}{dx} = \frac{dy/dr}{dx/dr} = \frac{\frac{dr}{d\theta}\sin\theta + r\cos\theta}{\frac{dr}{d\theta}\cos\theta - r\sin\theta}$$

Area Bounded by a Polar Curve

$$A = \frac{1}{2}\int_{\alpha}^{\beta} r^2\,d\theta$$

Area between Two Polar Curves

$$A = \frac{1}{2}\int_{\alpha}^{\beta} (r_2^2 - r_1^2)\,d\theta$$

Length of an Arc

$$L = \int \sqrt{r^2 + \left(\frac{dr}{d\theta}\right)^2}\,d\theta$$

Multiple Choice Strategies

The multiple choice section of the AP exam takes more than half the time of the test, and the number of questions—45 multiple choice as compared to six free response—make it feel even bigger. It's a good idea to have a plan. As noted on page 31, the best way to approach the multiple choice section is to do the easy questions first. For the more difficult questions, you can always guess if you can eliminate one or more answer choices. The best strategy, however, is to look for new, more efficient ways to find the right answer. Here are a few tested strategies for getting it right.

Don't Find What You Don't Need

It sounds obvious—don't do work you don't need to do—but it's easy to waste valuable time deriving, calculating, or evaluating things you don't actually need to know to answer the question. Read the question all the way through before you start to work. Focus on exactly what is necessary. The fact that something is mentioned in the question doesn't mean you have to calculate it. Consider this question on linear approximation.

Suppose $f(x) = x^2 - 3x + 2$, and the tangent line to the graph of $f(x)$ at $x = 1$ is used to approximate values of $f(x)$. Which of the

following is the largest value of x for which the error of that approximation will be less than 0.25?

A. 1.1   B. 1.3   C. 1.5   D. 1.7   E. 1.9

Don't spend time approximating the value of $f(x)$ for any of the
given values of x. You don't need to know what the approximation is.
You need to know what the error is. Keep your focus on the error. The
fastest way to do that is to work with the function and its tangent, rather
than specific values. The tangent line at $x = 1$ is $y = 1 - x$. The error of
the approximation at any point near $x = 1$ can be found by subtracting

$\left(x^2 - 3x + 2\right) - \left(1 - x\right) = x^2 - 2x + 1 = \left(x - 1\right)^2$. You want $\left(x - 1\right)^2 < 0.25$,

which means $-0.5 < x - 1 < 0.5$ or $0.5 < x < 1.5$. Note that x must be
less than 1.5, so B is the largest acceptable answer.

Don't Calculate When an Estimate Will Do

If you're working on a section for which calculators are not permitted,
you shouldn't be doing a lot of calculation. There's probably a better
way to do the problem. Don't be seduced into thinking you need your
calculator for every question on the calculator-permitted section either.
Often you can narrow down the answer choices without doing more
than an estimate of the arithmetic. Consider this volume question.

The base of a solid is a region in the first quadrant bounded by the x-
axis, the y-axis, and the line $x + 2y = 6$. If cross sections of the solid perpendicular to the x-axis are semicircles, what is the volume of the solid?

A. 3.524   B. 7.069   C. 14.137   D. 23.562   E. 29.274

You'll want to sketch this quickly, and then set up your integral. The
volume is the sum of the semicircular cross sections, each of which has a

radius of $\dfrac{y}{2}$ and an area of $\dfrac{1}{2}\pi r^2$, so $V = \int\limits_0^6 \left(\dfrac{1}{2}\pi\left(\dfrac{y}{2}\right)^2\right) dx = \dfrac{\pi}{8}\int\limits_0^6 y^2\, dx$

$= \dfrac{\pi}{8}\int\limits_0^6 \left(\dfrac{6-x}{2}\right)^2 dx = \dfrac{\pi}{8}\int\limits_0^6 \dfrac{(6-x)^2}{4}\, dx = \dfrac{\pi}{32}\int\limits_0^6 (6-x)^2\, dx = \dfrac{\pi}{32}\int\limits_0^6 (36 - 12x + x^2)\, dx$

$= \dfrac{\pi}{32}\left[36x - 6x^2 + \dfrac{x^3}{3}\right]_0^6$. The first thing to notice is that when $x = 0$, the entire expression is zero. Also note that when $x = 6$, $36x - 6x^2 = 0$, so you're only evaluating $\dfrac{\pi}{32} \cdot \dfrac{6^3}{3}$. Since $\dfrac{\pi}{32} \approx \dfrac{1}{10}$ and $\dfrac{6^3}{3} = 2 \cdot 6^2$, you're looking for an answer of approximately 7. Only one answer is reasonable.

Say it with Symbols

Sometimes you read a question and you immediately understand what work you need to do. Other times, nothing jumps out at you. To help you get going, translate the words and phrases of the question into symbols. Often that will be enough to make the rest of your work clear.

When $x = 7$, the rate at which $\sqrt[3]{x+1}$ is increasing is k times the rate at which x is increasing. What is the value of k?

A. $\dfrac{1}{12}$ B. $\dfrac{1}{3}$ C. 3   D. 6   E. 24

Approach the problem like a translation exercise. The phrase "the rate at which $\sqrt[3]{x+1}$ is increasing" becomes $\dfrac{d}{dt}\sqrt[3]{x+1}$ and "the rate at which x is increasing" is $\dfrac{dx}{dt}$, so you have the equation $\dfrac{d}{dt}\sqrt[3]{x+1} = k\dfrac{dx}{dt}$.

You know $\dfrac{d}{dt}\sqrt[3]{x+1} = \dfrac{1}{3\sqrt[3]{(x+1)^2}}\dfrac{dx}{dt}$, so $\dfrac{1}{3\sqrt[3]{(x+1)^2}}\dfrac{dx}{dt} = k\dfrac{dx}{dt}$, which means $\dfrac{1}{3\sqrt[3]{(x+1)^2}} = k$. All that's left to do is plug in $x = 7$, and

$k = \dfrac{1}{3\sqrt[3]{(7+1)^2}} = \dfrac{1}{3\sqrt[3]{64}} = \dfrac{1}{12}$.

Remember that there is a finite list of topics that can be covered on the test. The question, no matter how strange it may sound, will always ask you to do something from that list.

Understand the Relationship between the Graphs of *f*, *f'*, and *f"*

Whether analytically, numerically, or graphically, you'll be tested to see if you understand fundamental connections between a function and its derivative. The derivative as the slope of the tangent, with all that means for determining when the function is increasing or decreasing, where relative extrema occur, and what the graph looks like, is guaranteed to show up on the exam.

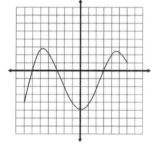

Let $g(x) = \int_{a}^{x} f(t)\,dt$, where $a \leq x \leq b$. The figure above shows the

graph of g on $[a,b]$. Which of the following could be the graph of *f*?

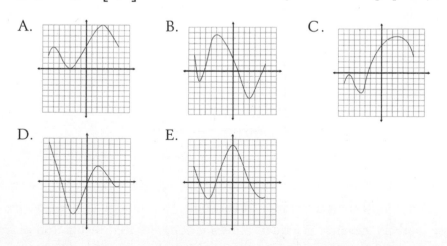

A.

B.

C.

D.

E.

Examine the graph of the derivative first to see where its x-intercepts fall. Each zero of the derivative should correspond to a turning point of the function. Then check where the derivative is negative and where it's positive. That will tell you whether those turning points are maxima or minima. You should be able to choose D as the graph of f quickly.

Understand the Relationship between Distance, Velocity, and Acceleration

Distance, velocity, and acceleration will show up on every AP exam. Particle motion problems are one common setting in which you'll encounter these ideas. Velocity is the change in distance over time, and the words "change in" should translate to derivative for you. So velocity is the derivative of distance or displacement, and acceleration is the change in, or derivative of, velocity. If you need to move up the ladder, integrate.

A particle starts from rest at the point $(1,0)$ and travels along the x-axis with a constant positive acceleration for time $t \ge 0$. Which of the following could be the graph of the distance of the particle from the origin over time?

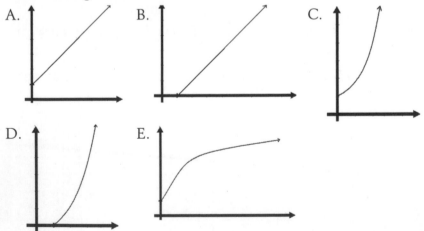

The derivative of distance is velocity and the derivative of velocity is acceleration. If the acceleration is constant, the velocity is a linear function, and the distance is a quadratic function, and that realization alone narrows the options to two. At time $t = 0$, the particle is one unit from the origin, so graph C with y-intercept (0, 1) is the best choice.

Do the Memory Work

You can't expect to score well on the AP exam by memorization alone, but there are some things that should be committed to memory. Common rules for derivatives and integrals should be habitual, and key identities from trigonometry can't be forgotten. In addition, if you're taking the BC exam, you'll want to memorize common series such as the Maclaurin series to save yourself from having to do everything from scratch.

The glossary of formulas will give you a good list of what you need to know. It has the most important trig identities, your basic derivatives and antiderivatives, rules for differentiation and integration, and key information about series. Remember that a Maclaurin series is just a Taylor series centered at $x = 0$. Be certain you know how to recognize the Maclaurin series for e^x, $\ln(1 \pm x)$, $\sin x$, and $\cos x$.

Know Key Theorems

While most of the multiple choice questions ask you to perform a calculation, you can expect some questions that test your understanding of important definitions and theorems. Almost every AP calculus exam has a question that hinges on your ability to recognize the definition of the derivative at a point, and most exams include questions that test whether you understand the Mean Value Theorem, Rolle's Theorem, the Intermediate Value Theorem, or the Fundamental Theorem of Calculus.

The hypotheses of the various theorems are similar. The function is continuous on a closed interval. You'll likely be given that, but you'll probably be left to determine for yourself whether the function is differentiable. You'll need to keep straight what the conclusion of each theorem promises, so organize them for yourself.

Theorem Name	Conditions	Conclusion
Rolle's Theorem	f is: differentiable on (a,b) continuous on $[a,b]$ $f(a) = f(b) = 0$	There is at least one point c in (a,b) for which $f'(c) = 0$.
Mean Value Theorem	f is: differentiable on (a,b) continuous on $[a,b]$	There is at least one point c in (a,b) for which $f'(c) = \dfrac{f(b)-f(a)}{b-a}$.
Intermediate Value Theorem	$f(x)$ is continuous on $[a,b]$. $d \in [f(a),f(b)]$	There is a $c \in [a,b]$ such that $f(c) = d$.
Fundamental Theorem of Calculus	f is continuous on $[a,b]$ F is any antiderivative for f on $[a,b]$	$\displaystyle\int_a^b f(t)\,dt = F(b) - F(a)$

THE BIG PICTURE: HOW TO PREPARE YEAR-ROUND

The AP Calculus Exam may be months away, but the time to start preparing is now. In this section, we'll help you get the head start you need to make the most of your class and study time. By the time crunch time arrives, all you'll need is a quick review to be ready to earn a top score on the exam.

Here are the key steps to focusing your attack for the coming months:

- Set your goals (page 239)—What score do you want to earn, and what are your obstacles to achieving it?

- Track your progress (page 243)—Is your class keeping up with the materials, or do you need to study some of the materials on your own?

- Follow a routine (page 249)—Use strategies to organize your work and take good notes.

- Practice, practice, practice (page 255)—Make the most of your time outside class.

Use these strategies as you prepare throughout the year. As the exam gets closer, begin working through the review materials and test-taking strategies in the Comprehensive Strategies and Review section earlier in this book. When you are just a few days out, go back to the Last-Minute Study Guide section, do a final review of the key concepts, and make sure you have everything you need for exam day. You're ready to go!

Setting Your Goals

It would be great to live in a world where everyone got a 5 on all their AP tests. In this world, you would take every AP test under the sun, participate in every extracurricular activity available, and have plenty of time for after-school jobs, hanging out with friends, and whatever else you wanted to do. Since we do not live in that world, it's important to set realistic but ambitious goals and find ways to achieve them.

Which Test Should You Take?

If your class covers all the materials in the Calculus BC curriculum (see page 246), the answer is simple—take the BC exam. The BC exam covers more topics than the AB exam, but it isn't necessarily harder. You are not asked to solve problems any more quickly, and many of the same multiple choice and free response questions are included on both tests.

Students who take the BC exam also receive an AB subscore based on their responses to AB problems. Even if you don't get the score you want on the BC exam, you may earn a high enough score on the AB subsection to earn college credit. If you decide to only take the AB exam, however, you'll never know if you could have received even more college credit by taking the BC exam.

If your class only covers AB materials, it will take self-discipline to learn the additional materials, but it can be done. You will need to carve out extra time to study the additional BC topics throughout the year. Before you decide to do this, however, think about your other obligations, including other AP tests and extracurricular activities. Will you be able to squeeze in the extra study time required to learn the additional topics? If so, great. If not, decide whether the chance for a high score on the BC exam is worth sacrificing another activity you have on your plate.

What Score Do You Need?

You want a 5, of course. If you're going into the exam planning to settle for less than that, adjust your attitude. Get more aggressive. Go for it.

That said, it's helpful to know how scores less than 5 can affect your future. If you are taking the exam in your senior year, check the policies of the schools you are considering attending. Many schools give credit for scores of 3 and above. By the time you get your scores, you should know what college you are attending, so your score will not affect your application. There's no harm in taking as many AP exams as you can.

What if your college application process is still a year or more away? When it comes to college admissions, nobody can tell for sure that this or that score on the AP exam will get you into College H or University P. The college admissions process is far too complicated to boil down to a few test scores. Students with straight A records, 800 SAT scores, and 5s on their APs get waitlisted or outright rejected. Other students are admitted to their wildest reaches.

When a college admission committee considers your application, they're looking at the whole package: grades, test scores, athletics, extracurricular activities, community involvement, your essays, teacher recommendations, your passions and special talents. So when you look at your record, think about how this AP score will work with the rest of the package. Did you write an essay about your love of mathematics, or are you applying to the school of engineering? If so, the admissions committee might be looking for a 4 or a 5. On the other hand, if you've made clear that literature is your life, taking AP Calculus may be seen as a sign of an ambitious and motivated student, and a 3 will seem quite respectable.

In the end, of course you want a 5. You always want to do the very best you can. Work for a 5. Study for a 5. Max your score. If the scores come back and you breathe a sigh of relief at your 3, that's fine, and no one has to know but you.

If You're Not Taking AP Calculus

If you are not taking an AP Calculus class, you are still welcome to take the test. You don't have much to lose, and college admissions officers will likely be impressed by your ambition to take the test without taking an AP class. (It might be wise to find a way to highlight this fact somewhere in your application.) If you choose to do so, you will need to carve out significant time to review materials you are not learning in class, perhaps by following the schedule on page 244. If you are not taking a calculus class at all, buy a calculus textbook, read it thoroughly, and do the practice problems. If you are planning on using your AP score to skip introductory calculus in college and move on to higher levels of math, don't just focus on what is in the AP test. There are likely to be other topics in introductory calculus that are not included in the test, but which you will need for future study.

Remember that the best way to learn the concepts on your own is to practice by doing lots of problems, and keep doing them until you get the hang of them. Take your first practice AP test at least a month before the test, and focus on the areas where you need further review.

Deciding Not to Take the Test

If you've gotten to the point of buying this book, you shouldn't be thinking about backing out now. Your nerves may be getting to you or you may feel unprepared. Take a deep breath and go study the content review chapters.

If you're still here, it probably means you feel that you can't earn a respectable score on the test. You don't want a poor score going out to potential colleges, and not taking the test seems the best way to avoid that.

Before you decide to bail, consider a couple of questions. Will your transcript show a course called AP Calculus? If colleges see AP Calculus on your transcript, but you never take the AP exam, you may have some explaining to do. Yes, a poor score will look bad, but do you want to send your college the message that when the going gets tough, you back out?

You have invested a lot of time in calculus. Are you sure you're not underestimating what you know? You don't have to be able to answer every question to earn a respectable score. If you start taking a practice test and you find you don't know the material, don't despair. Do the questions you know, skip the ones you don't, and try to get partial credit wherever you can on the free response. If you can get half the problems right, you're likely to earn a 3, which is perfectly respectable. If your score winds up being less than that, you're still in no worse shape than if you didn't take the exam at all—and you won't be left wondering what might have been.

Tracking Your Progress

Not all calculus classes are created equal. Courses labeled AP Calculus are committed to covering all the topics in the AP syllabus in time for you to take the exam in early May. If your class isn't labeled AP, it might not make that deadline, and even courses officially called AP can get bogged down, or lose time to unexpected circumstances such as snow days.

Use the following chart to track the pace of your class and ensure that you cover all the necessary materials by test time. Be warned, however, that there is no hard and fast timetable. Your course may tackle topics in a different sequence. Generally, you should expect to spend the first semester on differentiation, and the second semester on integration. The goal would be to finish the course by the end of April—earlier would be even better, but that's difficult—and leave whatever class time you have in May before the exam for review and practice tests.

AP Calculus AB	
September	Analysis of graphs Limits of functions Calculating limits using algebra Estimating limits from graphs or tables of data Asymptotic and unbounded behavior Continuity as a property of functions Intermediate Value Theorem Extreme Value Theorem (If you've had a strong precalculus course, you may skip some or all of this.)
October	Concept of the derivative Derivatives graphically, numerically, and analytically Derivative as the limit of the difference quotient Relationship between differentiability and continuity Derivative at a point Slope of a curve at a point Tangent line to a curve at a point Local linear approximation Instantaneous rate of change as the limit of average rate of change Approximate rate of change from graphs and tables of values
November	Derivative as a function Corresponding characteristics of graphs of $f(x)$ and $f'(x)$ Significance of the sign of $f'(x)$ for the increasing and decreasing behavior of $f(x)$ The Mean Value Theorem
December	Second derivatives Characteristics of the graphs of $f(x)$, $f'(x)$, and $f''(x)$ Significance of the sign of $f''(x)$ for the concavity of $f(x)$ Points of inflection Analysis of curves Absolute and relative extrema Rates of change, including related rates problems Implicit differentiation and inverse functions Applications of the derivative
January	Differential equations Slope fields and solution curves
February	Interpretations and properties of definite integrals Definite integral as a limit of Riemann sums Applications of integrals Fundamental Theorem of Calculus

March	Antiderivatives of basic functions Antiderivatives by u-substitution (including change of limits for definite integrals) Finding specific antiderivatives using initial conditions
April	Separable differential equations $y' = ky$ and exponential growth Riemann sums (left, right, and midpoint) Trapezoidal sums Approximating definite integrals of functions represented algebraically, graphically, and by tables of values
May	Final reviews for the exam

If you're worried that your class is falling behind schedule and you want to try to learn some of the later material on your own, the material on Riemann sums and trapezoidal sums is probably the most manageable for independent study. If you understand the integral as the area under a curve, Riemann sums and trapezoidal sums make sense as ways to approximate that area. You can probably also work on the separable differential equations independently once you have the basics of antiderivatives. And of course, you can start reviewing and taking practice tests whenever you wish. You may not know how to answer all the questions on a practice test yet, but the questions you do work on will give you both a review and practice with the style of question the AP exam is likely to ask.

Planning for the BC Exam

Establishing a timetable for the BC exam is more difficult. Some schools spread the course over more than two semesters, which sometimes leads to a more leisurely pace. Other schools expect students to take the AB exam one year and the BC exam the next. Since many of the same topics appear on both exams, the BC year includes both review and additional topics. Many schools try to introduce some basic calculus concepts in precalculus.

If you are preparing for the BC exam in one school year, with no prior experience with this material, the pace will need to be brisk, and little time will be given for review. You'll be expected to come into the course with a strong background in algebra and precalculus, and if you need to review concepts from earlier courses, you'll be expected to do it on your own.

AP Calculus BC	
September	Limits of functions Calculating limits using algebra Estimating limits from graphs or tables of data Asymptotic and unbounded behavior Continuity as a property of functions Intermediate Value Theorem Extreme Value Theorem Parametric, polar, and vector functions (Any of the above that was covered in precalculus may be treated as review material.)
October	Concept of the derivative Derivatives graphically, numerically, and analytically Derivative defined as the limit of the difference quotient Relationship between differentiability and continuity Derivative at a point Slope of a curve at a point Tangent line to a curve at a point Local linear approximation Instantaneous rate of change as the limit of average rate of change Approximate rate of change from graphs and tables of values
November	Derivative as a function Corresponding characteristics of graphs of $f(x)$ and $f'(x)$ Significance of the sign of $f'(x)$ for the increasing and decreasing behavior of $f(x)$. The Mean Value Theorem Second derivatives Characteristics of the graphs of $f(x)$, $f'(x)$, and $f''(x)$ Significance of the sign of $f''(x)$ for the concavity of $f(x)$ Points of inflection
December	Analysis of curves, including curves given in parametric form, polar form, and vector form Absolute and relative extrema Rates of change, including related rates problems Implicit differentiation and inverse functions Applications of the derivative

January	Derivatives of parametric, polar, and vector functions Slope fields and solution curves Numerical solution of differential equations using Euler's method
February	Interpretations and properties of definite integrals Definite integral as a limit of Riemann sums Applications of integrals Fundamental Theorem of Calculus Antiderivatives of basic functions Antiderivatives by u-substitution (including change of limits for definite integrals) Integration by parts Simple partial fractions (nonrepeating linear factors only) Using initial conditions
March	Improper integrals (as limits of definite integrals) Separable differential equations $y' = ky$ and exponential growth Logistic differential equations Riemann sums (left, right, and midpoint) Trapezoidal sums Approximating definite integrals of functions represented algebraically, graphically, and by tables of values L'Hôpital's Rule
April	Concept of series Geometric series with applications The harmonic series Alternating series with error bound The integral test P-series The ratio test Comparing series to test for convergence or divergence Taylor polynomial approximation Maclaurin series and the general Taylor series centered at $x = a$ Maclaurin series for the functions e^x, $\sin x$, $\cos x$, and $\dfrac{1}{1-x}$ Substitution, differentiation, antidifferentiation, and the formation of new series from known series Radius and interval of convergence of power series Lagrange error bound for Taylor polynomials
May	Final reviews for the exam

If your class is falling behind, work on the material on series (the topics scheduled for April in the chart above) independently. It's not easy, but most of it can be tackled once you understand limits. Of those topics, only the integral test will require that you know how to integrate. You can also expect to see a series question—probably focusing on Taylor series—in the free response section of the exam, and there will be multiple choice questions about series as well.

As with the AB exam, you'll probably find the material on Riemann sums and trapezoidal sums to be accessible for self-study. Separable differential equations can be done independently once you have the basics of antiderivatives, but you'll need integration by partial fractions before you tackle the logistic model.

Maximizing Your Time

The best way to prepare for the AP exam is to take your class seriously. That means focusing in class, doing the homework, and absorbing the key concepts before moving on to the next topic. Here are a few tips on how to get the most out of the time you put into class.

Focus in Class

When you're in class, you might as well make the most of it. Of course, that means not focusing your attention elsewhere. But it also means more than just scribbling down all the teacher's notes into your notebook. Taking notes is important, but even more important is paying attention to what the teacher is saying and how he or she is solving the problems. If you have to make a choice between taking detailed notes and absorbing the concepts, go for absorbing the concepts. You can probably go back to your textbook to find most of what your teacher is writing down. However, you can't ask your textbook a question if you don't understand. Don't be shy about asking questions as your teacher goes through the materials—chances are, your classmates have some of the same questions.

Take Useful Notes

There's no one right way to take notes—what works for one person may not work for another. If what you've been doing has been successful, keep doing it. However, there may be ways to improve your notetaking to tailor it to the AP exam. When preparing for in-class tests, you are tested on what was covered in class, so it makes sense to simply take notes on what was covered in class, and study those notes. What the AP exam covers, however, may be different from what you learned in class. In class, you may learn about the epsilon-delta definition of a limit. You may learn to find volumes by shells. You may prove new theorems when they're introduced. That's wonderful stuff, but it's not going to be on the AP exam.

So, as you're taking notes, you want a way to distinguish material you must know for the AP exam from material that won't be covered there. Whether you box it, color code it, or distill your notes later, find a method to highlight the essentials.

If you haven't already done so, go to the College Board website and download the course description. As you work through the course, compare what's covered in class to that description. Your teacher my tell you that a particular topic is not covered on the exam, but if she doesn't, and you don't see it in the course description, ask.

If you have time, go through your class notes each evening and copy into another notebook or a set of index cards, the essential information you need for the AP exam. The process of distilling your notes in this way is a good study aid, and rewriting the material reinforces it in your memory. When it's time to review for the test, you'll have a study guide all ready.

In your exam notes, be sure to include the whys as well as the whats. Examples of how to find second derivatives are great, but you also want reminders that second derivatives talk about concavity. When the second derivative is positive, the graph of the function is concave up, and when the second derivative is negative, concave down. Include the fact that you can use a second derivative test to distinguish a relative minimum from a relative maximum. Make a note that the second derivative will be equal to zero at inflection points, but also a reminder to check that there's actually a change in concavity.

The most important part of taking notes is what you do after you take them. Don't wait until right before the test to start looking at them. You'll be studying for class tests throughout the year, which is good, but often that focuses your attention on just a small block of material. Set a time, perhaps once a week or once a month, to go back through your notes. This is not just to remember what you've done, although that it one purpose. The larger goal is to start to get the big picture, to put all the topics and techniques together in an integrated whole. Look for connections to topics covered previously.

The AP exam will test you on the entire year's work, and questions, especially in the free response section, will call upon different topics and techniques. You won't be able to label one question a derivative question and another an integral question. One part of a question might ask for a rate of change (derivative) while another part of the same question asks for the average value of the function (integral). You need to break the compartmental thinking that's often present in class tests.

A skilled craftsperson has a variety of tools, clearly organized in a tool box, easily accessible when needed. The skills and concepts of calculus are your tools, and to score well on the exam you'll need to access them easily. Your exam notes are your tool box. Keep it full, keep it in good order, and visit it frequently.

Practice Your Skills

If there's one thing more important than reviewing the concepts of calculus, it's putting them into practice. While your homework is likely to give you lots of practice, be sure not to stop practicing until you get the concepts down. If you find that you struggle particularly with a topic, go back to it later in the year and try more problems until you feel comfortable with the topic.

As you do practice problems, try use a consistent way of organizing your work. This will help you save time and avoid mistakes. It will also help keep your work in order and maximize your score in the free response portion of the AP exam. Here are a few examples.

Example 1

t (sec)	0	2	4	6	8	10
a (ft/sec2)	3	5	6	4	3	2

The table above gives the data for the acceleration $a(t)$ of a motorcycle from 0 to 10 seconds. If the velocity at $t = 0$ seconds is 13 feet per second, then the approximate velocity at $t = 10$ seconds, found by a left-hand Riemann sum with five subintervals of equal length is

A. 6　　B. 13　　C. 19　　D. 42　　E. 55

　　The arithmetic of the Riemann sum is simple enough, but you want a system to get it done quickly and accurately. The system doesn't have to be elaborate, just enough to help you avoid common errors. You can work right over the table given, for example. Mark the width of each interval, add a row for the quantity you're calculating, and use an arrow or other notation to remind yourself whether you're doing a right-hand or left-hand sum. Make space for the initial value so you don't forget it.

	width of interval		2	2	2	2	2	
t	(sec)	0	2	4	6	8	10	
a	(ft/sec^2)	3	5	6	4	3	2	
v	(ft/sec)	13+	6+	10+	12+	8+	6=	55

Example 2

The approximate value of $y = \sqrt{3-x}$ at $x = -1.3$, obtained from the tangent to the graph at $x = -1$, is

A. –0.241　　B. 0.075　　C. 2.074　　D. 2.075　　E. 2.325

The tangent line approximation requires four steps: find the point of tangency, find the slope of the tangent by evaluating the derivative, write the equation of the tangent line, and make the approximation. Tick off the four steps in order every time.

Point of tangency: Evaluate y when $x = -1$ to find the point of tangency is $(-1, 2)$.

Slope: $y' = -\dfrac{1}{2\sqrt{3-x}}\Big|_{x=-1} = -\dfrac{1}{4}$. The slope of the tangent line is $-\dfrac{1}{4}$.

Point-slope form: $y - 2 = -\dfrac{1}{4}(x+1)$. You don't need to spend time simplifying.

Approximation: Plug in $x = -1.3$ to the tangent line equation. $y - 2 = -\dfrac{1}{4}(-1.3+1)$. Solve for y. $y = -\dfrac{1}{4}(-0.3) + 2 = 2.075$.

When you solve problems, write out your work just as you would when solving a free response problem on the test. You'll find that having an imaginary audience in mind sharpens the mind and helps you avoid skipping key steps and avoiding sloppy errors.

Resources for Further Study

Books

Barron's AP Calculus—For a thorough review that sticks to AP test material, pick up a Barron's. This classic brand features the most thorough content review around. Its practice tests (3 AB tests and 3 BC tests) are particularly challenging.

The Princeton Review: Cracking the AP Calculus AB and BC Exams—This popular review book includes clear, straightforward explanations. The tests (3 AB tests and 2 BC tests) are somewhat easier than those found in Barron's.

Online

www.mymaxscore.com/aptests—At this site, you can take another free AP practice test. Detailed answers and explanations are provided for both the multiple choice and free response sections.

www.collegeboard.com/student/testing/ap/sub_calab.html—You can find the College Board's AP curriculum, sample test questions, test strategies, and scoring information here. You can also buy previous exams from the College Board store for $25 each.

This book contains one AB practice test. Visit mymaxscore.com to download your free second practice test with answers and explanations.

AP Calculus AB Practice Test

CALCULUS AB

SECTION I, Part A

Time—55 minutes

Number of questions—28

A calculator may not be used on this part of the examination.

<u>Directions</u>: Solve each of the following problems. After examining the answer choices, select the best solution to the problem. No credit will be given for anything written in the test book.

<u>In this test</u>: Unless otherwise specified, the domain of a function f is assumed to be the set of all real numbers x for which $f(x)$ is a real number.

1. $\displaystyle\int_{2}^{5} (3x^2 - 4x)\,dx =$

    A. 91

    B. 75

    C. 59

    D. 191

    E. 325

2. If $f(x) = x\sqrt{2x^2 - 5}$, then $f'(x) =$

A. $\dfrac{x}{\sqrt{2x^2 - 5}}$

B. $\dfrac{2x}{\sqrt{2x^2 - 5}}$

C. $\dfrac{2x^2}{\sqrt{2x^2 - 5}}$

D. $\dfrac{4x^2 - 5}{\sqrt{2x^2 - 5}}$

E. $\dfrac{4x + \sqrt{2x^2 - 5}}{\sqrt{2x^2 - 5}}$

3. If $\displaystyle\int_a^b f(x)dx = 3a - 2b$, then $\displaystyle\int_b^a (2f(x) - 1)dx =$

A. $6a - 4b - 1$
B. $4b - 6a - 1$
C. $5b - 7a$
D. $5a - 3b$
E. $5a - 5b$

4. If $f(x) = 5x^4 - 3x^2 - \dfrac{8}{x}$, then $f'(-2) =$

A. -150

B. -156

C. -146

D. 170

E. 174

5.   The graph of $y = 2x^4 - 5x^3 + 3x^2 - x + 1$ is concave down for

A. $\dfrac{1}{4} < x < 1$

B. $x < \dfrac{1}{4}$

C. $x > \dfrac{1}{4}$

D. $x < 1$

E. $x > 1$

6. $\int e^{2x-1} dx =$

A. $e^{2x-1} + C$

B. $(2x-1)e^{2x-1} + C$

C. $(2x-1)e^{2x-2} + C$

D. $2e^{2x-1} + C$

E. $\dfrac{1}{2}e^{2x-1} + C$

7. $\dfrac{d}{dx}\sin^{2}\left(2x^{4}\right) =$

    A. $8x^{3}\sin\left(2x^{4}\right)\cos\left(2x^{4}\right)$

    B. $8x^{3}\sin\left(4x^{4}\right)$

    C. $8x^{3}\sin\left(4x^{4}\right)\cos\left(4x^{4}\right)$

    D. $\sin\left(4x^{4}\right)$

    E. $16x^{3}\sin\left(4x^{4}\right)\cos\left(4x^{4}\right)$

The graph below represents the velocity of an object over the time interval $0 \le t \le 5$. Use this graph for questions 8 and 9.

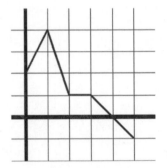

8. At what value of t does the object change direction?

    A. $t = 1$

    B. $t = 2$

    C. $t = 2.5$

    D. $t = 3$

    E. $t = 4$

9. What is the total distance traveled from $t = 0$ to $t = 5$?

    A. 7.5

    B. 7

    C. 6.5

    D. 6

    E. 5.5

10. An equation of the line tangent to the graph of $y = 1 - \sin\left(\frac{x}{2}\right)$ at $x = \pi$ is

A. $y = -\frac{1}{2}(x - \pi)$

B. $y = -2(x - \pi)$

C. $y = 1$

D. $y = 0$

E. $y - 1 = -\frac{1}{2}(x - \pi)$

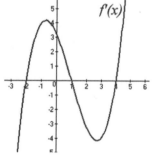

11. At what point(s) on the graph of $y = \frac{x^3}{3}$ is the tangent line parallel to the line $x - 4y = 2$?

A. $\left(\frac{1}{2}, \frac{1}{8}\right)$

B. $\left(-\frac{1}{2}, -\frac{1}{8}\right)$

C. $\left(\frac{1}{2}, \frac{1}{8}\right)$ and $\left(-\frac{1}{2}, -\frac{1}{8}\right)$

D. $(1,1)$ and $(-1,-1)$

E. $(1,1)$

12. The graph of the derivative of ƒ is shown in the figure above. Which of the following could be the graph of ƒ?

A.

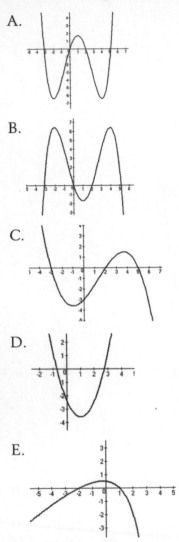

B.

C.

D.

E.

13. Let ƒ be a function defined for all real numbers x. If $f'(x) = \dfrac{\sqrt{x-3}}{9-x^2}$, then ƒ is decreasing on the interval

A. $x < 3$

B. $x > 3$

C. $x < -3$

D. $x > -3$

E. $-3 < x < 3$

14. Let f be a differentiable function such that $f(5) = 1$ and $f'(5) = -2$. If the tangent line to the graph of f at $x = 5$ is used to find an approximation to a zero of f, that approximation is

A. $x = 5.1$

B. $x = 5.2$

C. $x = 5.3$

D. $x = 5.4$

E. $x = 5.5$

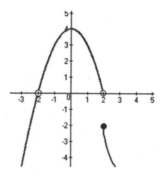

15. The graph of the function f is shown in the figure above. Which of the following statements about f is true?

A. $\lim\limits_{x \to -2} f(x) = 0$

B. $\lim\limits_{x \to 2} f(x) = 0$

C. $\lim\limits_{x \to 2} f(x) = -2$

D. $\lim\limits_{x \to -2} f(x) = \lim\limits_{x \to 2} f(x)$

E. $\lim\limits_{x \to -2} f(x)$ does not exist

16. The area of the region enclosed by the graph of $y = 4 - x^2$ and the line $y = 2x + 1$ is

    A. $\dfrac{32}{3}$

    B. $\dfrac{22}{3}$

    C. $-\dfrac{38}{3}$

    D. $\dfrac{38}{3}$

    E. $\dfrac{56}{3}$

17. If $x^2 + 2y^2 = 9$, what is the value of $\dfrac{d^2y}{dx^2}$ at the point $(1, -2)$?

    A. $-\dfrac{1}{2}$

    B. $\dfrac{5}{4}$

    C. $-\dfrac{9}{32}$

    D. $\dfrac{9}{32}$

    E. $-\dfrac{3}{16}$

18. $\displaystyle\int_{0}^{\pi/3} \frac{e^{\sec x}\sin x}{1-\sin^2 x}dx$ is

A. $e^2 - e$

B. $e^2 \tan e$

C. $e^2 \tan e - e$

D. $e - 1$

E. $e^2 - 1$

19. If $f(x) = \ln|9 - x^2|$, then $f'(x) =$

A. $\dfrac{1}{9-x^2}$

B. $\dfrac{x}{9-x^2}$

C. $\dfrac{2x}{9-x^2}$

D. $\dfrac{-2x}{9-x^2}$

E. $\dfrac{2x}{9+x^2}$

20. The average value of e^x on the interval $[1,3]$ is

A. $\dfrac{e}{3}\left(e^2 - 1\right)$

B. $\dfrac{e}{2}\left(e^2 - 1\right)$

C. $\dfrac{e}{3}\left(e^3 - 1\right)$

D. $\dfrac{1}{3}\left(e^2 - 1\right)$

E. $\dfrac{e^2}{2}$

21. $\displaystyle\lim_{x \to 3}\dfrac{2x}{\ln(x - 2)}$ is

A. 0

B. 6

C. ∞

D. $-\infty$

E. nonexistent

22. What are all values of x for which the function f defined by $f(x) = \left(x^2 - 1\right)e^{-x^2}$ is decreasing?

A. $(-\infty, 0)$

B. $(\sqrt{2}, \infty)$

C. $(-\sqrt{2}, 0) \cup (\sqrt{2}, \infty)$

D. $(0, \sqrt{2})$

E. $(-\infty, \infty)$

23. If the region in the first quadrant enclosed by the x-axis, the y-axis, the line $x = 3$, and the curve $y = e^x$ is revolved about the x-axis, the volume of the solid generated is

A. $\frac{\pi}{2}(e^6 - 1)$

B. $\frac{\pi}{2}(e^3 - 1)$

C. $\frac{\pi}{2}e^3$

D. $\pi(e^6 - 1)$

E. $2\pi(e^3 - 1)$

24. The expression $\frac{1}{30}\left(\sqrt{\frac{1}{30}} + \sqrt{\frac{2}{30}} + \sqrt{\frac{3}{30}} + ... + \sqrt{\frac{30}{30}}\right)$ is a Riemann sum approximation for

A. $\int_{1}^{30} \sqrt{x}\,dx$

B. $\int_{1}^{30} \sqrt{\frac{1}{x}}\,dx$

C. $\int_{0}^{20} \sqrt{x}\,dx$

D. $\int_{0}^{1} \sqrt{x}\,dx$

E. $\int_{0}^{1} \sqrt{\frac{1}{x}}\,dx$

25. $\int x\sin(x^2)dx =$

A. $2\cos(x^2)+C$

B. $\dfrac{1}{2}\cos(x^2)+C$

C. $-\dfrac{x^2}{2}\cos(x^2)+C$

D. $-2\cos(x^2)+C$

E. $-\dfrac{1}{2}\cos(x^2)+C$

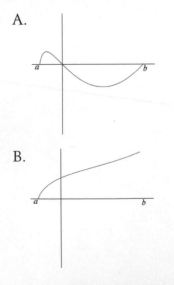

26. Let $f(x) = \int_{a}^{x} h(t)dt$, where h has the graph shown above. Which of the following could be the graph of f?

A.

B.

C.

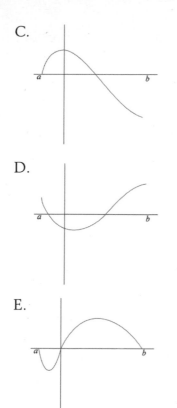

D.

E.

x	1.0	1.25	1.5	1.75	2.0	2.25	2.5	2.75	3.0
$f(x)$	3.0	2.5	1.75	1.25	1.0	0.75	1.25	1.75	3.0

27. A table of values for a continuous function f is shown above. If four equal subintervals of $[1,3]$ are used, which of the following is the trapezoidal approximation of $\int_1^3 f(x)dx$?

A. 10.75

B. 3.5

C. 16.75

D. 5.0

E. 12.625

28. Which of the following are derivatives of $F(x) = \sin^2 x \cos 2x$?

I. $f(x) = 2\sin x \cos x \cos 2x - 2\sin^2 x \sin 2x$

II. $f(x) = \sin 2x \cos 2x - 2\sin^2 x \sin 2x$

III. $f(x) = \sin 2x (3\cos^2 x - \sin^2 x - 2)$

    A. I only
    B. II only
    C. I and II
    D. I and III
    E. I, II, and III

CALCULUS AB
SECTION I, Part B
Time—50 Minutes
Number of Questions—17
A graphing calculator is required for some questions on this part of the examination.

Directions: Solve each of the following problems. After examining the answer choices, select the choice that best solves the problem. No credit will be given for anything written in the test book.

In this test:

1. The **exact** numerical value of the correct answer does not always appear among the answer choices. When this happens, select from among the choices the number that best approximates the exact numerical value.

2. Unless otherwise specified, the domain of a function f is assumed to be the set of all real numbers x for which $f(x)$ is a real number.

29. If $f(x) = \dfrac{e^{x^2}}{x^2}$, then $f'(x) =$

A. $\dfrac{e^{x^2}}{2x}$

B. $\dfrac{x^2 e^{x^2}}{2x}$

C. $\dfrac{2e^{x^2}(x^2-1)}{x}$

D. $\dfrac{2e^{x^2}(x^2-1)}{x^3}$

E. e^{x^2}

30. The graph of the function $y = 2x^3 + 5x^2 - 3x + 3\sin x$ changes concavity at $x =$

A. -1.5

B. -1.050

C. -1

D. -2.021

E. 0

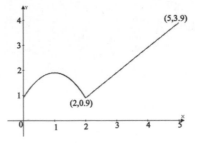

31. The graph of f is shown in the figure above. If $\int\limits_{0}^{2} f(x)dx = 3.1$ and $F'(x) = f(x)$, then $F(5) - F(0) =$

    A. 5.8
    B. 7.2
    C. 7.75
    D. 10.3
    E. 14.8

32. Let f be a function such that $\lim\limits_{h \to 0} \dfrac{f(3+h) - f(3)}{h} = 9$. Which of the following must be true?

    I. f is continuous at $x = 3$.
    II. f is differentiable at $x = 3$.
    III. The derivative of f is continuous at $x = 3$.

    A. II
    B. I and II
    C. I and III
    D. II and III
    E. I, II and III

33. Let f be the function given by $f(x) = 3e^{2x-1}$. For what value of x is the slope of the line tangent to the graph of f at $(x, f(x))$ equal to 2?

    A. 0.297
    B. 0.558
    C. –0.049
    D. –0.405
    E. –1.099

34. Two roads cross at right angles. An observer on the north-south road, $\frac{1}{8}$ of a mile south of the intersection, sees a car traveling east-bound at 60 miles per hour. How fast, in miles per hour, is the car moving away from the observer 10 seconds after it passes through the intersection?

A. 5 mph
B. 10 mph
C. 24 mph
D. 48 mph
E. 60 mph

35. If $y = 4 - 3x$, what is the maximum value of $x^2 y$ for $x > 0$?

A. 0

B. $\dfrac{8}{5}$

C. $\dfrac{8}{9}$

D. $-\dfrac{256}{125}$

E. $\dfrac{256}{243}$

36. What is the area of the region in the first quadrant enclosed by the graphs of $y = \sin x$, $y = 1 - x$ and the y-axis?

A. –0.253
B. 0.253
C. 0.508
D. –0.508
E. 0.247

37. The base of a solid, S, is the region enclosed by the graph of $y = \sqrt{e^x}$, the line $y = e$, and the y-axis. If the cross sections of S perpendicular to the x-axis are semicircles, then the volume of S is

    A. 1.926

    B. 7.704

    C. 3.902

    D. 3.294

    E. 0.975

38. If the derivative of f is given by $f'(x) = e^x - 4x^2$, at which of the following values of x does f have a relative maximum value?

    A. –0.408

    B. 0.144

    C. 0.715

    D. 3.262

    E. 4.307

39. Let $f(x) = \ln(x+3)$. If the rate of change of f at $x = c$ is three times its rate of change at $x = 0$, then $c =$

    A. –2

    B. –1

    C. 0

    D. 1

    E. 2

40. At time $t \geq 0$, the acceleration of a particle moving on the x-axis is $a(t) = t^2 - \cos t$. At $t = 0$, the velocity of the particle is 0. For what value of t will the velocity of the particle be 7?

    A. 0.756

    B. 1.790

    C. 2.491

    D. 2.702

    E. 2.916

SECTION II
GENERAL INSTRUCTIONS

You may wish to look over the problems before starting to work on them, since you may not have time to complete all parts of all problems. All problems are given equal weight, but the parts of a particular problem may not be given equal weight.

A graphing calculator is required for some problems on this section of the examination.

- Write all work for each part of each problem in the space provided for that part in the booklet. Be sure to write clearly and legibly. If you make an error, you may save time by crossing it out rather than erasing it.

- Show all your work. You will be graded on the correctness and completeness of your methods as well as your answers. Correct answers without supporting work may not receive credit.

- You may use your calculator to solve an equation, find the derivative of a function at a point, or calculate the value of a definite integral. However, be sure to clearly indicate the setup of your problem. If you use other calculator features or programs, show the mathematical steps necessary to produce your results.

- Your work must be expressed in standard mathematical notation rather than calculator syntax.

- Unless otherwise specified, answers (numeric or algebraic) need not be simplified. If your answer is given as a decimal approximation, it should correct to three places after the decimal point.

- Unless otherwise specified, the domain of a function f is assumed to be the set of all real numbers x for which $f(x)$ is a real number.

SECTION II, PART A

Time—30 minutes

Number of problems—2

A graphing calculator is required for some problems or parts of problems.
During the timed portion for Part A, you may work only on the problems in Part A.

On Part A, you may use your calculator to solve an equation, find the derivative of a function at a point, or calculate the value of an integral. However, you must clearly indicate the setup of your problem, namely the equation, function, or integral you are using. If you use other features or programs, be sure to show the mathematical steps necessary to produce your results.

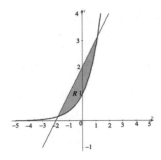

1. Let R be the shaded region bounded by the graph of $y = e^x$ and the line $y = x + 2$, as shown above.

a. Find the area of R.

b. Find the volume of the solid generated when R is rotated about the horizontal line $y = -1$.

c. Write, but do not evaluate, an integral expression that can be used to find the volume of the solid generated when the portion of R in the first quadrant is rotated about the y-axis.

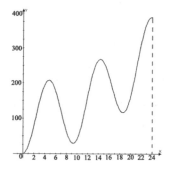

2. Commuters enter a subway station at the rate $P(t) = 200\sin^2\left(\dfrac{t}{3}\right) + \dfrac{t^2}{3}$

    people per hour over the time interval $0 \le t \le 24$. The graph of $y = P(t)$ is shown above.

a. To the nearest whole number, find the total number of people entering the station over the time interval $0 \le t \le 24$.

b. The city will install surveillance cameras in the station if there is at least one three-hour period during which $P(t) \ge 225$ people per hour and the average value of P over the 24-hour period is at least 150 people per hour. Find all values of t for which $P(t) \ge 225$ and compute the average value of P over $0 \le t \le 24$. Will the city install surveillance cameras in this station? Support your answer.

c. The city will assign a ticket agent to a ticket booth in the station for the eight-hour shift from $t = 4$ to $t = 12$ if the product of the total number of commuters entering the station and the total number exiting the station during that time is greater than 500,000. Over the time interval $4 \le t \le 12$, 80 commuters per hour exit the station. Does this station require a ticket agent? Explain the reasoning that leads to your conclusion.

PART B

Time—60 minutes

Number of problems—4

No calculator is allowed for these problems.

During the timed portion for Part B, you may continue to work on the problems in Part A without the use of any calculator.

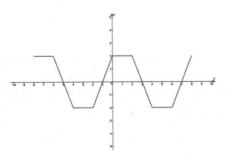

3.   The graph of the function f shown above consists of eight line segments. Let g be the function given by $g(x) = \int_0^x f(t)dt$.

a.   Find $g(7)$, $g'(7)$, and $g''(7)$.

b.   Write an equation for the line tangent to the graph of g at $x = 2$.

c.   Does g have a relative minimum, a relative maximum, or neither at $x = -5$? Justify your answer.

t	0	10	20	30	40	50	60	70	80	90
$v(t)$	800	1200	2500	3200	4000	3100	2500	2000	1500	900

4.   Two cars driven on a test track have positive velocity $v(t)$. At time $t = 0$ seconds, the cars are at a starting line, denoted as $s(0) = 0$. The velocity of the first car, in feet per minute, is recorded for selected values of t over the interval $0 \le t \le 90$ minutes, as shown in the table above.

a.   Find the average acceleration of the first car over the time interval $0 \le t \le 90$ minutes. Indicate units of measure.

b.   Using correct units, explain the meaning of $\int_{30}^{60} v(t)dt$ in terms of the first car's travel. Use a right-hand Riemann sum with 3 subintervals of equal length to approximate $\int_{30}^{60} v(t)dt$.

c.   The second car leaves the starting line with an acceleration of $a(t) = \dfrac{150}{\sqrt{t+4}}$ feet per minute per minute. At time $t = 0$ seconds, the initial position of the second car is 0 feet and the initial velocity is 1000 feet per minute. Which of the two cars is traveling faster at $t = 60$ minutes? Explain your answer.

5.   Consider the differential equation $\dfrac{dy}{dx} = \dfrac{1-x}{y^2}$, where $y \ne 0$.

a.   On the axes provided, sketch a slope field for the given differential equation at the points indicated.

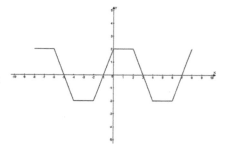

b.   Find the particular solution $y = f(x)$ to the differential equation with the initial condition $f(1) = 3$.

6. The twice-differentiable function f is defined for all real numbers and satisfies the following conditions: $f(3) = 2$, $f'(3) = 4$ and $f''(3) = -2$.

a. The function g is given by $g(x) = (x-4)^2 \cdot f(x)$. Find $g'(3)$ and $g''(3)$. Show the work that leads to your answers.

b. The function h is given by $h(x) = \sqrt{f(x)}$ for all real numbers. Find $h'(x)$ and write an equation for the line tangent to the graph of h at $x = 3$.

SOLUTIONS: AP Calculus AB Practice Test

Multiple Choice

Section I Part A

1. B. $\int_{2}^{5}(3x^2-4x)dx = x^3-2x^2\,\big|_2^5 = (125-50)-(8-8)=75$

2. D. If $f(x)=x\sqrt{2x^2-5}$, then $f'(x)=x\cdot\dfrac{4x}{2\sqrt{2x^2-5}}+\sqrt{2x^2-5}$

$= \dfrac{2x^2}{\sqrt{2x^2-5}}+\sqrt{2x^2-5} = \dfrac{2x^2+2x^2-5}{\sqrt{2x^2-5}}=\dfrac{4x^2-5}{\sqrt{2x^2-5}}$

3. C. If $\int_{a}^{b}f(x)dx = 3a-2b$, then

$\int_{b}^{a}(2f(x)-1)dx = 2\int_{b}^{a}f(x)dx-\int_{b}^{a}1dx = -2\int_{a}^{b}f(x)dx-\int_{b}^{a}1dx$

$= -2(3a-2b)-(a-b) = -6a+4b-a+b = 5b-7a$.

4. C. If $f(x)=5x^4-3x^2-\dfrac{8}{x}$, then $f'(x)=20x^3-6x+\dfrac{8}{x^2}$ and

$f'(-2) = 20(-8)-6(-2)+\dfrac{8}{4} = -160+12+2 = -146$.

5. A. The graph of $y=2x^4-5x^3+3x^2-x+1$ is concave down when the second derivative is negative. If $y=2x^4-5x^3+3x^2-x+1$, then $y'=8x^3-15x^2+6x-1$ and $y''=24x^2-30x+6$. Set the second derivative equal to zero and solve. If $24x^2-30x+6=0$, then $6(4x-1)(x-1)=0$ and $x=\dfrac{1}{4}$ or $x=1$. Evaluate the second derivative below $x=\dfrac{1}{4}$, between $x=\dfrac{1}{4}$ and $x=1$, and above $x=1$. $y''(0)=6>0$,

$y''\left(\frac{1}{2}\right) = 6 - 15 + 6 = -3 < 0$, and $y''(2) = 96 - 60 + 6 = 42 > 0$. The second derivative is negative between $x = \frac{1}{4}$ and $x = 1$.

6. E.   Use a u-substitution with $u = 2x - 1$, $du = 2dx$, and $\frac{1}{2}du = dx$. Then $\int e^{2x-1}dx = \frac{1}{2}\int e^u du = \frac{1}{2}e^{2x-1} + C$.

7. B.   Using the chain rule, $\frac{d}{dx}\sin^2(2x^4) = 2\sin(2x^4)\cos(2x^4)\cdot 8x^3$

$= 16x^3\sin(2x^4)\cos(2x^4)$. Apply the identity for $\sin 2x$ to get

$= 8x^3\sin(4x^4)$.

8. E.   The object changes direction when velocity changes from positive to negative at $t = 4$.

9. A.   The total distance traveled by the object from $t = 0$ to $t = 5$ is

$\left|\int_0^4 v(t)dt\right| + \left|\int_4^5 v(t)dt\right|$. You can calculate this by the area under the curve.

$\left|\int_0^4 v(t)dt\right| + \left|\int_4^5 v(t)dt\right| = 3 + 2.5 + 1 + 0.5 + 0.5 = 7.5$.

10. D.   If $y = 1 - \sin\left(\frac{x}{2}\right)$, at $x = \pi$ $y' = -\frac{1}{2}\cos\left(\frac{x}{2}\right) = -\frac{1}{2}\cos\left(\frac{\pi}{2}\right) = 0$. Since $y = 1 - \sin\left(\frac{\pi}{2}\right) = 0$, the point of tangency is $(\pi, 0)$, and the equation of the tangent is $y - 0 = 0(x - \pi)$ or $y = 0$.

11. C. The tangent line parallel to the line $x - 4y = 2$ or $y = \frac{1}{4}x - \frac{1}{2}$ when it has a slope of $\frac{1}{4}$. The slope of the tangent line is the first derivative, $y' = x^2$, which is equal to $\frac{1}{4}$ when $x = \pm\frac{1}{2}$. So the tangents at $\left(\frac{1}{2}, \frac{1}{8}\right)$ and $\left(-\frac{1}{2}, -\frac{1}{8}\right)$ are parallel to the line $x - 4y = 2$.

12. A.   The graph of the derivative has x-intercepts at $x = -2$, $x = 1$, and $x = 4$, so the graph of f should have these critical points. Graphs (a) and (b) have these critical points. At $x = -2$, the derivative changes from negative to positive, so the graph of f should change from decreasing to increasing. The graph of (a) has the appropriate minimum at $x = -2$, and the correct turning points at the other critical numbers.

13. B.   The function f is decreasing when $f'(x) = \dfrac{\sqrt{x-3}}{9-x^2} < 0$. Since the

derivative is defined for $x \geq 3$, and since $\sqrt{x-3} \geq 0$, $f'(x) < 0$ when $9 - x^2 < 0$, or $x > 3$.

14. E.   The tangent line to f at $(5,1)$ has a slope of –2, so the equation of the tangent line is $y - 1 = -2(x - 5)$ or $y = -2x + 11$. Using the tangent line to approximate where $y = 0$ gives you $0 = -2x + 11$ or $x = 5.5$.

15. A.   Although f is undefined for $x = -2$, $\lim\limits_{x \to -2^-} f(x) = 0$ and $\lim\limits_{x \to -2^+} f(x) = 0$, so $\lim\limits_{x \to -2} f(x)$ exists and $\lim\limits_{x \to -2} f(x) = 0$. $\lim\limits_{x \to 2^-} f(x) = 0$ and $\lim\limits_{x \to 2^+} f(x) = -2$. Since the limit from the left and the limit from the right are different, $\lim\limits_{x \to 2} f(x)$ does not exist.

16. A.   Find the points of intersection by solving $4 - x^2 = 2x + 1$. $x^2 + 2x - 3 = 0$ becomes $(x+3)(x-1) = 0$, so $x = -3$ and $x = 1$. The area of the region enclosed by the graph of $y = 4 - x^2$ and the line $y = 2x + 1$

is $\displaystyle\int_{-3}^{1} (4 - x^2) - (2x + 1)\,dx = \int_{-3}^{1} (-x^2 - 2x + 3)\,dx = -\frac{1}{3}x^3 - x^2 + 3x \Big|_{-3}^{1}$

$= \left(-\frac{1}{3} - 1 + 3\right) - \left(\frac{1}{3} \cdot 27 - 9 - 9\right) = \frac{5}{3} + 9 = \frac{32}{3}.$

17. D.   If $x^2 + 2y^2 = 9$, $2x + 4y\dfrac{dy}{dx} = 0$ and $\dfrac{dy}{dx} = \dfrac{-x}{2y}$.   Then

$$\dfrac{d^2y}{dx^2} = \dfrac{2y(-1) - (-x)2\dfrac{dy}{dx}}{4y^2} = \dfrac{-2y + 2x\dfrac{dy}{dx}}{4y^2} = \dfrac{-2y + 2x\dfrac{-x}{2y}}{4y^2} = \dfrac{-2y^2 - x^2}{4y^3}.$$

At the point $(1, -2)$, $= \dfrac{-8 - 1}{-32} = \dfrac{9}{32}$.

18. A. $\displaystyle\int_0^{\pi/3} \dfrac{e^{\sec x}\sin x}{1 - \sin^2 x}dx = \int_0^{\pi/3} \dfrac{e^{\sec x}\sin x}{\cos^2 x}dx = \int_0^{\pi/3} e^{\sec x}\sec x\tan x\,dx = e^{\sec x}\Big|_0^{\pi/3}$

$= e^2 - e$

19. D.   If $f(x) = \ln|9 - x^2|$, then $f'(x) = \dfrac{-2x}{9 - x^2}$

20. B.   The average value of e^x on the interval $[1, 3]$ is $\dfrac{1}{3 - 1}\displaystyle\int_1^3 e^x dx = \dfrac{1}{2}e^x\Big|_1^3$

$= \dfrac{1}{2}\left(e^3 - e^1\right) = \dfrac{e}{2}\left(e^2 - 1\right).$

21. E. $\displaystyle\lim_{x \to 3}\dfrac{2x}{\ln(x - 2)}$ is nonexistent since $\displaystyle\lim_{x \to 3}\ln(x - 2) = 0$ but

$\displaystyle\lim_{x \to 3} 2x \neq 0$.

22.   C. $f(x) = (x^2 - 1)e^{-x^2}$ is decreasing when $f'(x) < 0$.

$f'(x) = (x^2 - 1)(-2xe^{-x^2}) + e^{-x^2}(2x) = -2x^3 e^{-x^2} + 2xe^{-x^2} + 2xe^{-x^2}$

$= -2x^3 e^{-x^2} + 4xe^{-x^2}\ = 2xe^{-x^2}\left(2 - x^2\right)$. Then $2xe^{-x^2}\left(2 - x^2\right) < 0$ if

$2xe^{-x^2} < 0$, which occurs when $x < 0$, or if $2 - x^2 < 0$, which occurs

when $|x| > \sqrt{2}$. Note that for $x < -\sqrt{2}$, both factors are negative, so $f'(x)$

is positive. Thus $f'(x)$ is negative on the intervals $(-\sqrt{2}, 0)$ and $(\sqrt{2}, \infty)$.

23. A. If the region enclosed by the x-axis, the line $x = 3$, and the curve $y = e^x$ is revolved about the x-axis, the volume of the solid generated is $\pi \int_0^3 (e^x)^2 dx = \frac{\pi}{2} e^{2x} \Big|_0^3 = \frac{\pi}{2}(e^6 - 1)$.

24. D. $\Delta x = \dfrac{1}{30}$, $x_n = \dfrac{n}{30}$ and $f(x_n) = \sqrt{\dfrac{n}{30}} = \sqrt{x_n}$. These 30 terms represent $\int_0^1 \sqrt{x}\, dx$.

25. E. $\int x \sin(x^2) dx = \frac{1}{2} \int \sin u \, du = -\frac{1}{2} \cos(x^2) + C$

26. C. Since $f(x) = \int_a^x h(t) dt$, $f(a) = 0$, so (d) is not possible. For $a < x < 0$, f will be positive, so eliminate (e). For $x > 0$, the value of f will decrease because the area between h and the axis is negative. Choice (a) changes direction too soon, while (b) does not decrease. The best choice is (c).

27. B. $\int_0^2 f(x) dx \approx \frac{1}{2}(0.5)(3.0 + 2 \cdot 1.75 + 2 \cdot 1.0 + 2 \cdot 1.25 + 3.0)$

$\approx \frac{1}{2}(0.5)(3.0 + 3.5 + 2.0 + 2.5 + 3.0) \approx \frac{1}{2}(0.5)(14.0) \approx 3.5$

28. E. If $F(x) = \sin^2 x \cos 2x$, $F'(x) = (2 \sin x \cos x) \cos 2x + \sin^2 x(-2 \sin 2x)$

$= 2 \sin x \cos x \cos 2x - 2 \sin^2 x \sin 2x$. Apply the double angle identify to show that $f(x) = (2 \sin x \cos x) \cos 2x - 2 \sin^2 x \sin 2x$ $= \sin 2x \cos 2x - 2 \sin^2 x \sin 2x$. Factor and apply both the double angle identity and the Pythagorean identity to show that $f(x) = \sin 2x \cos 2x - 2 \sin^2 x \sin 2x = \sin 2x (\cos 2x - 2 \sin^2 x)$

$= \sin 2x (\cos 2x - 2(1 - \cos^2 x)) = \sin 2x (\cos 2x - 2 + 2 \cos^2 x)$

$= \sin 2x (\cos^2 x - \sin^2 x - 2 + 2 \cos^2 x) = \sin 2x (3 \cos^2 x - \sin^2 x - 2)$.

Section I Part B

29. D. If $f(x) = \dfrac{e^{x^2}}{x^2}$, then

$$f'(x) = \frac{x^2(2xe^{x^2}) - 2xe^{x^2}}{x^4} = \frac{2xe^{x^2}(x^2 - 1)}{x^4} = \frac{2e^{x^2} \cdot (x^2 - 1)}{x^3}.$$

30. B. The graph of the function $y = 2x^3 + 5x^2 - 3x + 3\sin x$ changes concavity when y'' changes sign. $y' = 6x^2 + 10x - 3 + 3\cos x$ and $y'' = 12x + 10 - 3\sin x = 0$ at $x \approx -1.050$, by finding the zero of the graph of y''. The graph confirms that y'' changes from negative to positive.

31. D.

$$F(5) - F(0) = \int_0^5 f(x)dx = \int_0^2 f(x)dx + \int_2^5 f(x)dx = 3.1 + \int_2^5 f(x)dx. \text{ The}$$

value of $\displaystyle\int_2^5 f(x)dx$ can be approximated by the area under the curve. The area under the graph of $f(x)$ from $x = 2$ to $x = 5$ is a trapezoid with area $\dfrac{1}{2}(3)(0.9 + 3.9) = 7.2$ so $F(5) - F(0) = 3.1 + 7.2 = 10.3$.

32. B. $\displaystyle\lim_{h \to 0} \frac{f(3 + h) - f(3)}{h} = 9$ indicates that $f'(3) = 9$. The derivative exists at $x = 3$, so the function is differentiable at $x = 3$, which implies that it is continuous at $x = 3$. To confirm that $f'(x)$ is continuous at $x = 3$, you must show $f'(3)$ exists, $\displaystyle\lim_{x \to 3} f'(x)$ exists, and $\displaystyle\lim_{x \to 3} f'(x) = f'(3)$. You know $f'(3)$ exists, but have no information about $\displaystyle\lim_{x \to 3} f'(x)$.

33. C.   If $f(x) = 3e^{2x-1}$, $f'(x) = 3e^{2x-1}(2) = 6e^{2x-1}$. Set $6e^{2x-1} = 2$ and

$e^{2x-1} = \dfrac{1}{3}$. Solve to find $x = \dfrac{1 - \ln 3}{2} \approx -0.049$.

34. D.   Ten seconds after it passes through the intersection, the vehicle

is $\dfrac{10}{3600} \cdot 60 = \dfrac{1}{6}$ of a mile east of the intersection, and the observer is $\dfrac{1}{8}$

of a mile south of the intersection. The distance between the observer and the vehicle completes the hypotenuse of a right triangle. The length

of the hypotenuse is $\sqrt{\left(\dfrac{1}{8}\right)^2 + \left(\dfrac{1}{6}\right)^2} = \sqrt{\dfrac{1}{64} + \dfrac{1}{36}} = \sqrt{\dfrac{100}{2304}} = \dfrac{10}{48} = \dfrac{5}{24}$

of a mile. Differentiate $a^2 + b^2 = c^2$ with respect to time, to

get $2a\dfrac{da}{dt} + 2b\dfrac{db}{dt} = 2c\dfrac{dc}{dt}$ and substitute known quantities.

$\dfrac{1}{8}(0) + \left(\dfrac{1}{6}\right)(60) = \dfrac{5}{24} \cdot \dfrac{dc}{dt}$ becomes $10 \cdot \dfrac{24}{5} = \dfrac{dc}{dt}$ or $48 = \dfrac{dc}{dt}$.

35. E.   To find the maximum value of $x^2 y$, consider the derivative

$x^2 \dfrac{dy}{dx} + 2xy$. Substitute for $\dfrac{dy}{dx}$ and for y, to get $x^2(-3) + 2x(4 - 3x)$

$= -3x^2 + 8x - 6x^2 = 8x - 9x^2$. The maximum value occurs when the de-

rivative is equal to zero, so solve $8x - 9x^2 = 0$ to get $x = 0$ or $x = \dfrac{8}{9}$. When

$x = 0$, $x^2 y = 0$ but when $x = \dfrac{8}{9}$, $x^2 y = \left(\dfrac{8}{9}\right)^2 \left(4 - 3 \cdot \dfrac{8}{9}\right) = \dfrac{64}{81}\left(\dfrac{4}{3}\right) = \dfrac{256}{243}$.

36. B.   Find the point of intersection of $y = \sin x$ and $y = 1 - x$ to determine the limits of integration. The graphs intersect at $x \approx 0.511$. The
area of the region in the first quadrant enclosed by the graphs of $y = \sin x$,

$y = 1 - x$ and the y-axis is $\displaystyle\int_0^{0.511} (1 - x - \sin x)\,dx = x - \dfrac{x^2}{2} + \cos x \Big|_0^{0.511}$
≈ 0.253.

37. E.   The diameter of each cross section is $e - \sqrt{e^x}$, so the radius is

$\dfrac{e - \sqrt{e^x}}{2}$. The volume is $\displaystyle\int_0^2 \frac{1}{2}\pi\left(\frac{e - \sqrt{e^x}}{2}\right)^2 dx = \frac{\pi}{8}\int_0^2 (e^2 - 2e\cdot e^{\frac{x}{2}} + e^x)dx$

$= \dfrac{\pi}{8}\displaystyle\int_0^2 (e^2 - 2e^{\frac{x}{2}+1} + e^x)dx = \frac{\pi}{8}(xe^2 - e^{\frac{x}{2}+1} + e^x)\Big|_0^2$

$= \dfrac{\pi}{8}[(2e^2 - 4e^2 + e^2) - (0 - 4e + 1)] = \dfrac{\pi}{8}(-e^2 + 4e - 1) \approx 0.975.$

38. C. The relative maximum will occur at the point where the first derivative changes from positive to negative. The zeros of $f'(x) = e^x - 4x^2 = 0$ occur at $x \approx -0.408$, $x \approx 0.715$, and $x \approx 4.307$. Test the first derivative in each of the intervals created by these critical numbers. $f'(-1) = e^{-1} - 4 < 0$, $f'(0) = 1 > 0$, $f'(2) = e^2 - 16 < 0$, and $f'(5) = e^5 - 100 > 0$. The derivative changes from positive to negative at 0.715.

39. A.   If $f(x) = \ln(x+3)$, $f'(x) = \dfrac{1}{x+3}$. If the rate of change of f at $x = c$ is three times its rate of change at $x = 0$, then $\dfrac{1}{c+3} = 3\left(\dfrac{1}{0+3}\right)$ or $\dfrac{1}{c+3} = 1$. Solve to find that $c = -2$.

40. D.   At time $t \geq 0$, the acceleration of a particle moving on the x-axis is $a(t) = t^2 - \cos t$ so the velocity is $v(t) = \dfrac{t^3}{3} + \sin t + C$. At $t = 0$, the velocity of the particle is 0 so $v(0) = C = 0$. The velocity of the particle will be 7 when $v(t) = \dfrac{t^3}{3} + \sin t = 7$ or $t \approx 2.702$.

Section II, Part A

1. First find the points of intersection by solving $x + 2 = e^x$. Use your graphing calculator to find $x \approx -1.841$ and $x \approx 1.146$.

a. The area of R is $\int_{-1.841}^{1.146} (x + 2 - e^x)dx = \frac{x^2}{2} + 2x - e^x \Big|_{-1.841}^{1.146} \approx 1.949$. Re-

member that you can use your graphing calculator to find the integral, but you must set it up with proper calculus notation.

b. The volume of the solid generated when R is rotated about the horizontal line $y = -1$ is $V = \pi \int_{-1.841}^{1.146} (-1 - x - 2)^2 - (-1 - e^x)^2 dx$

$= \pi \int_{-1.841}^{1.146} (x^2 + 6x + 9) - (1 + 2e^x + e^{2x})dx$

$= \pi \int_{-1.841}^{1.146} (x^2 + 6x + 8 - 2e^x - e^{2x})dx$

$= \pi \left[\frac{x^3}{3} + 3x^2 + 8x - 2e^x - \frac{1}{2}e^{2x} \right]_{-1.841}^{1.146} \approx 9.341$.

c. Solve each equation for x in terms of y. $x = y - 2$ and $x = \ln y$. Divide the region in two, the lower section from the y-intercept of $y = e^x$ to the y-intercept of $y = x + 2$. Determine the limits of integration, remembering that you want y-values. The limits are $y = 1$, the y-intercept of $y = e^x$, $y = 2$, the y-intercept of $y = x + 2$, and to $y \approx 3.146$, the y-coordinate of the point of intersection. $V = \pi \int_1^2 (\ln y)^2 dy + \pi \int_2^{3.146} (\ln y)^2 - (y - 2)^2 dy$

2. $P(t) = 200 \sin^2\left(\frac{t}{3}\right) + \frac{t^2}{3}$ people per hour over the time interval $0 \le t \le 24$.

a. The total number of people entering the station over the time interval $0 \le t \le 24$ is $\int_0^{24} \left(200 \sin^2\left(\frac{t}{3}\right) + \frac{t^2}{3} \right) dt \approx 3979$ people (by calculator).

b. $P(t) \ge 225$ when $200 \sin^2\left(\frac{t}{3}\right) + \frac{t^2}{3} \ge 225$. Use your calculator to find that this is when $12.929 \le t \le 15.857$ or when $20.895 \le t \le 24$. The average value of $P(t)$ over $0 \le t \le 24$ is $\frac{1}{24 - 0}\int_0^{24} \left(200 \sin^2\left(\frac{t}{3}\right) + \frac{t^2}{3} \right) dt \approx \frac{3979}{24} \approx 166$

people per hour. Surveillance cameras will be installed, because $P(t) \geq 225$ during the period $20.895 \leq t \leq 24$, which is more than 3 hours and the average rate for the 24-hour period is 166 people per hour, greater than the required 150 people per hour. (Note that $P(t) \geq 225$ when $12.929 \leq t \leq 15.857$, just shy of three hours.)

c. The product of the total number of commuters entering the station and the total number exiting the station in the period $4 \leq t \leq 12$

is $(8 \cdot 80) \int_{4}^{12} \left(200 \sin^2\left(\frac{t}{3}\right) + \frac{t^2}{3}\right) dt$ or $640 \int_{4}^{12} \left(200 \sin^2\left(\frac{t}{3}\right) + \frac{t^2}{3}\right) dt$

$\approx 640 \cdot 905 \approx 579,200$ people. Since this is greater than the required 500,000 people, this station will require a ticket agent.

Section II, Part B

3. $g(x) = \int_{0}^{x} f(t) dt$

a. $g(7) = \int_{0}^{7} f(x) dx = 4 + 1 - 1 - 4 - 1 = -1$, $g'(7) = f(7) = 0$, and

$g''(7) = f'(7) = \frac{4}{2} = 2$.

b. At $x = 2$, $g(2) = \int_{0}^{2} f(x) dx = 4$, and $g'(2) = f(2) = 2$, so the equation of the tangent line is $y - 4 = 2(x - 2)$ or $y = 2x$.

c. At $x = -5$, g has a relative maximum because f, the derivative of g, changes from positive to negative at $x = -5$, so g changes from increasing to decreasing.

4. $v(t) > 0$, $s(0) = 0$.

a. The average acceleration over the time interval $0 \leq t \leq 90$ minutes is

$\frac{v(90) - v(0)}{90 - 0} = \frac{900 - 800}{90} = \frac{10}{9}$ feet per minute per minute.

b. $\int_{30}^{60} v(t)dt$ is the distance, in feet, traveled by the car over the half-hour

time interval $30 \le t \le 60$. $\int_{30}^{60} v(t)dt \approx 10 \cdot 4000 + 10 \cdot 3100 + 10 \cdot 2500 \approx 96,000$

feet.

c. If $a(t) = \dfrac{150}{\sqrt{t+4}}$ feet per second per second, then $v(t) = \int \dfrac{150}{\sqrt{t+4}} dt$

$= 300\sqrt{t+4} + C$. At time $t = 0$ seconds, $300\sqrt{0+4} + C = 1000$,

so $C = 400$, and $v(t) = 300\sqrt{t+4} + 400$. At $t = 60$ minutes,

$v(60) = 300\sqrt{60+4} + 400 = 300 \cdot 8 + 400 = 2800$ feet per minute and

the velocity of the first car is 2500 feet per minute. The second car is

moving faster at $t = 60$ minutes.

5. $\dfrac{dy}{dx} = \dfrac{1-x}{y^2}$, $y \ne 0$.

a. Calculate the value of $\dfrac{dy}{dx}$ at each point in the region.

	y 2	1	0	−1	−2
x					
2	−¼	−1	undefined	−1	−¼
1	0	0	undefined	0	0
0	¼	1	undefined	1	¼
−1	½	2	undefined	2	½
−2	¾	3	undefined	3	¾

Draw a short line through each point with the corresponding slope.

b. To solve $\dfrac{dy}{dx} = \dfrac{1-x}{y^2}$, first separate the variables. $y^2 dy = (1-x)\,dx$.
Integrate both sides to get $\dfrac{y^3}{3} = x - \dfrac{x^2}{2} + C$. Since $f(1) = 3$, $\dfrac{3^3}{3} = 1 - \dfrac{1^2}{2} + C$
and $\dfrac{17}{2} = C$. The particular solution is $\dfrac{y^3}{3} = x - x^2 + \dfrac{17}{2}$.

6. $f(3) = 2$, $f'(3) = 4$ and $f''(3) = -2$

a. If $g(x) = (x-4)^2 \cdot f(x)$, then $g(3) = (3-4)^2 \cdot f(3) = 1 \cdot 2 = 2$, and

$g'(x) = (x-4)^2 \cdot f'(x) + 2(x-4) \cdot f(x)$, so

$g'(3) = (3-4)^2 \cdot f'(3) + 2(3-4) \cdot f(3) = 1 \cdot 4 - 2 \cdot 2 = 0$.

$g''(x) = (x-4)^2 f''(x) + 4(x-4)f'(x) + 2f(x)$

$g''(3) = (3-4)^2 f''(3) + 4(3-4)f'(3) + 2f(3)$

$= 1(-2) + 4(-1)4 + 2(2)$

$= -2 - 16 + 4$

$= -14$

b. If $h(x) = \sqrt{f(x)}$ then $h(3) = \sqrt{f(3)} = \sqrt{2}$, so the point of tangency is $\left(3, \sqrt{2}\right)$. $h'(x) = \dfrac{f'(x)}{2\sqrt{f(x)}}$ so the slope of the tangent line is

$h'(3) = \dfrac{f'(3)}{2\sqrt{f(3)}} = \dfrac{4}{2\sqrt{2}} = \sqrt{2}$. The equation of the tangent line is

$y - \sqrt{2} = \sqrt{2}\left(x - 3\right)$.

This book contains one BC practice test. Visit mymaxscore.com to download your free second practice test with answers and explanations.

AP Calculus BC Practice Test

CALCULUS BC

SECTION I, Part A

Time—55 minutes

Number of questions—28

A calculator may not be used on this part of the examination.

<u>Directions</u>: Solve each of the following problems. After examining the choices, select the answer that best solves the problem. No credit will be given for anything written in the test book.

<u>In this test</u>: Unless otherwise specified, the domain of a function f is assumed to be the set of all real numbers x for which $f(x)$ is a real number.

1. $\int_{0}^{3} x^2 \sqrt{x+1}\, dx =$

    A. 16.152

    B. 66

    C. 101.7

    D. 176

    E. 264

2. If $x = e^{t-\pi}$ and $y = \cos\left(\dfrac{t}{2}\right)$, then when $t = \pi$, $\dfrac{dy}{dx} =$

   A. $-\dfrac{1}{2}$

   B. -1

   C. -2

   D. 0

   E. $\dfrac{1}{2}$

3. The function f given by $f(x) = 2x^4 - 4x^3 + 2x^2$ has a relative maximum at

   A. $x = 1$

   B. $x = \dfrac{1}{2}$

   C. $x = 0$

   D. $x = -\dfrac{1}{2}$

   E. $x = -1$

4. $\dfrac{d}{dx}\left(x^2 \ln\left(e^{x^2-1}\right)\right) =$

   A. $2xe^{x^2-1}$

   B. $2x^3$

   C. $\dfrac{2x}{e^{x^2-1}}$

   D. $\dfrac{x^2}{x^2-1}$

   E. $2x\left(2x^2 - 1\right)$

5. If $f(x) = (x+4)^{5/2} + \dfrac{e^x}{3}$, then $f'(0) =$

A. $\dfrac{8}{3}$

B. 16

C. $\dfrac{16}{3}$

D. 20

E. $\dfrac{61}{3}$

6. The line normal to the curve $y = \sqrt{4-3x}$ at the point $(1,1)$ has slope

A. $-\dfrac{3}{2}$

B. $-\dfrac{2}{3}$

C. -3

D. $\dfrac{2}{3}$

E. $\dfrac{3}{2}$

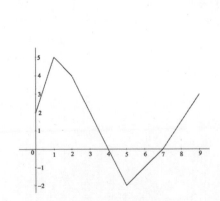

7. The function f is defined on the closed interval $[0, 9]$. The graph of its derivative f' is shown above.

The point $(3,11)$ is on the graph of $y = f(x)$. An equation of the line tangent to the graph of f at $(3,11)$ is

A. $y = x + 8$

B. $y = 2x + 5$

C. $y = 2x - 19$

D. $y = -2x + 17$

E. $y = -2x + 25$

8. How many points of inflection does the graph of f have?

    A. 0

    B. 1

    C. 2

    D. 3

    E. 4

9. At what value of x does a relative maximum of f occur?

    A. $x = 1$

    B. $x = 4$

    C. $x = 5$

    D. $x = 7$

    E. $x = 9$

10. If $2y = x^2 y + y^2 - 3$, then when $x = 2$ and y is positive, $\dfrac{dy}{dx}$ is

    A. $-\dfrac{1}{2}$

    B. -1

    C. -2

    D. -3

    E. $-\dfrac{3}{2}$

11. $\int\limits_{2}^{\infty} \dfrac{2x}{(3-x^2)^2}\,dx$ is

A. −1

B. 0

C. 1

D. $\dfrac{4}{3}$

E. ∞

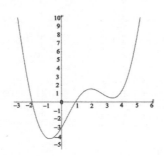

12. The graph of f', the derivative of f, is shown in the figure above. Which of the following describes all relative extrema of f on the open interval (a,b)?

A. One relative maximum

B. One relative minimum

C. One relative maximum and one relative minimum

D. Two relative maxima and one relative minimum

E. One relative maximum and two relative minima

13. A particle moves along the x-axis so that its acceleration at any time t is $a(t) = 3t - 5$. If the initial velocity of the particle is 4, and the initial position is the origin, at what time t during the interval $0 \le t \le 10$ is the particle farthest to the left?

A. $t = \dfrac{4}{3}$

B. $t = \dfrac{5}{3}$

C. $t = 2$

D. $t = \dfrac{10}{3}$

E. $t = 10$

14. The sum of the infinite geometric series $\dfrac{2}{5} + \dfrac{4}{25} + \dfrac{8}{125} + \dfrac{16}{625} + \dots$ is

A. 0

B. $\dfrac{2}{5}$

C. $\dfrac{2}{3}$

D. 1

E. $\dfrac{4}{3}$

15. The length of the path described by the parametric equations $x = \sin^2 t$ and $y = \cos t$ for $0 \le t \le \dfrac{\pi}{4}$ is given by

A. $\displaystyle\int_0^{\pi/4} \sqrt{\sin^2 t - \cos t}\, dt$

B. $\displaystyle\int_0^{\pi/4} \sqrt{\cos^2 t - \sin^4 t}\, dt$

C. $\displaystyle\int_0^{\pi/4} \sqrt{\sin^4 t - \cos^2 t}\, dt$

D. $\displaystyle\int_0^{\pi/4} \sqrt{\sin^4 t + \cos^2 t}\, dt$

E. $\displaystyle\int_0^{\pi/4} \sqrt{\sin^2 t + \cos t}\, dt$

16. $\lim\limits_{h \to 0} \dfrac{\ln(1+h)}{3h}$ is

   A. 0

   B. $\dfrac{1}{3}$

   C. 1

   D. $\ln\left(\dfrac{1}{3}\right)$

   E. nonexistent

17. Let f be the function given by $f(x) = e^{2x-3}$. The fourth degree Taylor polynomial for f about $x = 2$ is

   A. $e + 2e^2(x-2) + 4e^2(x-2)^2 + 8e^2(x-2)^3 + 16e^2(x-2)^4$

   B. $e + 2e^2(x-2) + 2e^2(x-2)^2 + \dfrac{4e^2}{3}(x-2)^3 + \dfrac{2e^2}{3}(x-2)^4$

   C. $e + 2e(x-2) + \dfrac{2e}{3}(x-2)^2 + \dfrac{4e}{3}(x-2)^3 + \dfrac{8e}{3}(x-2)^4$

   D. $e + 2e(x-2) + 3e(x-2)^2 + 8(x-2)^3 + 16(x-2)^4$

   E. $e + 2e(x-2) + 2e(x-2)^2 + \dfrac{4e}{3}(x-2)^3 + \dfrac{2e}{3}(x-2)^4$

18. For what values of t does the curve given by the parametric equations $x = 2t^3 - 3t^2 + 4$ and $y = t^3 - t^2 - t$ have a horizontal tangent?

   A. $t = 0$

   B. $t = 1$

   C. $t = -1$

   D. $t = \dfrac{1}{3}$

   E. $t = -\dfrac{1}{3}$

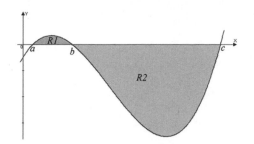

19. The graph of $y = f(x)$ is shown in the figure above. If R_1 and R_2 are the areas of the shaded regions as indicated, then in terms of R_1 and R_2, $\int_a^c f(x)dx - 3\int_c^b f(x)dx =$

A. R_1

B. R_2

C. $R_1 + R_2$

D. $R_1 + 2R_2$

E. $R_1 + 4R_2$

20. What are all values of x for which the series $\displaystyle\sum_{n=1}^{\infty} \frac{(x-1)^n}{n \cdot 2^n}$ converges?

A. $-1 < x \le 3$

B. $-1 < x < 3$

C. $-1 \le x < 3$

D. $-1 \le x \le 3$

E. All reals

21. Which of the following is equal to the area of the region inside the polar curve $r = 2\sin\theta$ and outside the polar curve $r = \sin\theta$?

A. 0

B. 2

C. $\frac{\pi}{4}$

D. $\frac{3\pi}{4}$

E. 2π

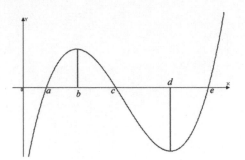

22. The graph of f is shown in the figure above. If $g(x) = \int_a^x f(t)\,dt$, for what value of x does $g(x)$ have a maximum?

    A. a
    B. b
    C. c
    D. d
    E. e

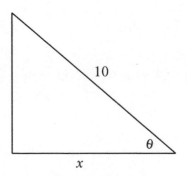

23. In the triangle shown above, if θ increases at a constant rate of 3 radians per minute, at what rate is x changing in units per minute when x equals 6 units?

    A. 24
    B. 18
    C. 12
    D. –18
    E. –24

24. The Taylor series for e^x about $x = 0$ is $1 + x + \dfrac{x^2}{2} + \dfrac{x^3}{6} + ... + \dfrac{x^n}{n!} + ...$ If

f is a function such that $f'(x) = e^{x^2}$, then the coefficient of x^5 in the

Taylor series for $f(x)$ about $x = 0$ is

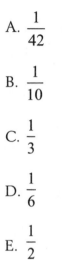

A. $\dfrac{1}{42}$

B. $\dfrac{1}{10}$

C. $\dfrac{1}{3}$

D. $\dfrac{1}{6}$

E. $\dfrac{1}{2}$

25. The closed interval $[a, b]$ is partitioned into n equal subintervals, each of width Δx, by the numbers $x_0, x_1, ..., x_n$ where

$a = x_0 < x_1 < x_2 < ... < x_{n-a} < x_n = b$. What is $\displaystyle\lim_{n \to \infty} \sum_{i=0}^{n} \dfrac{1}{x_i} \cdot \Delta x$?

A. $\ln(a - b)$

B. $\ln(b - a)$

C. $\ln(a + b)$

D. $\ln\left(\dfrac{a}{b}\right)$

E. $\ln\left(\dfrac{b}{a}\right)$

26. Which of the following sequences converge?

I. $\left\{ \dfrac{3n}{n+2} \right\}$

II. $\left\{ \dfrac{2^n}{n-1} \right\}$

III. $\left\{ \dfrac{2^n}{2^n+1} \right\}$

    A. I
    B. II
    C. III
    D. I and III
    E. I, II, and III

27. When the region enclosed by the graphs of $y = 2x$ and $y = 3x - x^2$ is revolved about the x-axis, the volume of the solid generated is given by

    A. $\dfrac{\pi}{30}$

    B. $\dfrac{\pi}{6}$

    C. $\dfrac{2\pi}{15}$

    D. $\dfrac{11\pi}{30}$

    E. $\dfrac{22\pi}{15}$

28. $\lim\limits_{h \to 0} \dfrac{\cos(\pi + h) + 1}{h} =$

A. 0

B. −1

C. 1

D. 2

E. Undefined

CALCULUS BC

SECTION I, Part B

Time—50 Minutes

Number of Questions—17

A graphing calculator is required for some questions on this part of the examination.

Directions: Solve each of the following problems. After examining the form of the choices, select the choice that best solves the problem. No credit will be given for anything written in the test book.

In this test:

1. The **exact** numerical value of the correct answer does not always appear among the answer choices. When this happens, select from among the choices the number that best approximates the exact numerical value.

2. Unless otherwise specified, the domain of a function f is assumed to be the set of all real numbers x for which $f(x)$ is a real number.

29. The position of an object moving along the y-axis is given by $y(t) = \sin t + \dfrac{1}{2}\cos(2t)$, where t is time in seconds. In the first 5 seconds, how many times does the object change direction?

   A. 1

   B. 2

   C. 3

   D. 4

   E. 5

30. Let f be the function given by $f(x) = \sin\dfrac{x}{2} + \ln\dfrac{x}{2}$. What is the smallest value of x at which the graph of f changes concavity?

   A. –2.844

   B. 0

   C. 2.844

   D. 5.804

   E. 6.474

31. Let f be a continuous function on the closed interval $[-1,4]$, which is differentiable on the open interval $(-1,4)$. If $f(-1)=0$ and $f(4)=3$, then the Mean Value Theorem guarantees that

A. $f'(x) = \dfrac{3}{4}$ for some value of x in the interval $[-1,4]$.

B. $f(x) = \dfrac{3}{5}$ for some value of x in the interval $[-1,4]$.

C. $f(x) = \dfrac{3}{2}$ for some value of x in the interval $[-1,4]$.

D. $f'(x) = \dfrac{3}{5}$ for some value of x in the interval $[-1,4]$.

E. $f'(x) = \dfrac{3}{2}$ for some value of x in the interval $[-1,4]$.

32. If $0 \le x \le 5$, of the following, which is the greatest value of x such that $\displaystyle\int_{2}^{x}(t^2 + 3t)dt \le \int_{0}^{x} t\,dt$?

A. 2.404

B. 2.596

C. 2.833

D. 4.167

E. 5.778

33. If $\dfrac{dy}{dx} = \left(2 + \sqrt{x}\right)y^2$ and if $y = 3$ when $x = 1$, then $y =$

A. $e^x \sqrt[3]{e^{x^{3/2}}}$

B. $-2x - \dfrac{2}{3}x^{3/2} + 3$

C. $27 - 18x - 6x\sqrt{x}$

D. $\dfrac{1}{27 - 18x - 6x\sqrt{x}}$

E. $\dfrac{3}{9 - 6x - 2x\sqrt{x}}$

34. $\int x^2 \cos 2x \, dx =$

A. $\dfrac{1}{2}x^2 \sin 2x + \dfrac{1}{2}x \cos 2x - \dfrac{1}{4}\sin 2x + C$

B. $\dfrac{1}{2}x^2 \sin 2x + \dfrac{1}{2}x \cos 2x + \dfrac{1}{4}\sin 2x + C$

C. $\dfrac{1}{2}x^2 \sin 2x + \dfrac{1}{2}x \cos 2x - \dfrac{1}{2}\cos 2x + C$

D. $\dfrac{1}{2}x^2 \sin 2x + \dfrac{1}{2}x \cos 2x + \dfrac{1}{2}\cos 2x + C$

E. $\dfrac{1}{2}x^2 \sin 2x - x \sin 2x + C$

35. Let f be a continuous, twice differentiable function such that $f(0) = 2$ and $f(4) = -1$. Which of the following must be true for the function f on the interval $0 \le x \le 4$?

I. The average rate of change of f is $-\dfrac{3}{4}$.

II. The average value of f is $-\dfrac{3}{4}$.

III. $f'(c) = -\dfrac{3}{4}$ for some value c in the interval $(0,4)$.

A. I only

B. II only

C. III only

D. I and III

E. I, II, and III

36. $\int \dfrac{dx}{(x-1)(x+3)} =$

A. $\dfrac{1}{3}[\ln(x-1)+\ln(x+3)]+C$

B. $\dfrac{1}{4}[\ln(x-1)+\ln(x+3)]+C$

C. $\dfrac{1}{4}\ln\left[\dfrac{1}{(x-1)(x+3)}\right]+C$

D. $\dfrac{1}{4}\ln\left|\dfrac{x-1}{x+3}\right|+C$

E. $\dfrac{1}{3}\ln\left|\dfrac{x-1}{x+3}\right|+C$

37. The base of a solid is the region in the first quadrant enclosed by the graph of $y=4-x^2$ and the coordinate axes. If every cross section of the solid perpendicular to the x-axis is a semicircle, the volume of the solid is given by

A. $\dfrac{128\pi}{15}$

B. $\dfrac{64\pi}{15}$

C. $\dfrac{32\pi}{15}$

D. $\dfrac{16\pi}{15}$

E. π

38. Let $f(x) = \int\limits_{0}^{2x} \sin t\, dt$. At how many points in the closed interval $[0, \pi]$ does the instantaneous rate of change of f equal the average rate of change of f on that interval?

    A. 0
    B. 1
    C. 2
    D. 3
    E. 4

39. If f is the antiderivative of $\dfrac{x^3}{1+x^4}$ such that $f(0) = 0$, then $f(3) =$

    A. 0.614
    B. 1.102
    C. 1.457
    D. 2.457
    E. 4.407

40. A force of 12 pounds is required to stretch a spring 3 inches beyond its natural length. Assuming Hooke's Law applies, how much work is done in stretching the spring from its natural length to 12 inches beyond its natural length?

    A. 288
    B. 216
    C. 144
    D. 54
    E. 18

SECTION II
GENERAL INSTRUCTIONS

You may wish to look over the problems before starting to work on them, since you may not have time to complete all parts of all problems. All problems are given equal weight, but the parts of a particular problem may not be given equal weight.

A graphing calculator is required for some problems on this section of the examination.

- Write all work for each part of each problem in the space provided for that part in the booklet. Be sure to write clearly and legibly. If you make an error, you may save time by crossing it out rather than erasing it.

- Show all your work. You will be graded on the correctness and completeness of your methods as well as your answers. Correct answers without supporting work may not receive credit.

- You may use your calculator to solve an equation, find the derivative of a function at a point, or calculate the value of a definite integral. However, be sure to clearly indicate the setup of your problem. If you use other calculator features or programs, you must show the mathematical steps necessary to produce your results.

- Your work must be expressed in standard mathematical notation rather than calculator syntax.

- Unless otherwise specified, answers (numeric or algebraic) need not be simplified. If your answer is given as a decimal approximation, it should correct to three places after the decimal point.

- Unless otherwise specified, the domain of a function f is assumed to be the set of all real numbers x for which $f(x)$ is a real number.

SECTION II, Part A

Time—30 minutes

Number of problems—2

A graphing calculator is required for some problems or parts of problems. During the timed portion for Part A, you may work only on the problems in Part A.

On Part A, you may use your calculator to solve an equation, find the derivative of a function at a point, or calculate the value of an integral. However, you must clearly indicate the setup of your problem, namely the equation, function, or integral you are using. If you use other features or programs, be sure to show the mathematical steps necessary to produce your results.

1. Let R be the region in the first and second quadrants bounded above by the graph of $y = \dfrac{2}{\sqrt{1+x^2}}$ and below by the horizontal line $y = 1$.

a. Find the area of R.

b. Find the volume of the solid generated when R is rotated about the x-axis.

c. The region R is the base of a solid. For this solid, the cross sections perpendicular to the x-axis are squares. Set up, but do not evaluate, an integral that could be used to find the volume of this solid.

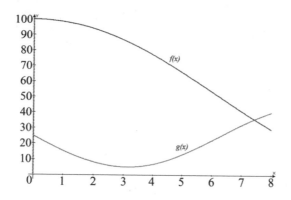

2. Faucets are turned on to allow water to flow into a bathtub, but the drain is not closed. The amount of water in the tub, in liters, is modeled by a continuous function $W(t)$ on the time interval $0 \le t \le 8$, where t is measured in minutes. The rate at which water enters the tub is $f(t) = 50\cos\dfrac{x}{4} + 50$ liters per minute for $0 \le t \le 10$. The rate at which water drains from the tub, in liters per minute, is $g(t) = 25 - 20\sin\dfrac{x}{2}$. The graphs of f and g are shown in the figure above.

a. How many liters of water enter the tank during the time interval $0 \le t \le 10$? Round your answer to the nearest liter.

b. For $0 \le t \le 10$, find the time intervals during which the amount of water in the tank is decreasing. Give a reason for each answer.

c. For $0 \le t \le 10$, at what time t is the amount of water in the tank greatest? To the nearest gallon, compute the amount of water at this time. Justify your answer.

Part B

Time—60 minutes

Number of problems—4

No calculator is allowed for these problems.

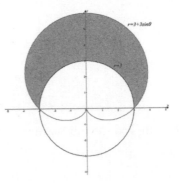

3. The graphs of the polar curves $r = 3$ and $r = 3 + 3\sin\theta$ are shown in the figure.

a. Let R be the region that is inside the graph of $r = 3 + 3\sin\theta$ and outside the graph of $r = 3$, as shaded in the figure. Find the area of R.

b. A particle moving with nonzero velocity along the polar curve given by $r = 3 + 3\sin\theta$ has position $(x(t), y(t))$ at time t, with $\theta = 0$ when $t = 0$. The particle moves along the curve so that $\dfrac{dr}{dt} = \dfrac{dr}{d\theta}$. Find the value of $\dfrac{dr}{dt}$ at $\theta = \dfrac{\pi}{3}$ and interpret your answer in terms of the motion of the particle.

c. For the particle described in part (b), $\dfrac{dx}{dt} = \dfrac{dx}{d\theta}$. Find the value of $\dfrac{dx}{dt}$ at $\theta = \dfrac{\pi}{3}$ and interpret your answer in terms of the motion of the particle.

4. Let f be the function defined for $0 < x < 2\pi$ with $f\left(\dfrac{\pi}{2}\right) = 1$ and f', the first derivative of f, given by $f'(x) = e^{\cos x}(\cos^2 x + \cos x - 1)$.

a. Write an equation for the line tangent to the graph of f at the point $\left(\frac{\pi}{2}, 1\right)$.

b. Find the x-coordinates of any inflection points of f on the interval $0 < x < 2\pi$.

c. Is the graph of f increasing or decreasing on the interval $\frac{\pi}{3} < x < \frac{2\pi}{3}$? Give a reason for your answer.

t	10	20	30	50	65	70	80
$v(t)$	1200	2500	3200	4000	3100	2500	2000

5. A car travels along a straight road at a velocity $v(t)$ in feet per minute. The table above gives selected values of the velocity $v(t)$ over the time interval $0 < t < 10$, where t is measured in minutes. The position of the car is modeled by a twice-differentiable function $s(t)$ of time t. For $0 < t < 10$, the graph of $s(t)$ is concave down. The position of the car is 2500 when $t = 20$ minutes. The fuel consumed by the car, in milliliters, is given by the function $f(t) = 0.0002s(t)v(t)$.

a. Estimate the position of the car when $t = 21$ minutes using the tangent line approximation at $t = 20$ minutes. Is your estimate greater than or less than the true value? Give a reason for your answer.

b. Find the rate of change of the fuel consumption of the car with respect to time when $t = 20$. Indicate units of measure.

c. Use a right Riemann sum with three subintervals to approximate $\int_{10}^{80} v(t)dt$. Using correct units, explain the meaning of $\int_{10}^{80} v(t)dt$ in terms of the movement of the car.

6. Let f be the function given by $f(x) = xe^x$

a. Write the first four nonzero terms and the general term of the Taylor
series for f about $x = 0$.

b. Use your answer to part (a) to find $\lim\limits_{x \to 0} \dfrac{x - f(x)}{x^2}$

c. Write the first four nonzero terms of the Taylor series for $\displaystyle\int_0^x f(t)\,dt$.

3. B.   If $f(x) = 2x^4 - 4x^3 + 2x^2$, then $f'(x) = 8x^3 - 12x^2 + 4x$. A rela-

tive maximum will occur when $f'(x) = 0$.

Solve $4x(2x^2 - 3x + 1) = 4x(2x - 1)(x - 1) = 0$ to find possible rela-

tive extrema at $x = 0$, $x = \frac{1}{2}$, and $x = 1$. A first derivative test shows

$f'(-1) = -24 < 0, f'\left(\frac{1}{4}\right) = \frac{3}{8} > 0, f'\left(\frac{3}{4}\right) = -\frac{3}{8} < 0$, and $f'(2) = 24 > 0$.

Since the derivative changes from positive to negative at $x = \frac{1}{2}$, the func-

tion changes from increasing to decreasing, and there is a relative maxi-

mum at $x = \frac{1}{2}$.

4. E.

$$\frac{d}{dx}(x^2 \ln(e^{x^2-1})) = \frac{d}{dx}(x^2(x^2 - 1)) = x^2 \cdot 2x + (x^2 - 1) \cdot 2x = 2x(2x^2 - 1)$$

5. E. If $f(x) = (x + 4)^{5/2} + \frac{e^x}{3}$,   then $f'(x) = \frac{5}{2}(x + 4)^{3/2} + \frac{e^x}{3}$ and

$f'(0) = 20 + \frac{1}{3} = \frac{61}{3}$.

6. D. The curve $y = \sqrt{4 - 3x}$ has derivative $y' = \frac{-3}{2\sqrt{4 - 3x}}$. Evaluate at

the point $(1,1)$ for a slope of the tangent of $y'(1) = \frac{-3}{2}$. The normal is

perpendicular to the tangent, and so has a slope of $\frac{2}{3}$.

7. B. The point $(3,11)$ is on the graph of $y = f(x)$. The slope of the

tangent line is $f'(3) = 2$. An equation of the line tangent to the graph

of f at $(3,11)$ is $y - 11 = 2(x - 3)$ or $y = 2x + 5$.

SOLUTIONS: AP Calculus BC Practice Test

Multiple Choice

Section I Part A

1. A. Use integration by parts with $u = x^2$, $dv = \sqrt{x+1}\,dx$, $du = 2x\,dx$ and $v = \frac{2}{3}(x+1)^{\frac{3}{2}}$.

$$\int x^2 \sqrt{x+1}\,dx = x^2 \cdot \frac{2}{3}(x+1)^{\frac{3}{2}} - \int \frac{2}{3}(x+1)^{\frac{3}{2}} \cdot 2x\,dx = \frac{2}{3}x^2(x+1)^{\frac{3}{2}} - \frac{4}{3}\int x(x+1)^{\frac{3}{2}}\,dx.$$

Repeat parts, this time with $u = x$, $dv = (x+1)^{3/2}\,dx$, $du = dx$, and $v = \frac{2}{5}(x+1)^{\frac{5}{2}}$.

$$\int x^2 \sqrt{x+1}\,dx = \frac{2}{3}x^2(x+1)^{\frac{3}{2}} - \frac{4}{3}\left[\frac{2}{5}x(x+1)^{\frac{5}{2}} - \frac{2}{5}\int (x+1)^{\frac{5}{2}}\,dx\right]$$

$$= \frac{2}{3}x^2(x+1)^{\frac{3}{2}} - \frac{4}{3}\left[\frac{2}{5}x(x+1)^{\frac{5}{2}} - \frac{4}{35}(x+1)^{\frac{7}{2}}\right]$$

$$= \frac{2}{3}(x+1)^{\frac{3}{2}}\left[x^2 - \frac{4}{5}(x+1) + \frac{8}{35}(x+1)^2\right]$$

$$= \frac{2}{105}(x+1)^{\frac{3}{2}}(15x^2 - 12x + 8)\Big|_0^3 = \frac{1696}{105} \approx 16.152.$$

2. A. If $x = e^{t-\pi}$, then $\frac{dx}{dt} = e^{t-\pi}$, and if $y = \cos\left(\frac{t}{2}\right)$, $\frac{dy}{dt} = -\frac{1}{2}\sin\left(\frac{t}{2}\right)$.

Divide to find $\frac{dy}{dx} = \dfrac{-\frac{1}{2}\sin\left(\frac{t}{2}\right)}{e^{t-\pi}} = \dfrac{-\sin\left(\frac{t}{2}\right)}{2e^{t-\pi}}$ and evaluate at $t = \pi$ to

find $\frac{dy}{dx} = \dfrac{-\sin\left(\frac{\pi}{2}\right)}{2e^0} = -\frac{1}{2}$.

8. C. The function f has 2 inflection points. Points of inflection occur when the second derivative changes sign, or when the first derivative changes from increasing to decreasing at $x = 1$ or decreasing to increasing at $x = 5$.

9. B. The critical numbers of f are $x = 4$ and $x = 7$, the zeros of f'. A maximum occurs when the graph of f changes from increasing to decreasing, so the derivative changes from positive to negative. This happens at $x = 4$.

10. B. Differentiate implicitly. If $2y = x^2 y + y^2 - 3$, then $2\dfrac{dy}{dx} = x^2 \dfrac{dy}{dx} + 2xy + 2y\dfrac{dy}{dx}$. Isolate $\dfrac{dy}{dx}$ to get $\dfrac{dy}{dx} = \dfrac{-2xy}{x^2 + 2y - 2}$.

Find the y-value that corresponds to $x = 2$ by substituting 2 for x

in $2y = x^2 y + y^2 - 3$ and solving for y. $2y = 4y + y^2 - 3$ becomes

$y^2 + 2y - 3 = 0$ so $y = -3$ or $y = 1$. When $x = 2$ and $y = 1$, $\dfrac{dy}{dx} = \dfrac{-4}{4} = -1$.

11. C. $\displaystyle\int_2^\infty \dfrac{2x}{(3 - x^2)^2}\,dx = \lim_{x\to\infty}\int_2^x \dfrac{2t}{(3 - t^2)^2}\,dt$. Integrate using a u-substitution

with $u = \left(3 - t^2\right)$ and $du = -2t\,dt$. Then $-\displaystyle\int u^{-2}\,du = u^{-1} + C$ becomes

$\displaystyle\int_2^x \dfrac{2t}{(3 - t^2)^2}\,dt = \dfrac{1}{3 - t^2}\bigg|_2^x = \dfrac{4 - x^2}{3 - x^2} \cdot \lim_{x\to\infty}\dfrac{4 - x^2}{3 - x^2} = 1$.

12. C. The graph of f', the derivative of f, has two x-intercepts. The first, slightly greater than -2, shows the derivative changing from positive to negative, indicating a maximum. The second, slightly less than 1, shows the derivative changing from negative to positive, indicating a minimum. The function f has one relative maximum and one relative minimum.

13. C. A particle moves along the x-axis so that its acceleration at any time t is $a(t) = 3t - 5$. Integrate to find $v(t) = \frac{3}{2}t^2 - 5t + C$. Because $v(0) = C = 4$, $v(t) = \frac{3}{2}t^2 - 5t + 4$. The particle will be farthest to the left at a time when it changes direction from moving left to moving right. When this happens, velocity will be zero, so solve $\frac{3}{2}t^2 - 5t + 4 = 0$ or $3t^2 - 10t + 8 = 0$, to find that the velocity is zero when $t = \frac{4}{3}$ and when $t = 2$. Test the velocity at points below, between, and above these values. $v(0) = 4$, $v\left(\frac{3}{2}\right) = -\frac{1}{8}$, and $v(10) = 104$, so the change from negative to positive indicates that the particle is farthest left at $t = 2$.

14. C. The infinite geometric series

$$\frac{2}{5} + \frac{4}{25} + \frac{8}{125} + \frac{16}{625} + \dots = \sum_{n=1}^{\infty} \left(\frac{2}{5}\right)^n = \frac{\frac{2}{5}}{1 - \frac{2}{5}} = \frac{\frac{2}{5}}{\frac{3}{5}} = \frac{2}{3}.$$

15. D. The length of the path described by the parametric equations $x = \sin^2 t$ and $y = \cos t$ for $0 \le t \le \frac{\pi}{4}$ is given by $\int_0^{\pi/4} \sqrt{\sin^4 t + \cos^2 t}\, dt$.

16. B. By L'Hôpital's rule,

$$\lim_{h \to 0} \frac{\ln(1+h)}{3h} = \lim_{h \to 0} \frac{\frac{1}{(1+h)}}{3} = \lim_{h \to 0} \frac{1}{3(1+h)} = \frac{1}{3}.$$

17. E. Find the first four derivatives of $f(x)$ and evaluate at $x = 2$.

$$f(x) = e^{2x-3} \qquad f(2) = e$$
$$f'(x) = 2e^{2x-3} \qquad f'(2) = 2e$$
$$f''(x) = 4e^{2x-3} \qquad f''(2) = 4e$$
$$f'''(x) = 8e^{2x-3} \qquad f'''(2) = 8e$$
$$f^{(4)}(x) = 16e^{2x-3} \qquad f^{(4)}(2) = 16e$$

The fourth degree Taylor polynomial for f about $x = 2$ is

$$f(x) \approx f(a) + f'(a)(x - a) + \frac{f''(a)}{2!}(x - a)^2 + \frac{f'''(a)}{3!}(x - a)^3 + \frac{f^{(4)}(a)}{4!}(x - a)^4$$

or $f(x) \approx e + 2e(x - 2) + 2e(x - 2)^2 + \frac{4e}{3}(x - 2)^3 + \frac{2e}{3}(x - 2)^4$.

18. E.   If $x = 2t^3 - 3t^2 + 4$ then $\dfrac{dx}{dt} = 6t^2 - 6t$ and if $y = t^3 - t^2 - t$,

$\dfrac{dy}{dt} = 3t^2 - 2t - 1$. The tangent will be horizontal when $\dfrac{dy}{dx} = 0$. Divide

to find $\dfrac{dy}{dx} = \dfrac{3t^2 - 2t - 1}{6t^2 - 6t}$ and solve $\dfrac{(3t + 1)(t - 1)}{6t(t - 1)} = \dfrac{3t - 1}{6t} = 0$. The tangent

line is horizontal when $t = 0$.

19. E. $\displaystyle\int_a^c f(x)dx = R_1 + R_2$ and $\displaystyle\int_c^b f(x)dx = -R_2$ so

$$\int_a^c f(x)dx - 3\int_c^b f(x)dx = R_1 + R_2 - 3(-R_2) = R_1 + R_2 + 3R_2 = R_1 + 4R_2.$$

20. C. $\displaystyle\sum_{n=1}^{\infty} \frac{(x-1)^n}{n \cdot 2^n}$ converges when $\left| \dfrac{(x-1)^{n+1}}{(n+1)\cdot 2^{n+1}} \div \dfrac{(x-1)^n}{n \cdot 2^n} \right| < 1$. Simplify

$\dfrac{(x-1)^{n+1}}{(n+1)\cdot 2^{n+1}} \cdot \dfrac{n \cdot 2^n}{(x-1)^n} = \dfrac{n(x-1)}{2(n+1)}$, and $\left| \dfrac{n(x-1)}{2(n+1)} \right| < 1$ or $-1 < \dfrac{n(x-1)}{2(n+1)} < 1$.

Solve for x.

$$\frac{-2(n+1)}{n} < x-1 < \frac{2(n+1)}{n}$$

$$-2-\frac{2}{n} < x-1 < 2+\frac{2}{n}$$

$$-1-\frac{2}{n} < x < 3+\frac{2}{n}$$

$$-1 < x < 3$$

Test for convergence at the endpoints of the interval. When $x = -1$,

$\displaystyle\sum_{n=1}^{\infty} \frac{(-2)^n}{n2^n} = \sum_{n=1}^{\infty} \frac{(-1)^n}{n}$ is the alternating harmonic series, which converges.

When $x = 3$, $\displaystyle\sum_{n=1}^{\infty} \frac{(2)^n}{n2^n} = \sum_{n=1}^{\infty} \frac{1}{n}$ is the harmonic series, which diverges. So

the interval of convergence is $-1 \le x < 3$.

21. D. The area of the region inside the polar curve $r = 2\sin\theta$ and outside the polar curve $r = \sin\theta$ is

$$\frac{1}{2}\int_0^\pi (2\sin\theta)^2 - (\sin\theta)^2 \, d\theta = \frac{1}{2}\int_0^\pi 3\sin^2\theta \, d\theta = \frac{3}{2}\int_0^\pi \frac{1}{2}(1-\cos 2\theta)\,d\theta$$

$$= \frac{3}{4}\left(\theta - \frac{1}{2}\sin 2\theta\right)\Big|_0^\pi = \frac{3}{4}[\pi - 0] = \frac{3\pi}{4}$$

22. C. If $g(x) = \displaystyle\int_a^x f(t)\,dt$ is interpreted as the area under the curve,

$g(x) = \displaystyle\int_a^a f(t)\,dt = 0$ and $g(x) = \displaystyle\int_a^b f(t)\,dt$ is positive. $g(x)$ continues

to increase until $x = c$, after which additional area is negative. Since

$g(x)$ changes from increasing to decreasing at $x = c$, the maximum oc-

curs at $x = c$.

23. E. If θ increases at a constant rate of 3 radians per minute, then

$\dfrac{d\theta}{dt} = 3$. Because $\cos\theta = \dfrac{6}{10}$, $\sin\theta = \dfrac{\sqrt{100-36}}{10} = \dfrac{8}{10}$. Using $\cos\theta = \dfrac{x}{10}$,

differentiate with respect to time to get $-\sin\theta\dfrac{d\theta}{dt} = \dfrac{1}{10}\dfrac{dx}{dt}$. Substitute

known values and solve for $\dfrac{dx}{dt}$. We have $-\dfrac{8}{10}\cdot 3 = \dfrac{1}{10}\dfrac{dx}{dt}$ so $-24 = \dfrac{dx}{dt}$.

24. B. Use $e^x = 1 + x + \dfrac{x^2}{2} + \dfrac{x^3}{6} + \ldots + \dfrac{x^n}{n!} + \ldots$ to find

$e^{x^2} = 1 + x^2 + \dfrac{x^4}{2} + \dfrac{x^6}{6} + \ldots + \dfrac{x^{2n}}{n!} + \ldots$. This represents $f'(x)$, the derivative of the desired function. Use antidifferentiation to find

$f(x) = x + \dfrac{x^3}{3} + \dfrac{x^5}{10} + \dfrac{x^7}{42} + \ldots + \dfrac{x^{2n+1}}{n!(2n+1)} + \ldots$. The coefficient of x^5 in

the Taylor series for $f(x)$ about $x = 0$ is $\dfrac{1}{10}$.

25. E. $\displaystyle\lim_{n\to\infty}\sum_{i=0}^{n-1}\dfrac{1}{x_i}\cdot\Delta x = \int_a^b \dfrac{dx}{x} = \ln x\Big|_a^b = \ln b - \ln a = \ln\left(\dfrac{b}{a}\right)$.

26. D. The sequence $\left\{\dfrac{3n}{n+2}\right\} = \left\{1, \dfrac{3}{2}, \dfrac{9}{5}, 2, \dfrac{15}{7}, \ldots\right\} = \left\{3 - \dfrac{6}{n+2}\right\} \to 3$ as

$n\to\infty$. The sequence $\left\{\dfrac{2^n}{n+1}\right\} = \left\{1, \dfrac{4}{3}, 2, \dfrac{16}{5}, \dfrac{16}{3}, \ldots\right\} \to \infty$ as $n\to\infty$ be-

cause 2^n grows so much more quickly than $n+1$. The sequence

$\left\{\dfrac{2^n}{2^n+1}\right\} = \left\{\dfrac{2}{3}, \dfrac{4}{5}, \dfrac{8}{9}, \dfrac{16}{17}, \dfrac{32}{33}, \ldots\right\} = \left\{1 - \dfrac{1}{2^n+1}\right\} \to 1$ as $n\to\infty$.

27. D. First find the points of intersection of the curves by solving $2x = 3x - x^2$. The curves intersect at $x = 0$ and $x = 1$. The volume of the solid generated is given by $V = \pi \int_0^1 (3x - x^2)^2 - (2x)^2 dx$

$$= \pi \int_0^1 (9x^2 - 6x^3 + x^4 - 4x^2)dx = \pi \int_0^1 (5x^2 - 6x^3 + x^4)dx$$

$$= \pi \left[\frac{5}{3}x^3 - \frac{3}{2}x^4 + \frac{1}{5}x^5 \right]_0^1 = \frac{11\pi}{30}.$$

28. A. $\displaystyle\lim_{h \to 0} \frac{\cos(\pi + h) + 1}{h} = \lim_{h \to 0} \frac{\cos(\pi + h) - \cos(\pi)}{h} = -\sin(\pi) = 0.$

Section I Part B

29. D. When the object changes direction, the velocity will be zero. The position of the object is $y(t) = \sin t + \frac{1}{2}\cos(2t)$ so the velocity is $y'(t) = \cos t - \sin(2t)$. Solve $\cos t - 2\sin t \cos t = \cos t(1 - 2\sin t) = 0$ to find that the velocity is zero when $\cos t = 0$ and when $\sin t = \frac{1}{2}$. Because of the periodic nature of the functions, $\cos t = 0$ at $t \approx 1.571$ and $t \approx 4.712$, and $\sin t = \frac{1}{2}$ at $t \approx .524$, and $t \approx 2.618$. In the first 5 seconds, the object changes direction four times.

30. E. If $f(x) = \sin\frac{x}{2} + \ln\frac{x}{2}$, then $f'(x) = \frac{1}{2}\cos\frac{x}{2} + \frac{1}{x}$ and

$f''(x) = -\frac{1}{4}\sin\frac{x}{2} - \frac{1}{x^2}$. A change in concavity will occur when the second derivative is zero, so solve $-\frac{1}{4}\sin\frac{x}{2} - \frac{1}{x^2} = 0$ or $x^2 \sin\frac{x}{2} = -4$ by calculator. Since the domain of f is positive reals, consider only positive solutions. The smallest positive value of x at which the graph of f changes concavity is 6.474.

31. D. The Mean Value Theorem guarantees that $f'(x) = \dfrac{3-0}{4+1} = \dfrac{3}{5}$ for some value of x in the interval $[-1,4]$.

32. A. $\displaystyle\int_{2}^{x}(t^2+3t)dt = \dfrac{t^3}{3}+\dfrac{3t^2}{2}\Big|_{2}^{x} = \dfrac{x^3}{3}+\dfrac{3x^2}{2}-\dfrac{26}{3}$ and $\displaystyle\int_{0}^{x}t^2 dt = \dfrac{t^3}{3}\Big|_{0}^{x} = \dfrac{x^3}{3}$.

The greatest value of x in the interval $0 \le x \le 5$ such that $\dfrac{x^3}{3}+\dfrac{3x^2}{2}-\dfrac{26}{3} \le \dfrac{x^3}{3}$ is found by solving $2x^3 + 9x^2 - 52 \le 2x^3$ or

$9x^2 - 52 \le 0$. The greatest value is $x \approx 2.404$.

33. E. To solve $\dfrac{dy}{dx} = \left(2+\sqrt{x}\right)y^2$, first separate the variables

$\dfrac{dy}{y^2} = \left(2+\sqrt{x}\right)dx$. Then find the antiderivative, $-\dfrac{1}{y} = 2x+\dfrac{2}{3}x^{3/2}+C$,

and use the initial condition to find C. $-\dfrac{1}{3} = 2\cdot 1+\dfrac{2}{3}+C$ means that

$C = -3$. Replace the constant and solve for y. $-\dfrac{1}{y} = 2x+\dfrac{2}{3}x^{3/2}-3$ be-

comes $\dfrac{3}{y} = 9-6x-2x\sqrt{x}$ and $y = \dfrac{3}{9-6x-2x\sqrt{x}}$.

34. A. Use integration by parts with $u = x^2$, $du = 2xdx$, $dv = \cos 2xdx$

and $v = \dfrac{1}{2}\sin 2x$. Then $\displaystyle\int x^2 \cos 2xdx = \dfrac{1}{2}x^2\sin 2x - \displaystyle\int x\sin 2xdx$.

Apply parts again, this time with $u = x$, $du = dx$, $dv = \sin 2xdx$,

and $v = -\dfrac{1}{2}\cos 2x$. The integral becomes $\displaystyle\int x^2 \cos 2xdx$

$= \dfrac{1}{2}x^2\sin 2x - \left[-\dfrac{1}{2}x\cos 2x + \dfrac{1}{2}\displaystyle\int \cos 2xdx\right]$. After the final integration,

$\displaystyle\int x^2 \cos 2xdx = \dfrac{1}{2}x^2 \sin 2x + \dfrac{1}{2}x\cos 2x - \dfrac{1}{4}\sin 2x + C$.

35. D. Statements I and III are true.

The average rate of change of f is $\dfrac{-1-2}{4-0} = -\dfrac{3}{4}$.

The average value of f is $\dfrac{1}{4-0}\int_0^4 f(x)dx$ but there is not enough information to evaluate this.

The Mean Value Theorem guarantees that $f'(c) = -\dfrac{3}{4}$ for some c in the interval $(0,4)$.

36. D. Use a partial fraction decomposition.

$\int \dfrac{dx}{(x-1)(x+3)} = \int\left(\dfrac{A}{x-1} + \dfrac{B}{x+3}\right)dx$. Finding a common denominator

gives a numerator of $A(x+3)+B(x-1)=1$, which leads to the system

of equations $A+B=0$ and $3A-B=1$. Solve the system to find that

$A = \dfrac{1}{4}$ and $B = -\dfrac{1}{4}$. Then $\int\left(\dfrac{\frac14}{x-1} + \dfrac{-\frac14}{x+3}\right)dx = \dfrac14\int\dfrac{dx}{x-1} - \dfrac14\int\dfrac{dx}{x+3}$

$= \dfrac14\ln|x-1| - \dfrac14\ln|x+3| + C = \dfrac14\ln\left|\dfrac{x-1}{x+3}\right| + C$.

37. C. $V = \int_0^2 \dfrac{\pi(r(x))^2}{2}dx = \dfrac{\pi}{2}\int_0^2\left(\dfrac{4-x^2}{2}\right)^2 dx = \dfrac{\pi}{2}\int_0^2\left(\dfrac{16-8x^2+x^4}{4}\right)dx$

$= \dfrac{\pi}{8}\int_0^2 (16-8x^2+x^4)dx = \dfrac{\pi}{8}\left[16x - \dfrac{8}{3}x^3 + \dfrac{x^5}{5}\right]_0^2 = \dfrac{\pi}{8}\left(\dfrac{256}{15}\right) = \dfrac{32\pi}{15}$.

38. D. Find $f(x) = \int_0^{2x} \sin t\,dt = -\cos t\,\big|_0^{2x} = -\cos 2x + \cos 0 = 1 - \cos 2x$

and evaluate at 0 and π. $f(0) = 1-1 = 0$ and $f(\pi) = 1-1 = 0$. The

average rate of change is $\dfrac{0-0}{\pi-0} = \dfrac{0}{\pi}$. The instantaneous rate of change is given by the derivative $f'(x) = \sin 2x$. Solve $\sin 2x = 0$, which has three solutions on the interval $[0, \pi]$, namely $x = 0, \frac{\pi}{2}, \pi$.

39. B. Find f by integrating, using a u-substitution with $u = 1 + x^4$ and $du = 4x^3 dx$.

Then $f(x) = \int \frac{x^3}{1 + x^4} = \frac{1}{4} \int \frac{du}{u} = \frac{1}{4} \ln|u| + C = \frac{1}{4} \ln(1 + x^4) + C$.

Because $\frac{1}{4} \ln(1 + 0) + C = 0$, $C = 0$ and $f(x) = \frac{1}{4} \ln(1 + x^4)$.

Evaluate $f(3) = \frac{1}{4} \ln(82) \approx 1.102$.

40. A. Hooke's Law says $F(x) = kx$, so $12 = 3k$ and $k = 4$. Then

$$W = \int_0^{12} 4x \, dx = 2x^2 \Big|_0^{12} = 288.$$

Free Response

Section II, Part A

1. Let R be the region in the first and second quadrants bounded above by the graph of $y = \dfrac{2}{\sqrt{1 + x^2}}$ and below by the horizontal line $y = 1$.

a. Find the limits of integration. Solve $\dfrac{2}{\sqrt{1 + x^2}} = 1$ to get $2 = \sqrt{1 + x^2}$ or

$4 = 1 + x^2$ and $x = \pm\sqrt{3}$. Then the area is $A = \displaystyle\int_{-\sqrt{3}}^{\sqrt{3}} \left(\frac{2}{\sqrt{1 + x^2}} - 1 \right) dx \approx 1.804$.

b. The volume of the solid generated when R is rotated about the x-axis is

$$V = \pi \int_{-\sqrt{3}}^{\sqrt{3}} \left[\left(\frac{2}{\sqrt{1 + x^2}} \right)^2 - 1^2 \right] dx = \pi \int_{-\sqrt{3}}^{\sqrt{3}} \left(\frac{4}{1 + x^2} - 1 \right) dx = \pi \int_{-\sqrt{3}}^{\sqrt{3}} \left(\frac{3 - x^2}{1 + x^2} \right) dx$$

$= 4.913\pi \approx 15.436$.

c. Each square has a side length equal to $\dfrac{2}{\sqrt{1+x^2}}+1$ so

$$V = \int_{-\sqrt{3}}^{\sqrt{3}} \left(\frac{2}{\sqrt{1+x^2}}-1\right)^2 dx.$$

2. a. The number of gallons of water that enter the tub during the

time interval $0 \le t \le 10$ is $\int_0^{10}\left(50\cos\frac{t}{4}+50\right)dt = \left[200\sin\frac{t}{4}+50t\right]\Big|_0^{10}$

$= 200\sin\dfrac{10}{4}+500 \approx 620$ liters.

b. The amount of water in the tub is decreasing when the rate at which water drains from the tub exceeds the rate at which water enters the tub, or when $50\cos\frac{t}{4}+50-\left(25-20\sin\frac{t}{2}\right)<0$. Solve

$50\cos\dfrac{t}{4}+20\sin\dfrac{t}{2}+25<0$ by calculator. The water in the tub is decreasing when $7.431 < t < 14.749$.

c. When W changes from increasing to decreasing, the amount of water in the tub is at a maximum. This corresponds to the rate of change, $50\cos\dfrac{t}{4}+20\sin\dfrac{t}{2}+25$, changing from positive to negative. The maximum amount of water is in the tub at $t = 7.431$. The volume at this time is $\int_0^{7.431} 50\cos\frac{t}{4}+20\sin\frac{t}{2}+25\,dt \approx 451$ gallons.

Section II, Part B

3. a. $A = \dfrac{1}{2}\int_0^{\pi}(3+3\sin\theta-3)^2\,d\theta = \dfrac{1}{2}\int_0^{\pi}(3\sin\theta)^2\,d\theta = \dfrac{9}{2}\int_0^{\pi}\sin^2\theta\,d\theta$

$= \dfrac{9}{2}\cdot\dfrac{1}{2}(\theta\frac{-1}{2}\sin 2\theta)\Big|_0^{\pi} = \dfrac{9\pi}{4}$

b. If $r = 3 + 3\sin\theta$, then $\dfrac{dr}{d\theta} = -3\cos\theta$, and $\dfrac{dr}{d\theta}\Big|_{\theta=\frac{\pi}{3}} = -3\left(\dfrac{1}{2}\right) = -\dfrac{3}{2}$.

Because $\dfrac{dr}{dt} = \dfrac{dr}{d\theta}, \dfrac{dr}{dt} = -\dfrac{3}{2}$. The particle is moving toward the origin at

$\theta = \dfrac{\pi}{3}$, because $\dfrac{dr}{dt}$ is negative.

c. To find $\dfrac{dx}{dt}$, first find x, using the polar conversion $x = r\cos\theta$.

$x = (3 + 3\sin\theta)\cos\theta = 3\cos\theta + 3\sin\theta\cos\theta$ so

$\dfrac{dx}{d\theta} = -3\sin\theta - 3\sin^2\theta + 3\cos^2\theta$. Because $\dfrac{dx}{dt} = \dfrac{dx}{d\theta}$,

$\dfrac{dx}{dt} = -3\sin\theta - 3\sin^2\theta + 3\cos^2\theta\big|_{\theta=\frac{\pi}{3}}$ or $= -3\left(\dfrac{\sqrt{3}}{2}\right) - 3\left(\dfrac{3}{4}\right) + 3\left(\dfrac{1}{4}\right)$

$= -\dfrac{3\sqrt{3} - 3}{2}$.

At $\theta = \dfrac{\pi}{3}$, the value of $\dfrac{dx}{dt}$ is $-\dfrac{3\sqrt{3} - 3}{2}$, which indicates that the particle

is moving toward the y-axis.

4. a. To find an equation for the line tangent to the graph of f at the point

$\left(\dfrac{\pi}{2}, 1\right)$, first find the slope at $\left(\dfrac{\pi}{2}, 1\right)$ $f'\left(\dfrac{\pi}{2}\right) = e^0(0 + 0 - 1) = -1$, then

use point-slope form $y - 1 = -1\left(x - \dfrac{\pi}{2}\right)$.

b. Inflection points will occur when the second derivative is zero. If
$f'(x) = e^{\cos x}(\cos^2 x + \cos x - 1)$,

$f''(x) = e^{\cos x}(-2\cos x\sin x - \sin x) - e^{\cos x}\sin x(\cos^2 x + \cos x - 1)$
$= e^{\cos x}(-2\sin x\cos x - \sin x - \sin x\cos^2 x - \sin x\cos x + \sin x)$
$= e^{\cos x}(-\sin x\cos^2 x - 3\sin x\cos x)$
$= e^{\cos x}(-\sin x)\cos x(\cos x + 3)$

Set the second derivative equal to zero and solve. Since $e^{\cos x} \neq 0$, and $\cos x \neq -3$, find the zeros of the other factors.

$$-\sin x = 0 \;\Big|\; \cos x = 0$$
$$x = \pi \;\Big|\; x = \frac{\pi}{2}, x = \frac{3\pi}{2}$$

Test the second derivatives at values between these zeros to be certain there is a change in sign, and therefore a change in concavity. $f''\left(\frac{\pi}{6}\right) < 0$,

$f''\left(\frac{5\pi}{6}\right) > 0$, $f''\left(\frac{7\pi}{6}\right) < 0$, and $f''\left(\frac{11\pi}{6}\right) > 0$, so the function has in-

flection points at $x = \frac{\pi}{2}$, $x = \pi$, and $x = \frac{3\pi}{2}$.

c. Evaluate $f'(x) = e^{\cos x}(\cos^2 x + \cos x - 1)$ at a point in the interval.

$f'\left(\frac{\pi}{2}\right) = e^{\cos \frac{\pi}{2}}\left(\cos^2 \frac{\pi}{2} + \cos \frac{\pi}{2} - 1\right) = e^0(-1) = -1$. Since the derivative

is negative, the function is decreasing.

5. a. The tangent line at $t = 20$ is $y - 2500 = 2500(t - 20)$. When $t = 21$, $y = 2500(1) + 2500 = 5000$. Since the graph of $s(t)$ is concave down, the tangent line sits above the graph, so this estimate will be larger than the actual value.

b. Because $f(t) = 0.0002s(t)v(t)$, the rate of consumption is

$f'(t) = 0.0002(s(t)v'(t) + s'(t)v(t))$ or $f'(t) = 0.0002(s(t)v'(t) + (v(t))^2)$.

Calculate $v'(t) \approx \dfrac{3200 - 1200}{30 - 10} = \dfrac{2000}{20} = 100$ and then evaluate

$f'(t) = 0.0002(s(t)v'(t) + (v(t))^2) = 0.0002(2500 \cdot 100 + 2500^2) = 1300$.

c. $\displaystyle\int_{10}^{80} v(t)dt \approx 20 \cdot 3200 + 35 \cdot 3100 + 15 \cdot 2000 \approx 202,500$. The integral

$\displaystyle\int_{10}^{80} v(t)dt$ represents the total distance, in feet, traveled by the car in the

70-minute period from $t = 10$ to $t = 80$.

6. a. Find the first four derivatives of f and evaluate f and its derivatives

at $x = 0$.

$$f(x) = xe^x \qquad\qquad f(0) = 0$$
$$f'(x) = xe^x + e^x \qquad f'(0) = 1$$
$$f''(x) = xe^x + 2e^x \qquad f''(0) = 2$$
$$f'''(x) = xe^x + 3e^x \qquad f'''(0) = 3$$
$$f^{(4)}(x) = xe^x + 4e^x \qquad f^{(4)}(0) = 4$$

Then $f(x) \approx 0 + 1x + \dfrac{2}{2!}x^2 + \dfrac{3}{3!}x^3 + \dfrac{4}{4!}x^4 + \ldots + \dfrac{nx^n}{n!} + \ldots$ or

$$f(x) \approx x + x^2 + \frac{x^3}{2} + \frac{x^4}{6} + \ldots + \frac{x^n}{(n-1)!} + \ldots .$$

b. $x - \left(x + x^2 + \dfrac{x^3}{2} + \dfrac{x^4}{6} + \ldots + \dfrac{x^n}{(n-1)!} + \ldots \right) = -\left(x^2 + \dfrac{x^3}{2} + \dfrac{x^4}{6} + \ldots + \dfrac{x^n}{(n-1)!} + \ldots \right).$

Dividing by x^2,

$$\frac{-\left(x^2 + \dfrac{x^3}{2} + \dfrac{x^4}{6} + \ldots + \dfrac{x^n}{(n-1)!} + \ldots \right)}{x^2} = -1 - \left(\frac{x}{2} + \frac{x^2}{6} + \ldots + \frac{x^{n-2}}{(n-1)!} \right),$$

therefore, $\displaystyle\lim_{x \to 0} \frac{x - f(x)}{x^2} = -1$.

c. The first four nonzero terms of the Taylor series for

$$\int_0^x f(t)dt = \int_0^x \left(t + t^2 + \frac{t^3}{2} + \frac{t^4}{6} \right)dx = \frac{t^2}{2} + \frac{t^3}{3} + \frac{t^4}{8} + \frac{t^5}{30} \Big|_0^x = \frac{x^2}{2} + \frac{x^3}{3} + \frac{x^4}{8} + \frac{x^5}{30}.$$

About the Author

Carolyn Wheater teaches middle school and upper school mathematics at the Nightingale-Bamford School in New York City. Educated at Marymount Manhattan College and the University of Massachusetts, Amherst, she has taught math and computer technology for thirty years to students from preschool through college.

Notes

Notes

Notes

Notes

Notes

Notes

Also Available

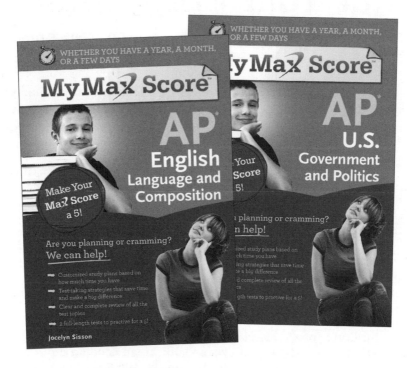

Essentials from
Dr. Gary Gruber
and the creators of My Max Score

*"Gruber can ring the bell on any number
of standardized exams."*
—Chicago Tribune

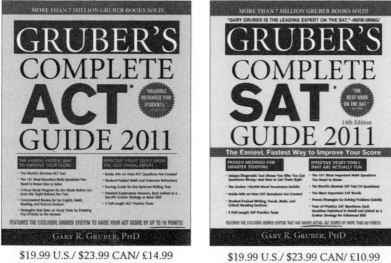

$19.99 U.S./ $23.99 CAN/ £14.99
978-1-4022-4307-3

$19.99 U.S./ $23.99 CAN/ £10.99
978-1-4022-3777-5

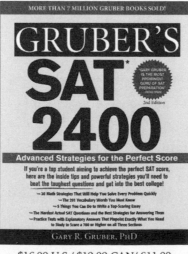

$16.99 U.S./ $19.99 CAN/ £11.99
978-1-4022-4308-0

$13.99 U.S./ $16.99 CAN/ £7.99
978-1-4022-3859-8

"Gruber's methods make the questions
seem amazingly simple to solve."
—*Library Journal*

"Gary Gruber is the leading expert on the SAT."
—*Houston Chronicle*

$14.99 U.S./ $15.99 CAN/ £7.99
978-1-4022-1846-0

$14.99 U.S./ $15.99 CAN/ £7.99
978-1-4022-1847-7

$14.99 U.S./ $15.99 CAN/ £7.99
978-1-4022-1848-4

$12.99 U.S./ $15.99 CAN/ £6.99
978-1-4022-2010-4